The European Union:
Annual Review 1999/2000

Edited by

Geoffrey Edwards
and
Georg Wiessala

General Editors: Iain Begg and John Peterson

Copyright © Blackwell Publishers Ltd

ISBN 0-631-22183-2

First published 2000

Blackwell Publishers Ltd
108 Cowley Road, Oxford OX4 1JF, UK

Blackwell Publishers Inc.
350 Main Street,
Malden, MA 02148, USA

British Library Cataloguing in Publication Data
A catalogue record for this book is available from the British Library

Library of Congress
Cataloging in Publication Data applied for

This journal is printed on acid free paper
Printed in the UK by J.W. Arrowsmith Ltd, Bristol

CONTENTS

Journal of Common Market Studies

Volume 38, Annual Review
September 2000

Editorial: Revolution Beyond Reform?

GEORG WIESSALA
University of Central Lancashire
and
GEOFFREY EDWARDS
University of Cambridge

I. Reform, Horizontal and Vertical

The last year of the old millennium became another turning point for the EU and its executive. Issues of democratic legitimacy, accountability, transparency and political responsibility were never far from public view or political limelight. The resignation *en masse* of the discredited Santer Commission early in the year threw into stark relief the urgent need for overhaul and a more precise definition of the Union's still indeterminate collective identity. It may be for future assessments to decide how far the Santer College was, indeed, a 'remarkably proficient bureaucracy' (Peterson, 1997, 1999) but the focus in 1999 was clearly on its disastrous downfall. Just how comprehensive the processes of change should be, remained a bone of contention throughout the year. The credibility of the Union and its attempts at reform if not reformation, in areas ranging from foreign policy and the much-heralded 'common defence policy', to a more solid grounding in human rights, have determined perceptions in both Brussels and the Member States and influenced domestic, transnational and intergovernmental expectations.

Although debates have tended to focus on the new Commission, the mass resignation of its predecessor body in March 1999 had the effect of a stone cast into muddy water. The circles produced by the first shock wave expanded, and questions of root-and-branch reform quickly spread to other institutions. As a result, disputes about issues such as the publication of the minutes of the Council's meetings or those of the European Central Bank (ECB), even of the new Commission President's private correspondence, became more protracted. A more vigorous leadership role, enhanced control of the future Commission and a right of initiative beyond codecision were debated more vociferously by a newly elected European Parliament (EP), which found itself with a European People's Party (EPP) majority. In return for the EPP's support, Commission President Romano Prodi agreed to a five-point agenda, designed to put further limitations on the Commission's future room for manœuvre. Desmond Dinan points to many of the reforms undertaken by Prodi, whether in continuation of the reform programme set in train by Santer, in response to the proposals set out by the Committee of Independent Experts in their Second Report, or those derived from his own assessment (supplemented by those of Neil Kinnock whom Prodi chose to become Commissioner for Reform). Prodi sought from the outset to link reform, irreversibly and convincingly, to the grand historical project of further enlargement and has continued to make the case of the latter not working without the former. In pressing for the reforms he wants, as well as the changing personnel within the higher echelons, he has been regarded – not wholly accurately or even fairly perhaps – as moving the Commission's culture from what was perceived as a continental-French approach to a more British-influenced one.

    Reforms were not, however, to be limited to the Commission, but encompassed other institutions, including the Council. In the interests of effectiveness, further institutional changes were envisaged, with the Heads of State or Government (HOSG) approving the 'comprehensive review' of the Council's working methods at Helsinki. The reforms and operational changes recommended were not particularly new, though in the interests of improving 'the coherence and consistency of the Council's work', the Council was restricted to a maximum of only 15 different manifestations and only five 'informals' in any one Presidency – which presumably will leave a good number of ministers (other than foreign and finance ministers) fighting it out for a luxury weekend in yet another Schloss. The General Affairs Council (GAC), the Presidency and COREPER were all reaffirmed in their central co-ordinating roles, despite the criticisms of the capacity of the GAC to exercise control horizontally, the prospective post-enlargement difficulties facing any Presidency in fulfilling its political responsibilities, and the tensions surrounding the role of COREPER in organizing vertically all the 'multidisciplinary and interpillar dossiers' (as well as the possible tensions created by the proposed increased role of the Council General Secretariat). One aspect that fits a growing trend within the EU is the agreement that each Member State will review its own internal co-ordination procedures in order to ensure 'the optimum functioning of the

Council'. There is no recommendation that Member governments should begin to approximate their national arrangements or that there should be convergence on a single model, but the idea of benchmarking, and examining different if not best practices, used in relation to particular policy areas, seems now to be used for institutional procedures. Perhaps 'fusion' lives after all! (Wessels, 1997).

II. Nice and Ready?

The references at Helsinki as at Cologne were frequently to the need to meet the challenge of enlargement. There seems to have been (finally?) a recognition that further enlargement was unlikely to be postponed for too long. There may have been complaints from some of the candidate countries that not all the existing Member States had yet begun to take the accession negotiations seriously, but awareness of the possible repercussions of enlargement were, at last, being taken on board by Member governments. Many of the problems facing the institutions could be settled by such procedural reforms mentioned above, without treaty revision – as the Dehaene Report of October 1999 suggested (Dehaene, 1999). But Dehaene and his co-authors (the former Belgian Prime Minister together with Richard von Weizsäcker, the former President of Germany, and the former British Minister for European Trade, Lord Simon) urged more extensive institutional reform (though for the most part they eschewed specific proposals), which were the possible remit of the Intergovernmental Conference (IGC).

The Cologne Council suggested an agenda for the IGC largely limited to the 'Amsterdam leftovers' (number of Commissioners, reweighting of Council votes and the extension of qualified majority voting or QMV). But while it was clear that the IGC would be convened under the Portuguese Presidency in early 2000, it was perhaps less obvious, notwithstanding French ambitions, that it would have completed its work by December 2000 for the prospective Nice European Council. Not all Member States were prepared for the minimalist agenda of the Amsterdam leftovers. Certainly France, Germany, Spain and the UK aligned themselves in favour of the 'leaner', and therefore less time-consuming process. Even so, there were some variations as to whether any additional items might be included such as revisiting flexibility or closer co-operation (which the Germans among others seemed to favour), the possibility of a charter on fundamental rights (another German favourite, though this time, Green, as Maurer points out in his review of the German Presidency) and splitting the Treaty, dividing it up between 'basic provisions' and 'implementation rules' (as suggested by Dehaene). The incoming Commission President, who was clearly unwilling to settle for minimal reform, saw the IGC as an 'historical' opportunity, not to be missed. However, as the year progressed, Member States increasingly poured cold water over the idea of a more fundamental, treaty-changing, 'constitutionalized' reform of the EU. The Helsinki Council Conclusions left the door ajar by allowing the Presidency to propose any additional issues. But the pressures have been strong to restrict the agenda in order to complete by December in Nice.

III. Defence and the Three 'Ds'

One issue left off the agenda, in part so as not to create complications was that of security and defence. Whether the agreement reached at Helsinki to set up a military force 'of up to 50–60,000 persons capable of the full range of Petersberg tasks' and the related decisions taken at the European Council requires treaty amendment were left for the Portuguese Presidency to report on. But, as our keynote article by John Roper suggests, the decisions are potentially of major significance. What has been intriguing in the assessments of the year's discourse has been uncertainty of quite what their potential might be. On the one hand, one can trace fairly straightforwardly, a development from the Franco–British bilateral at St Malo, through the various NATO and EU Councils to Helsinki. There is also the clear impetus given to a European role provided by the Kosovo crisis, during which the EU15 maintained a remarkable solidarity, as Dave Allen and Mike Smith point out, especially in view of hostile public opinion in several Member States. And yet, however interconnected and 'wired-up' the various (frequently confusing) elements of EU activity in the Balkans might be, they did not win the battle. NATO, led by the United States, did that. It may be that there is now a consensus – unlike ten years ago after the Iraqi invasion of Kuwait – that the lesson to be learned is that Europe needs to pursue a serious Common European Security and Defence Policy (CESDP). But, on the other hand, ambiguities still abound. The military force, according to the Helsinki Council Conclusions, for example, 'does not imply the creation of a European army', and the autonomous capacity 'to launch and conduct EU-led military operations' appears to be only 'where NATO as a whole is not engaged'. One gauge of Europe's seriousness might be the way in which the US has responded to the latest moves. In what can only be described as a battle of the soundbite, the American Secretary of State, Madeleine Albright, warned Europe in April 1999 that America could only welcome closer European co-operation in defence if there is 'no duplication, no decoupling, no discrimination', a reaction echoed by Deputy Secretary Strobe Talbot in December (Albright, 1999; Talbot, 1999). In turn, British commitment could perhaps be measured in the counter three 'Ds' addressed to the US of 'no disengagement, no delegation, no domination' (House of Commons, 2000).

But however ambiguous the evidence, one factor was of particular interest in the policy's development – the debt the development owes to bilateral discussions. The revived impetus provided by St Malo and much of the subsequent momentum was provided by negotiations between rather than simply among governments. Bilateralism is not, of course, a new phenomenon; Franco–German initiatives have long been of vital importance even if they have appeared increasingly forced and/or empty over the last decade. Nor, perhaps, is the new emphasis on bilaterals solely one sparked by Tony Blair in an effort to break into the Franco–German 'duumvirate', though there have been many who have sought to do so in the past – with little success. But it is clearly the case that Blair is fond of bilaterals – there seem to be few visits to or from fellow Prime Ministers which have not resulted in the establishment of a new bilateral agreement – and that he uses personal contacts extensively – whether via the PMNet or telephone. However, while noting the phenomenon, whether it should be seen in a transnational or an intergovernmental perspective should possibly be left to the reader's own predilections.

IV. Acknowledgements

The *Annual Review* this year has a number of new faces. With enormous gratitude for all their work over probably more years than they bargained for at the outset, we had to allow Brigid Laffan and John Redmond to escape. It points up the extent of our indebtedness to others. But we are delighted to welcome Hussein Kassim, Lee Miles and Alison Cottrell, and hope that they will all join the ranks of long-term contributors. We have been extremely fortunate in gaining John Roper to write the keynote article (ennobled since we asked him to undertake it – which only goes to confirm the high esteem in which either he or the *Annual Review* is held), and Andreas Maurer and Alexander Stubb to report on the German and Finnish Presidencies. The latter's is a particularly intriguing piece given Alexander's intimate involvement in his government's activities. Finally, we owe particular thanks to Julie Smith (and Chatham House) for allowing us to prevail on her to bowdlerize her Chatham House Briefing Paper on enlargement when Chris Preston found commuting between England, Lithuania and Romania just too time-consuming to be able to write his contribution.

References

Albright, M. (1999) 'Press Briefing at the End of the NATO Summit in Washington'. 25 April.

Dehaene, J-L. (1999) *The Institutional Implications of Enlargement – Report to the European Commission* (Dehaene Report), 18 October.

House of Commons 8th Defence Report, 19th April 2000.

Peterson, J. (1997) 'The European Union: Pooled Sovereignty, Divided Accountability'. *Political Studies,* Vol. 45, No. 3, p. 562.

Peterson, J. (1999) 'Jacques Santer: The EU's Gorbachev'. *ECSA Review*, Fall, p. 4.

Talbot, S. (1999) Brussels, 15 December.

Wessels, W. (1997) 'An Ever Close Fusion? A Dynamic Macropolitical View on Integration Processes'. *Journal of Common Market Studies*, Vol. 35, No. 2, pp. 267–99.

Journal of Common Market Studies

Volume 38, Annual Review
September 2000

Keynote Article: Two Cheers for Mr Blair? The Political Realities of European Defence Co-operation*

JOHN ROPER
House of Lords

I. Politics is the Art of the Possible

1999 saw significant changes in the discourse on European Defence Co-operation and the development of a Common European Security and Defence Policy (CESDP). It was also – and this was not totally coincidental – a year in which the forces of many European Union Member States were involved alongside the United States in a major military operation in south eastern Europe. It is, therefore, a moment to try to evaluate what progress has been made, what constraints have been removed and which remain. What is now possible that might have been considered impossible or improbable a year ago?

There is a perennial problem in trying to assess trends when the process appears to be moving rapidly but when, as often in political affairs, there are conflicting signals. On the one hand, developments from the Franco-British Declaration of St Malo in December 1998, through the NATO Washington summit in April 1999, the Bremen ministerial meeting of WEU in May 1999, and the European Council meeting at Cologne in June 1999, the latter both held under German Presidencies, and concluding with the European Council meeting in Helsinki in December 1999, show that there has been a clear

* John Roper is a Professor at the College of Europe, Bruges, and an Honorary Professor of the University of Birmingham. He was from 1990–95 the first Director of the Institute for Security Studies of Western European Union. He became a member of the House of Lords in 2000.

political acceptance of the European Union assuming enhanced responsibilities in the fields of defence. The Cologne and Helsinki documents are particularly clear in this respect, although the formal decisions will only be fully made within the course of 2000. Thus while there is some cause for optimism, not too much should be taken for granted.

On the other hand, the 11-week air campaign against Serbia and the subsequent installation of the Kosovo Force (KFOR) sent rather uncertain signals. The very modest participation by European forces in the air actions illustrates the current serious limitations of European force structures for this sort of involvement, as does the long delay in assembling the 50,000 troops required in Kosovo. More seriously, there was far from consensus among major European countries about the critical decisions during the war, including the overall targeting strategy, the use of ground troops, and the timing and format of negotiations. Fortunately, Milosevic accepted a settlement before these differences became too acute, but the lack of a common European approach, and the relatively limited European force contribution, meant that too many of the critical decisions were taken in Washington.

Some have argued that the experience of Kosovo demonstrates the impossibility now, or in the foreseeable future, of Europe being able to act as anything other than as a junior partner within a NATO action. This view may be disputed, and assumes a continuing American willingness to act as the policeman of Europe, if not of the world. The preponderance of usable American forces, particularly for the air actions, also means that decisions as to whether or not to use military force will be made in Washington, largely independently of European views. So, too, consequential decisions, e.g. what constraints will be imposed on the force used, whether there is a reluctance to use ground troops because of risks of casualties, or a reluctance to fly below 15,000 feet for similar reasons (even if this reduced the effectiveness of the air action and increased collateral civilian casualties), meant that Kosovo was an important reality check and showed the present limits on European policy.

Finally, in the area of European armaments co-operation, it is difficult to call 1999 a particularly encouraging year. The long-discussed amalgamation between European aerospace companies was realized in part on 14 October 1999 when the German Dasa and the French Aerospatiale Matra agreed to merge their aerospace and defence activities into the European Aeronautic, Defense and Space Company (EADS), which will be the world's third largest aerospace company. However, British Aerospace (BAe Systems) was too busy with its own national merger with the defence sectors of GEC Marconi to participate, which proved a serious limitation on the project.

One of the major naval collaborative projects, the 'Horizon' frigate, collapsed in May 1999 when the UK dropped out of the project. On the other hand, France has left the Multi Role Armoured Vehicle Programme (MRAV), preferring to pursue a national programme, the VC1. The French, along with the UK and Germany, had signed an agreement in 1998 for the development and initial production of the family of vehicles. The MRAV will be one of the first managed by OCCAR, the new European Armaments Agency. Thus, while there were some bilateral mergers, both internal to some countries and between countries, there was no real sign, in spite of another fall in aggregate European defence expenditure, that armaments co-operation would be the motor pushing European defence co-operation, from defence industries, from within ministries of defence, or from political sources.

II. A Sea Change in London

The most important factor was the radical change in the attitude towards European Defence Co-operation demonstrated by the British Prime Minister, Tony Blair. From it followed the developments set out in the series of meetings from St Malo to Helsinki. From the summer of 1998 he indicated that he had realized that, in the field of defence as elsewhere, there is no contradiction between being a good European and being a good Atlanticist. He is probably the first British Prime Minister to accept this, and it has been a major factor driving the change in British policy. Thus one of the major constraints to building an effective defence dimension to the EU's Common Foreign and Security Policy (CFSP) has been removed. As his Conservative opponents in the House of Commons do not hesitate to point out, it has been a fairly dramatic change.[1] In June 1997 on his return from the Amsterdam IGC, Blair reported to the House:

> Getting Europe's voice heard more clearly in the world will not be achieved through merging the European Union and the Western European Union or developing an unrealistic Common Defence Policy. We therefore resisted unacceptable proposals from others. Instead, we argued for – and won – the explicit recognition, written into the treaty for the first time, that NATO is the foundation of our and other allies' common defence.[2]

By December 1999, when he reported to the House of Commons on the Helsinki European Council, the Prime Minister's position had clearly evolved. He said:

> It would be a tragic mistake – repeating mistakes of British European policy over the past few decades – if Britain opted out of the debate on European Defence Policy and left the field to others. This is a debate that we must shape

[1] House of Commons, *Hansard*, 20 February 2000, Col 1413.
[2] House of Commons, *Hansard*, 18 June 1997, Col 314.

© Blackwell Publishers Ltd 2000

and influence from the start, because our vital strategic interests are affected by it.[3]

Reporting on the decision to develop European capabilities, he continued:

> We also all made the decision that our continent of Europe, which twice this century has lost millions of its citizens in the two most bloody wars in human history, should now co-operate in defence where the object is to help keep the peace.[4]

The appointment of the British Defence Minister, George (now Lord) Robertson, one of the most committed Europeans in the Labour government, as Secretary-General of NATO may facilitate the task of ensuring that this European development will not be seen as being in competition with NATO.

III. What Do We Want?

One of the continuing problems for the advocates of the inclusion of defence within the ambit of the European Union is to define what is wanted and, more important, how it should be attained. Politics, like war, requires both strategy and tactics. There is a need to define the objective and the stages by which it is to be achieved. The history of European integration in the last half century has been the adoption of a phased approach, whereby confidence in the process of integration is reinforced by success in intermediate steps towards the final objective. This is almost certainly also true in the area of defence, where national identification with armed forces is still strong, even for those countries where many essential decisions have been subordinated to those made at the level of NATO.

The UK's Strategic Defence Review (SDR) completed in the summer of 1998 was designed from the outset to be 'foreign policy led', in an attempt to distinguish it from most previous British defence reviews which had been perceived as being driven by a wish to cut the defence budget. The same principle could be applied to defining the shared requirements for European defence capabilities. It is only possible to work out what armed forces are required in Europe if Europe has defined the sort of external role it wants to play. The traditional requirements for the defence of national territorial borders have been significantly changed with the end of the Cold War. They retain an important residual role and provide the justification for the retention of nuclear weapons by the UK and France, who thereby continue to provide an element of deterrent protection for their European partners. However, the main uses of European armed forces in the last ten years have been, and most

---

[3] House of Commons, *Hansard,* 13 December 1999, Col 22.
[4] House of Commons, *Hansard*, 13 December 1999, Col 23.

probably will continue to be, in executing the 'Petersberg' tasks, of peacekeeping, humanitarian actions and crisis management. In defining common defence requirements, Europe needs to define the limits for these, both in terms of their geographical scope and the size of force that might be deployed. Europe's sense of its own responsibilities in these fields may evolve over time, but the experience of Kosovo might help the definition of some initial minimal targets for capabilities, with their related logistic, communication and sustainability requirements.

Trying to develop a consensus on Europe's external role, faces the problem of the best being the enemy of the good, a fear that arguing for a global role for Europe may provoke negative reactions from minorities in some countries and from majorities in others, and that this will in turn make it more difficult to achieve more modest objectives for European defence. Some argue that it is impossible for Europeans to come to a common position on issues of this sort in the abstract; they need to be dealing with specific crises before they can manage it. This amounts to a counsel of despair. Unless effective decisions have been made and action taken to achieve European defence capabilities well in advance of such a crisis, the range of options open to decision-makers will be very limited. However, only a phased policy of developing capabilities for force projection is probable for, apart from the political problems of going too far too fast, only limited financial resources are likely to be available. Even if Member States begin by developing capabilities for relatively limited missions, they need to build in 'stretchability', so that the initial force structures – as well as being useful in themselves – could also provide the foundations for larger forces with a longer reach at a later stage.

IV. What has Been Achieved

Beginning with the December 1998 Franco–British meeting at St Malo, these concepts were developed through various meetings in 1999 up to the European Council of December 1999 in Helsinki. Following the St Malo Declaration, which pointed the way towards an effective European defence, the NATO Washington summit of April 1999 responded very positively to the future role of the European Union. It picked up much of the language of the Declaration, particularly in its summit communiqué. Meeting shortly afterwards in Bremen, the foreign and defence ministers of the WEU countries took the debate further. But most important was the report submitted by the German Presidency to the European Council meeting in Cologne in June 1999, together with the European Council 'Declaration on Strengthening the Common European Policy on Security and Defence' adopted at Cologne and the subsequent reports approved by the European Council at Helsinki.

One of the most important developments in the St Malo Declaration was the assertion that the EU 'must have the capacity for autonomous action'.[5] This had long been a French objective and it was important that it was accepted by Britain. Even more importantly, it was also accepted by NATO as a whole. As the Washington communiqué put it: 'We acknowledge the resolve of the European Union to have the capacity for autonomous action so that it can take decisions and approve military action where the Alliance as a whole is not engaged'.[6] Thus, already in April, before the EU had formally come to its conclusion in Cologne, NATO had accepted the European right to autonomy and had broken with the view of some that NATO wished to maintain a monopoly in this field. This was in turn confirmed in the EU's Cologne Declaration which stated:

> In pursuit of our Common Foreign and Security Policy objectives and the progressive framing of a common defence policy, we are convinced that the Council should have the ability to take decisions on the full range of conflict prevention and crisis management tasks defined in the Treaty on European Union, the 'Petersberg tasks'. To this end, the Union must have the capacity for autonomous action, backed up by credible military forces, the means to decide to use them, and a readiness to do so, in order to respond to international crises without prejudice to actions by NATO.[7]

Parallel to this right of Europe to autonomy was the acceptance, by France as well as Britain, that:

> In strengthening the solidarity between the Member States of the European Union, in order that Europe can make its voice heard in world affairs, while acting in conformity with our respective obligations in NATO, we are contributing to the vitality of a modernised Atlantic Alliance which is the foundation of the collective defence of its members.[8]

This recognition of the centrality of NATO for collective (i.e. territorial) defence was important insofar as it removed any ambiguity about French attitudes. It was, of course, echoed in NATO documents; the Washington summit communiqué confirmed that 'a stronger European role will help contribute to the vitality of our Alliance for the 21st century, which is the foundation of the collective defence of its members'.[9]

This was then re-echoed in the EU's Cologne Declaration which stated that 'the Alliance remains the foundation of the collective defence of its Member

---

[5] Joint Declaration issued at the British–French summit, St Malo, France 3–4 December 1998, para. 2.
[6] Washington summit communiqué issued by the Heads of State or Government participating in the meeting of the North Atlantic Council in Washington, D.C. on 24 April 1999, para. 9a.
[7] European Council Declaration on Strengthening the Common European Policy on Security and Defence, Cologne 3–4 June, 1999, para. 1.
[8] Joint Declaration, St Malo, 3–4 December 1998, para 2.
[9] Washington summit communiqué, 24 April 1999, para. 9.

States.'[10] This was in fact only developing the assertion in the Amsterdam Treaty that:

> The policy of the Union ... shall respect the obligations of certain Member States which see their common defence realised in NATO, under the North Atlantic Treaty and be compatible with common security and defence policy established within that framework.[11]

which, in turn, echoed Art. J.4.4 of the Maastricht Treaty.

Autonomy implies the necessity for Europe to develop its own capabilities in the fields of intelligence, strategic transport, and command and control, and this was recognized in the St Malo document. '[The European] Union must be given appropriate structures and a capacity for analysis of situations, sources of intelligence, and a capability for relevant strategic planning, without unnecessary duplication'.[12] The Cologne European Council Declaration put the issue into a wider context, but picked up the same points, when the Member State committed themselves:

> to further develop more effective European military capabilities from the basis of existing national, bi-national and multinational capabilities and to strengthen our own capabilities for that purpose. This requires the maintenance of a sustained defence effort, the implementation of the necessary adaptations and notably the reinforcement of our capabilities in the field of intelligence, strategic transport, command and control.[13]

It is significant that this declaration was agreed by all 15 Member States including the four 'neutral' countries, and that it was developed further at the Helsinki European Council. The Presidency Conclusions reported that, 'Member States have also decided to develop rapidly collective capability goals in the fields of command and control, intelligence and strategic transport'.[14] The Conclusions also returned to the need to avoid 'unnecessary duplication' which, however, implies that some duplication is necessary, and reflects the fears of many Europeans of relying on an American monopoly in specific components of defence.

The issue of whether the EU should be solely reliant on NATO for the military structures it may require in any significant action, with the risk that the United States (or, in theory, any other non-EU alliance member) could prevent the use of NATO assets has been frequently raised. France, in particular, has been concerned that European autonomy required that Europe should not be

---

[10] European Council Declaration, 3–4 June 1999, para. 5.
[11] Treaty on European Union (Amsterdam) Art. 17.1 (J7.1).
[12] Joint Declaration, St Malo, 3–4 December 1998, para. 3.
[13] European Council Declaration, 3–4 June, 1999, para. 2.
[14] European Council, Presidency Conclusions, Helsinki, 10–11 December 1999.

reliant on an American decision. The need for a European alternative is addressed in the St Malo Declaration, which made clear that:

> In order for the European Union to take decisions and approve military action where the Alliance as a whole is not engaged ... the European Union will ... need to have recourse to suitable military means (European capabilities pre-designated within NATO's European pillar or national or multinational European means outside the NATO framework).[15]

The NATO approach was clearly described in the Washington summit communiqué:

> We therefore stand ready to define and adopt the necessary arrangements for ready access by the European Union to the collective assets and capabilities of the Alliance, for operations in which the Alliance as a whole is not engaged militarily as an Alliance. The Council in Permanent Session will approve these arrangements, which will respect the requirements of NATO operations and the coherence of its command structure, and should address:
>
> (a) assured EU access to NATO planning capabilities able to contribute to military planning for EU-led operations;
>
> (b) the presumption of availability to the EU of pre-identified NATO capabilities and common assets for use in EU-led operations;
>
> (c) [the] identification of a range of European command options for EU-led operations, further developing the role of DSACEUR in order for him to assume fully and effectively his European responsibilities;
>
> (d) the further adaptation of NATO's defence planning system to incorporate more comprehensively the availability of forces for EU-led operations.[16]

This goes much further than earlier NATO statements, firstly by referring throughout to the EU rather than WEU, thus taking for granted the new responsibilities of the EU. The reference in sub-section (b) of the presumption of the availability of pre-identified NATO capabilities and assets for use in EU-led operations also picks up the St Malo call for 'European capabilities pre-designated within NATO's European pillar'.

WEU ministers at Bremen referred to the progress that had been made between WEU and NATO when 'they welcomed the agreement with NATO of a framework document on the release of assets to WEU, and of improved consultation arrangements in the event of a WEU-led operation using NATO assets and capabilities'.[17]

The report of the German Presidency to the EU's Cologne summit returned to the issue of the two alternative approaches of using or not using NATO. The summit Declaration stated:

[15] Joint Declaration, St Malo, France 3–4 December 1998, para 3.
[16] Washington summit communiqué, 24 April 1999, para. 10.
[17] WEU Ministerial Meeting, Bremen 10–11 May 1999, Bremen Declaration, para. 6.

For the effective implementation of EU-led operations the European Union will have to determine, according to the requirements of the case, whether it will conduct:

– EU-led operations using NATO assets and capabilities, or
– EU-led operations without recourse to NATO assets and capabilities.

For EU-led operations without recourse to NATO assets and capabilities, the EU could use national or multinational European means pre-identified by Member States. This will require either the use of national command structures providing multinational representation in headquarters or drawing on existing command structures within multinational forces. Further arrangements to enhance the capacity of European multinational and national forces to respond to crises situations will be needed.

For EU-led operations having recourse to NATO assets and capabilities, including European command arrangements, the main focus should be on the following aspects:

Implementation of the arrangements based on the Berlin decisions of 1996 and the Washington NATO summit decisions of April 1999. The further arrangements set out by NATO at its summit meeting in Washington should address in particular: assured EU access to NATO planning capabilities able to contribute to military planning for EU-led operations; the presumption of availability to the EU of pre-identified NATO capabilities and common assets for use in EU-led operations.[18]

These statements indicate both the practical way in which the EU's substantive military options have developed and the efforts made by European members of NATO, particularly the UK and Germany, to ensure that the Washington NATO and EU Cologne documents were consistent.[19] That is not to suggest that everything went smoothly: the fact that the Cologne document dealt with 'EU-led operations *without* recourse to NATO assets and capabilities' ahead of 'EU-led operations *having recourse to* NATO assets and capabilities', thereby reversing the order initially used, led to a certain overreaction from some in Washington who suggested that this implied the marginalization of NATO. There were cries that Europe should act only if NATO were not prepared to act. The third paragraph of the Finnish Presidency's Conclusions from the Helsinki European Council responded to this and also, in its final phrase, addressed a particular British neurosis:

The European Council underlines its determination to develop an autonomous capacity to take decisions and, where NATO as a whole is not engaged, to launch and conduct EU-led military operations in response to international

---

[18] Report from the German Presidency on strengthening the common European policy on security and defence submitted to the European Council, Cologne, June 1999, para. 4.
[19] This close co-operation has been confirmed by senior British and German officials.

crises. This process will avoid unnecessary duplication and does not imply the creation of a European army.[20]

V. The Problems of Asymmetry

One of the issues which has caused most anxiety in the discussions on the EU's assumption of the WEU's defence responsibilities has been the position of the six European members of NATO who are not members of the EU. While the three countries that joined NATO in March 1999 – Hungary, Poland and the Czech Republic – are due to become members of the EU and thus present only a transitional problem, of the other three, Turkey was only accepted at Helsinki as a candidate for membership (and no date has been set for entry negotiations to begin), and Norway and Iceland are not even applicants. Each of the last three have had associate member status in WEU since 1993. The most difficult problems relate to Turkey which, until Helsinki at least, felt rejected by the EU. Both the Washington and Cologne documents reflect the fact that some of the most difficult discussions at the NATO Washington summit turned on the issue of the prospective position of Turkey.

The Washington NATO summit communiqué makes clear that NATO attaches 'the utmost importance to ensuring the fullest possible involvement of non-EU European Allies in EU-led crisis response operations, building on existing consultation arrangements within the WEU'.[21] The WEU ministers at their Bremen meeting made an interim response to this, noting 'the need for WEU to be operationally effective with the involvement and participation of all WEU nations in accordance with their status and to continue its co-operation with the EU and NATO, in preparation for any new arrangements which may be agreed in light of ongoing developments'.[22] The reference to 'all WEU nations' is interesting in that it implies not only the ten members of WEU and the five observers (who are, of course, the other members of the EU), but also the six associate members and seven associate partners.[23] The EU Cologne Declaration was even more specific, saying:

> We want to develop an effective EU-led crisis management in which NATO members, as well as neutral and non-allied members, of the EU can participate fully and on an equal footing in the EU operations. We will put in place arrangements that allow non-EU European allies and partners to take part to the fullest possible extent in this endeavour.[24]

---

[20] European Council, Presidency Conclusions, Helsinki, 10–11 December 1999.
[21] Washington summit communiqué, 24 April 1999, para. 9d.
[22] WEU Ministerial Meeting, Bremen 10–11 May 1999, Bremen Declaration, para. 4.
[23] Bulgaria, Estonia, Latvia, Lithuania, Romania, Slovakia and Slovenia.
[24] European Council Declaration, Cologne 3–4 June, 1999, para. 3.

The German Presidency Report itself went further:

> The successful creation of a European policy on security and defence will require in particular:
> * the possibility of all EU Member States, including non-allied members, to participate fully and on an equal footing in EU operations;
> * satisfactory arrangements for European NATO members who are not EU Member States to ensure their fullest possible involvement in EU-led operations, building on existing consultation arrangements within WEU;
> * arrangements to ensure that all participants in an EU-led operation will have equal rights in respect of the conduct of that operation, without prejudice to the principle of the EU's decision-making autonomy, notably the right of the Council to discuss and decide matters of principle and policy;
> * the need to ensure the development of effective mutual consultation, co-operation and transparency between NATO and the EU;
> * the consideration of ways to ensure the possibility for WEU Associate Partners to be involved.[25]

This rather complex statement indicates the persistent nature of the problem facing the EU, which wishes to preserve the clear position of the EU Council in decision-making but, nonetheless, wants to respond to the legitimate concerns of other European allies and partners. The Helsinki Presidency Conclusions returned to the problem:

> Modalities will be developed for full consultation, co-operation and transparency between the EU and NATO, taking into account the needs of all EU Member States; appropriate arrangements will be defined that would allow, while respecting the Union's decision-making autonomy, non-EU European NATO members and other interested States to contribute to EU military crisis management.[26]

The Helsinki Conclusions illustrate a further important issue that both the Washington NATO documents and the Cologne EU documents had begun to address – the actual relationship between the EU and NATO. The two organizations may be based in the same city, but they have had very little interaction, at any level. The WEU has attempted to act as a bridge, but without any very great success. It was therefore important that the Washington NATO summit communiqué should say that, 'NATO and the EU should ensure the development of effective mutual consultation, co-operation and transparency, building on the mechanisms existing between NATO and the WEU'.[27] The EU

[25] Report from the German Presidency on strengthening the common European policy on security and defence submitted to the European Council, Cologne, June 1999, para. 5.
[26] European Council, Presidency Conclusions, Helsinki, 10–11 December 1999.
[27] Washington summit communiqué, 24 April 1999, para. 9b.

Cologne Declaration responded to this by saying that, 'in implementing this process launched by the EU, we shall ensure the development of effective mutual consultation, co-operation and transparency between the European Union and NATO'.[28]

This further example of the two organizations using almost exactly the same formulation is of course encouraging but, given the ingrained habits and cultures of the two institutions, putting this into practice will not be easy.

VI. Implementation

As the Cologne Declaration said:

> We are now determined to launch a new step in the construction of the European Union. To this end we task the General Affairs Council to prepare the conditions and the measures necessary to achieve these objectives, including the definition of the modalities for the inclusion of those functions of the WEU which will be necessary for the EU to fulfil its new responsibilities in the area of the Petersberg tasks. In this regard, our aim is to take the necessary decisions by the end of the year 2000. In that event, the WEU as an organisation would have completed its purpose.[29]

In fact, the Helsinki European Council made considerable progress in setting operational targets, a 'headline goal', by agreeing:

> They [the Member States] will be able to deploy rapidly and then sustain forces capable of the full range of Petersberg tasks as set out in the Amsterdam Treaty, including the most demanding, in operations of up to corps level (up to 15 brigades or 50,000–60,000 persons). These forces should be militarily self-sustaining with the necessary command, control and intelligence capabilities, logistics, other combat support services, and additionally, as appropriate air and naval elements. Member States should be able to deploy in full at this level within 60 days, and within this to provide smaller rapid response elements available and deployable at very high readiness. They must be able to sustain such a deployment for at least one year. This will require an additional pool of deployable units (and supporting elements) at lower readiness to provide replacements for the initial forces.[30]

The Helsinki Conclusions went on:

> Member States have also decided to develop rapidly collective capability goals in the fields of command and control, intelligence and strategic transport.[31]

---

[28] European Council Declaration, Cologne, 3–4 June 1999 para. 3.
[29] European Council Declaration, Cologne, 3–4 June 1999, para. 5.
[30] European Council, Presidency Conclusions, Helsinki, 10–11 December 1999.
[31] European Council, Presidency Conclusions, Helsinki, 10–11 December 1999.

In some ways this was more significant because these are the three areas in which, in the past, the Europeans have been dependent on the Americans and which have inhibited European autonomy.

The Helsinki Council also took important decisions on the institutional side:

new political and military bodies and structures will be established within the Council to enable the Union to ensure the necessary political guidance and strategic direction to such operations, while respecting the single institutional framework;

modalities will be developed for full consultation, co-operation and transparency between the EU and NATO, taking into account the needs of all EU Member States;

appropriate arrangements will be defined that would allow, while respecting the Union's decision-making autonomy, non-EU European NATO members and other interested States to contribute to EU military crisis management;

the General Affairs Council is invited to begin implementing these decisions by establishing as of March 2000 the agreed interim bodies and arrangements within the Council, in accordance with the current Treaty provisions.[32]

The details of these three new bodies were set out in the Finnish Presidency's 'Progress Report to the Helsinki European Council ...':

(a) A standing Political and Security Committee (PSC) in Brussels will be composed of national representatives of senior/ambassadorial level. The PSC will deal with all aspects of the CFSP, including the CESDP, in accordance with the provisions of the EU Treaty and without prejudice to Community competence. In the case of a military crisis management operation, the PSC will exercise, under the authority of the Council, the political control and strategic direction of the operation. For that purpose, appropriate procedures will be adopted in order to allow effective and urgent decision taking. The PSC will also forward guidelines to the Military Committee.

(b) The Military Committee (MC) will be composed of the Chiefs of Defence, represented by their military delegates. The MC will meet at the level of the Chiefs of Defence as and when necessary. This committee will give military advice and make recommendations to the PSC, as well as provide military direction to the Military Staff. The Chairman of the MC will attend meetings of the Council when decisions with defence implications are to be taken.

(c) The Military Staff (MS) within the Council structures will provide military expertise and support to the CESDP, including the conduct of EU-led military crisis management operations. The Military Staff will perform

---

[32] European Council, Presidency Conclusions, Helsinki, 10–11 December 1999.

early warning, situation assessment and strategic planning for Petersberg tasks including identification of European national and multinational forces.[33]

Thus at the beginning of March 2000 the interim Political and Security Committee (PSC) [34] began meeting on a weekly basis, and each Member State seconded a serving military officer to work in the Council Secretariat and form the nucleus of the European Union's future military staff.[35] The Military Committee, made up of the military representatives of the Chiefs of Defence Staff of Member States also met for the first time in March.

Another important, though less commented on development of Helsinki was a second report on the EU's work on the non-military dimensions of crisis management. The EU's comparative advantage is that it has the possibility of responding to crises using a range of instruments. As the High Representative for CFSP, Javier Solana said at the launch of the PSC in Brussels:

> Our aim is to equip the Union to respond effectively to international crises using all the tools at its disposal: diplomacy, economic measures, humanitarian assistance and, ultimately, the use of military forces. The ability to integrate these measures will set the EU apart and allow it to play an international role consistent with its responsibilities and the expectations of its citizens.[36]

Thus the EU has the potential to have a full range of external policies, whereas NATO is limited in being only an instrument of its members for the military dimension of their policy. During the Cold War, when the collective defence of Member States was the principal objective of foreign policy, NATO was central, but post-Cold War, external policy requires a more subtle mix of instruments, of which military force may be one, but is not exclusively so. Now that it has been agreed that the CFSP will have a military component, which was not done at Maastricht or Amsterdam but at Cologne and Helsinki, the European Union has potentially a more complete range of instruments to develop its Foreign and Security Policy.

VII. The Remaining Problems

That said, there is a risk of confusion over the two words 'common' and 'defence'. The CFSP is not 'common' in the same way as policies in Pillar One, where common policies such as the Common Agricultural Policy or Common

---

[33] Annex 1 to Annex IV of the Presidency Progress Report to the Helsinki European Council on Strengthening the Common European Policy on Security and Defence.
[34] More frequently known by its French acronym (COPS).
[35] The head of the military experts is the UK Brigadier Graham Messervy-Whiting, a former Deputy Director of WEU and Military Adviser to Lord Owen when he was co-chairman of the International Conference on Former Yugoslavia (Secretary General/High Representative Press Release 08/03/2000).
[36] Secretary General/High Representative Press Release 01/03/2000.

Commercial Policy are developed by the Commission and agreed by the Council. In Pillar Two, foreign security and defence policies are developed intergovernmentally, although the High Representative, with his Policy Unit and Military Staff in the Council Secretariat might be seen as proto-Commission. However, the policy developed is not yet seen by Member States, and least of all by Britain and France, as a substitute for national policies.

Secondly, 'defence' also produces problems. While the EU is developing a military dimension, it is not yet taking on responsibilities for the territorial defence of its Member States, which most citizens would assume to be the essence of defence. It seems very unlikely that Art. V of the Modified Brussels Treaty (the legal basis for WEU), which provides a collective defence commitment among its members and parallels Art. 5 of NATO's Washington Treaty will be transferred to the EU at the end of 2000. This is for three reasons: first, the four non-members of NATO – Austria, Ireland, Finland and Sweden – as well as Denmark, are at present opposed to the EU becoming what they would consider to be a military alliance. Secondly, there would be problems if the EU were to assume the functions of collective defence when countries like Estonia and Slovenia which are, at present, outside NATO became members of the EU. It would be difficult to prevent them from being covered by this part of the *acquis*. And yet, it would be extremely complicated for the military planners of NATO member states to implement collective defence guarantees for countries that were not members of NATO, irrespective of the effect this would have on EU–Russian relations. Assuming such a function would mean that the EU was in some sense duplicating NATO's collective defence role and would suggest a decoupling of the two bodies. The third reason for not incorporating Art. V of the Brussels Treaty into the Treaty on European Union is that it would be seen by some as an attempt to compete with NATO, which would counter the wishes of the Member States. Fortunately, in practice, collective territorial defence is no longer as central a question as it was in the Cold War for the existing EU members.

In spite of these reservations, much progress has been made. But there are three sets of problems that must be resolved before there can be an effective European defence component of the Common Foreign and Security Policy: the conceptual problems of the objectives of European defence, operational problems of force structures and resources, and institutional problems linked to effective decision-making. All three sets of problems need to be resolved, but that does not mean that all three have to be fully resolved before anything can be done, nor that, as has been outlined, we cannot take any useful steps. The development of a Common Defence Policy for the European Union will be like other dimensions of EU policy, something that will develop over time.

The conceptual problems involve answering the question of what we want a European defence capability to be able to do. It is generally agreed that it needs to be well grounded in a common foreign policy and, like the 1997–98 British Strategic Defence Review, the EU's Common Defence Policy should be foreign policy-led. The problem here is that the EU has not yet really defined what sort of actor it wants to be in world affairs. While few still argue for its limitation to a 'civilian power', there is a continued open question as to whether Europe should behave as a 'regional power', worried primarily about trouble in its immediate neighbourhood. Certainly much of current European foreign policy is driven less by humanitarian motives than by an aversion to refugees. Or again, there are those who would say that Europe has wider, global security responsibilities and should envisage becoming a strategic partner of the United States.

Europe's role in the world is likely to be defined, in part, by doing, but it will be difficult to have a common foreign policy in the absence of a common political culture. There are still very different national reactions to different situations and it has been much more difficult to define a CFSP for Europe in the post-Cold War world than was probably envisaged. In the Cold War, the external challenge imposed common objectives. Now, it is more difficult to define what we want instruments of foreign policy for, including armed forces.

Taking Germany as an example, there has in the decade since the end of the Cold War, been a remarkable movement in the readiness to use armed forces for purposes other than territorial defence. But there is still a much greater reluctance to see the military dimension of European foreign policy having a global role, and the claims here of the French and – to the extent they exist – British are seen as post-imperial delusions. Germany does not seem yet to have absorbed the American wish to have Europe contributing to global security responsibilities. There is potential here for tension, not only with the more globally-inclined British and French, but also with the USA.

The second group of problems are 'operational ones that arise from the question of how Europe is going to acquire the capabilities needed for effective force projection'. It is unlikely that there will be more resources available for defence, hence the only way forward is national restructuring and the development of more pooled European forces. This would bring about economies of scale and the removal of the absurd duplication between the support, training and logistic elements of the armed forces of European countries. It can be argued that the only way the European taxpayer can get value for money will be to operate in common many of the force elements now deployed on a national basis. This is already done in the case of most European members of NATO for airborne early warning and control aircraft (AWACS). This may be easier to extend for air forces, but there are clearly elements of naval support and logistic support for ground forces where the same approach could be used.

The funding of such common elements is linked to the third set of problems for European defence, which are institutional. From the time the three pillars were introduced at Maastricht, Britain and France have insisted that CFSP and, *a fortiori*, any Common Defence Policy should remain intergovernmental rather than *communautaire*. This has implied the virtual exclusion of the Commission, Parliament and European Court of Justice from defence matters. There is always a sensitive balance in the EU between intergovernmentalism and supranationality, but the CFSP is an area where there is need for quick and effective decision- making. There is therefore perhaps a case for re-examining the pillar structure. This is unlikely to take place at the Intergovernmental Conference of 2000 since a number of Member States have been determined to limit the agenda. But a further IGC may be necessary in 2003–04 when more substantial changes might be examined. In the absence of change, however, the CFSP and Defence Policy are likely to be dominated by informal *directoires*. In the meantime, the intergovernmental character of Pillar Two also removes one of the useful potential levers to achieving more effective defence co-operation, the EU's budget. This could be used to fund pooled force capacities and would avoid the problem of free-riders, countries who enjoy the benefits without making an appropriate contribution. It has been suggested that even under Pillar Two, a European defence fund could be created, on a basis comparable to the existing European development fund, outside the budget and therefore removed from the intervention of the European Parliament.

These problems demonstrate that, in spite of the remarkable progress since the end of 1998 to develop a defence dimension for the European Union, a number of key questions are still to be addressed. That they are on the agenda indicates that there has been progress. Tony Blair, therefore, deserves at least two cheers for his energetic reopening of this dossier, a European accolade rarely, if ever received, by a British prime minister since the UK's accession in 1973.

Journal of Common Market Studies

Volume 38, Annual Review
September 2000

Governance and Institutions 1999: Resignation, Reform and Renewal

DESMOND DINAN
George Mason University

I. Introduction

1999 will long be remembered as the year of the Commission's collapse. Already on shaky ground once the European Parliament (EP) refused to grant a budget discharge in 1998, the Commission's position became untenable in March 1999, following the release of a damning investigation into its activities. The report of a group of independent experts confirmed in embarrassing detail what many had long suspected: that 'fraud, irregularities or mismanagement' were widespread in a Commission beyond political control. The Commission's resignation triggered an institutional upheaval. Building on work begun by the old Commission, the new Commission President, Romano Prodi, and Vice-President Neil Kinnock launched a 'root and branch' overhaul of the Brussels bureaucracy. Their ambitious goal was to alter not only administrative procedures and practices, but also the culture of the Commission itself.

Although it had a widespread impact beyond the Commission, the resignation crisis did not undermine the EU system or profoundly alter the EU's vaguely defined interinstitutional balance. Even while the disgraced College remained in office in a caretaker capacity for six more months, the EU did not grind to a halt. And if the Commission's weakness under Jacques Santer, the outgoing President, had been exaggerated, its strength under his successor, Romano Prodi, was equally exaggerated. For a variety of reasons stretching back to the early 1990s, the Commission's political influence was as circumscribed at the beginning of 1999 as it was at the end the year. The quality of Commission leadership matters less in an inauspicious political climate than it does when circumstances favour Commission entrepreneurship. Regardless of who was President and regardless of the political climate, the Commission continued to play a leading role in those areas for which it was primarily responsible, such as conducting commercial policy and managing the single market.

The EP's assertion of accountability did not so much tip the institutional balance as redress an institutional imbalance. In principle, the Commission has always been accountable to the Parliament, in practice it must now behave accordingly. This did not make the Commission unduly deferential to the EP, as Prodi gently but firmly showed, for instance, during the investiture of his Commission and in his strategy towards the Intergovernmental Conference (IGC). Fear of parliamentary censure should help to keep the Commission's house in order, and internal reform is likely to enhance the Commission's conduct of legislative and executive affairs. This, in turn, should bolster the Commission's position in its day-to-day dealings with the Council and the Parliament.

The EP also experienced an upheaval, but of a much less traumatic kind. The elections of June 1999 resulted in the centre-right European People's Party (EPP) displacing the Party of European Socialists (PES) as the largest group in the EP, for the first time since the advent of direct elections 20 years before. More important, the EPP decided not to renew its joint management agreement with the PES, under which the EP's two biggest groups had monopolized parliamentary affairs to the detriment of the other groups and, arguably, also to the detriment of parliamentary democracy in the EU. The falling out of the EPP and the PES, which originated in part in their respective handling of the Commission crisis, introduced a keener edge into the conduct of parliamentary business at a time when the Amsterdam Treaty greatly extended the range of the codecision procedure.

The Commission crisis overshadowed implementation of the Treaty on 1 May, although this would have been a low-key affair in any case. Few of the Treaty's provisions were particularly eye-catching, and most were put into effect quickly and quietly once it was legally permissible to do so, at the end of a lengthy ratification procedure. The appointment of Javier Solana as 'Mr CFSP', in June 1999, was an exception. This highly publicized event drew attention to the EU's rapidly developing security and defence identity. A special summit in Tampere in Finland in October 1999, devoted to Justice and Home Affairs (JHA), drew attention to another policy area significantly altered by the Amsterdam Treaty, a policy area for which there appeared to be considerable public support.

Notwithstanding the Commission crisis, 1999 was a year of big decisions for the EU, notably on *Agenda 2000*, the Common European Security and Defence Policy (CESDP), enlargement, and Turkey's candidacy for membership. Decision-making in these highly politicized areas required skill on the part of the Council Presidency and a heavy investment of time and effort by the Heads of State or Government (HOSG). The European Council met unusually often in 1999: in addition to the regular end-of-presidency summits and the Tampere summit, there was a special summit in Berlin in March 1999 to conclude *Agenda 2000*, a special summit in Brussels the previous month to pave the way for an agreement in Berlin, and a special summit in Brussels the following month to discuss the Commission crisis (although Kosovo dominated that meeting).

The European Council therefore showed itself again in 1999 to be an indispensable forum for making decisions, setting agendas and giving strategic direction. European Councils are the tip of an iceberg: innumerable preparatory meetings, at all levels, lie beneath the surface and help shape a summit's outcome. Nevertheless, relations between EU leaders inevitably affect a European Council's conduct and results. 1999 was noteworthy in that respect with Santer's presence as acting Commission President an embarrassment to the other summiteers. Prodi's arrival was greeted with relief (the Tampere summit was Prodi's first as Commission President). Yet goodwill and bonhomie were not sufficient to put a strong Commission imprint on the European Council. Personal considerations notwithstanding, Prodi's potential influence may be significant but in 1999 was relatively limited because the Commission's influence was somewhat restrained in the rarefied realm of big decision-making, especially on issues relating to JHA and CESDP, where intergovernmentalism continued to reign supreme.

II. The Commission Resignation Crisis

The new year could not have opened on a more dramatic note. Following a bruising encounter at the EP's plenary session in December 1998 over allegations of corruption and cronyism in the EU executive, Parliament and the Commission were on a collision course. Yet the Commission escaped censure and removal from office during a showdown on 14 January because the EP's two main political groups were divided among and within themselves. The PES, then in a majority, backed away from its own vote of censure for fear of provoking an institutional crisis. The EPP seemed more interested in targeting the Commission's two most vulnerable members – both socialists – than in ousting the Commission as a whole. In the circumstances, only 232 MEPs voted in favour of censure, with 292 voting against and 27 abstaining.

The unsuccessful effort to censure the Commission represented a setback for the EP and especially for the PES, whose leader, Pauline Green, found her position seriously weakened. Lack of co-operation between the PES and EPP over the censure motion contributed to the breakdown, after direct elections, of the parties' monopoly of EP affairs, a minor upheaval that may have important repercussions for the institution's future.

The Commission had survived the censure battle, but would soon lose the accountability war. In return for the main political groups' willingness not to recommend censure, the Commission acquiesced in the establishment of a committee of independent experts to inquire into prevailing allegations. As the Committee set about its work, interviewing Commissioners and examining Commission files, and as new allegations of Commission egregiousness surfaced, it became clear that the Committee's report would be devastating. Such, indeed, was the case. One widely reported sentence in the lengthy report, published on 15 March, proved especially injurious: 'It is becoming difficult to find anyone [in the Commission] who has even the slightest sense of responsibility'.

The Commission might still have survived had it been able to sack Edith Cresson, who had been singled out in the report for blatant cronyism, and who for the EP personified all that was wrong with the Commission. Although Santer initially pressed her to leave, legally Cresson could not be fired and, politically, she retained the French government's support. Once the EP made it clear that a Commission that still included Cresson would not survive another vote of censure, the Commission had no choice but to accept the consequences of collegiality and resign as a body.

Far from being the result of a calculated parliamentary manœuvre, the Commission's collapse was the culmination of a series of mistakes and misjudgements in both institutions. But the widespread perception was that Parliament had finally come of age and asserted its authority over an arrogant and corrupt Commission. As perception shapes political reality, the events of March 1999, indeed, represented a major institutional advance for Parliament, although not necessarily a major institutional reversal for the Commission. By 'throwing the rascals out' (even though the rascals jumped before they were pushed), the EP was seen to have asserted its right to hold the Commission accountable.

Ironically, and awkwardly for everyone concerned, the Commission remained in place for a further six months, in an acting capacity. Whereas the Treaty provided for the Commission's removal, it did not stipulate a timetable for dissolving a caretaker administration. Emboldened by the credit accruing to it for the Commission's resignation, and eager to avert institutional drift, the EP sought to install a new, interim Commission to complete the outgoing

Commission's statutory period in office (until January 2000), and then to install a successor Commission for the next five years (until January 2005). Largely uninvolved so far in the crisis, the Council now took control. Within a week, the Heads of State or Government nominated Prodi to succeed Santer until January 2005, not January 2000. Because it would take them more time to nominate the other Commissioners, and because the EP would be caught up in the elections and their aftermath in June and July, the Council set a timetable whereby the new Commission could not be confirmed until September. The only way for the EP to have thwarted the Council would have been to delay confirmation of the Commission even further or not to confirm the new Commission at all. These were politically unpalatable alternatives. As a result, the Council effectively tied the EP's hands.

In January 1999, Prodi, whose name had surfaced the previous year as a possible successor to Santer (see last year's EU *Review of Activities*), told *Le Monde* that he was definitely not a candidate for the job. Three months later he was drafted by the HOSG because he was the right man (a senior, centrist politician) in the right place (a southern Member State) at the right time (currently unemployed). Thus, the once and possibly future Italian Prime Minister became the Commission President-designate. In view of his proclamation to *Le Monde* and the state of interinstitutional relations in Brussels, Prodi may well have preferred to be the *current* Italian Prime Minister; the Italian government enthusiastically supported Prodi's nomination for a job in Brussels partly for that reason.

The EP overwhelmingly ratified Prodi's nomination on 5 May (392 votes to 72, with 41 abstentions). Acting under the provisions of the newly implemented Amsterdam Treaty, Prodi set about selecting his team of Commissioners 'in common accord' with national governments. In fact, most national governments acted largely as they had done in the past, paying only lip-service to Prodi. German Chancellor Schröder's nomination of one Commissioner from each of the governing coalition parties (in keeping with tradition) infuriated the EPP which, having just become the largest group in Parliament, interpreted the results as a popular mandate for a majority of EPP members in the new Commission. Considering that the Euro-elections were second-order elections and that the turnout was low, this was a bold claim. Understandably, Schröder gave it short shrift.

The Prodi Commission included four leftovers from the Santer Commission – four too many, as far as some MEPs were concerned. Politically, most of the Commissioners were from the left, as were most governments in the Council. Prodi managed to maintain the gender balance of the old Commission, which in fact was a gender imbalance of five women and 15 men. The allocation of portfolios proved less contentious than on previous occasions, with Prodi having considerable latitude to organize Commissioners' areas of responsibility. At the end of the process, he was proud to proclaim that 'each member of the new team has a real job'.

While putting his team together, Prodi sought to assert his authority vis-à-vis the Parliament, as well as the Council. Specifically, he refused to jettison any Commissioner not to the Parliament's liking, unless the EP uncovered evidence of a candidate's unsuitability for office. Here Prodi walked a delicate line, on the one hand somewhat beholden to a resurgent EP and, on the other hand, trying to maintain his own and the Commission's independence. In the event, the EP's investiture proceedings were uneventful. Candidate Commissioners' questionnaires and auditions threw some light on the new Commission's strategy and preferences, but the procedure was otherwise uninspiring. Empty threats by the EPP not to confirm the Prodi Commission had a lot to do with domestic German politics (the EPP's new political leader was a German Christian Democrat who deeply resented Schröder's decision not to appoint a Christian Democratic Commissioner). In a series of votes on 15 September, the EP overwhelmingly approved the new Commission.

The Prodi Commission was finally installed on 17 September. Santer had left office four weeks earlier to become an MEP (of all things). In a fitting footnote to the entire débâcle, Manuel Marin, one of the Commissioners at the heart of the crisis, became acting President until Prodi's assumption of office. The acting Commission had launched no new initiatives, but had not shirked from conducting essential EU activities either.

Overall, the crisis can only have helped the Commission. Radical internal reform, long overdue, rightly became a priority. Accountability, for long a vague concept, became a meaningful political instrument. The Commission's role and responsibilities nevertheless remained unchanged. The outcome of the resignation crisis would probably strengthen, rather than weaken, the Commission's potential political influence, which would ultimately depend on a wide range of prevailing circumstances. The EP emerged a winner from the crisis in the sense that one of its powers – control over the Commission – was greatly enhanced. The Council also emerged triumphant as the arbiter of a bitter interinstitutional dispute.

III. The Prodi Reformation

For obvious reasons, internal Commission reform was at the top of the new President's agenda. Commission reform was not a new issue: Santer had launched a reform programme when he became President in 1995. In January 1999, when the Commission narrowly escaped censure and agreed to the establishment of an experts' committee, Santer had tried to appease the EP by announcing a new reform programme covering issues such as the structure of Directorates-General (DGs) and services; the responsibilities of Commissioners, *cabinets* and senior officials; the fight against fraud; and the strengthening of financial management. At the end of January, Santer outlined an accelerated reform schedule, setting deadlines for various actions to be taken throughout the year. Speaking before the storm broke, Santer used Prodi-like language when he declared that 'we are laying the foundation of a truly European administrative culture based on independence, efficiency and transparency'. Ironically, it was Santer's reform initiatives – notably the 'screening exercise' (staff stocktaking) undertaken as part of *Designing the Commission of Tomorrow*, and the far-reaching *Sound and Efficient Management 2000* project – that laid a solid foundation for the Prodi reformation.

Prodi, himself, was in no doubt about the urgency of reform. No sooner was he nominated as President than he announced his intention to take numerous steps going well beyond what Santer had envisioned to overhaul the Commission. These included strengthening recently approved codes of conduct for Commissioners and senior officials; denationalizing and slimming down the *cabinets*; launching a major shake-up of portfolios and Directorates-General; allocating responsibility for reform to one of the two Commission Vice-Presidents; and preparing a comprehensive reform strategy for release in February 2000.

Apart from changes in his own *cabinet*, the first manifestations of the Prodi reformation were the configuration of Commissioners' portfolios and the staffing of Directorates-General at the highest level. Commission portfolios have changed with every new presidency, but rarely as much as when Prodi took over. To some extent Prodi's reorganization merely reflected changes in the EU itself, especially since the implementation of the Amsterdam Treaty. Thus, for instance, Prodi established new portfolios and corresponding DGs exclusively for JHA and enlargement. To a greater extent, however, Prodi used the reform momentum to overcome Member State resistance to a rationalization of portfolios and DGs. Thus, for instance, he reorganized the external affairs portfolios along thematic lines, merged agriculture and fisheries, and brought bits of existing portfolios together in a new enterprise portfolio. In the course of these changes, Prodi reduced the number of Commission DGs and services from 42 to 36.

Prodi also insisted that Commissioners move out of the Commission's headquarters (the Breydel building) and into the buildings scattered throughout Brussels where their DGs were located. In addition, he made a small but important symbolic change: instead of being known by number, as had been the case throughout the EU's history, DGs would henceforth be known by function, e.g. DG Agriculture or DG Energy and Transport (TREN). This has meant a painful relearning process for professors of European integration.

One of the most dramatic events of the Prodi reformation was the shake-up of top Commission positions (at the A1 and A2 levels) that took place on 29 September. The reconfiguration of portfolios and services required a reallocation of senior staff in any case, but the urgency of reform gave the Commission an opportunity to attack entrenched national positions. In doing so, the Commission broke up France's lock on agriculture and Italy's lock on economic and financial affairs. The Commission also got rid of poor performers (an almost unheard-of occurrence) and announced that some senior positions would be filled by outside candidates (another unprecedented move).

The Commission's attempt to end the practice of attaching national flags to senior positions highlighted the problems of nationality in a multinational bureaucracy. Promotion to the Commission's senior ranks had long depended on nationality as much as, or even more than, merit. This sapped the morale of able and ambitious mid-level officials who belonged to the 'wrong' nationality. While recognizing the importance of having a multinational staff (at all levels) in a multinational EU, the new Commission sought to strike a balance between experience, ability and country of origin. The Commission could not have attempted this without Member States' support. Nevertheless the continuing, if not increasing, sensitivity of the nationality question was demonstrated by blatant pressure from the Spanish Prime Minister to appoint more Spaniards to senior Commission positions, and a growing debate in Germany about the country's under-representation in the Brussels bureaucracy.

Perhaps because the British government was so bullish for reform, Prodi chose Neil Kinnock – ironically one of the leftovers from the disgraced Commission – to head the new reform portfolio. This led to accusations that Prodi was too enamoured of the 'Anglo-Saxon' approach to public administration. Implicit in the Prodi/Kinnock approach, according to its critics, was a rejection of the predominant French imprint on the institution's development since the days of the High Authority. Others advocated the 'Nordic model' of public administration (a variation of the Anglo-Saxon model that emphasized individual responsibility, transparency and modern management practices). The debate about contending models and approaches further highlighted the challenge of reforming such a heterogeneous, multinational body as the Commission.

Working with a Reform Group of seven Commissioners, and heading a Task Force for Administrative Reform (TFAR), Kinnock threw himself energetically into the fray. Even before the task force was established, the need for major reform was once again highlighted, this time by the publication in early September of a second report by the Group of Independent Experts.

© Blackwell Publishers Ltd 2000

Unlike the first report, which had examined specific allegations against the Commission, the second report was more reflective and less incendiary (much to the disappointment of the EP). In it, the independent experts described in great detail the Commission's structural and cultural inadequacies, and recommended numerous changes. These ranged from the general (such as a complete overhaul of personnel policy, including recruitment, promotion and career development), to the specific (such as the establishment of a Committee of Standards in Public Life and an EU Public Prosecutor's Office). On a topical note, the report recommended greater protection for whistle-blowers (this was a covert criticism of how the new Commission had treated an official who had blown the whistle on the previous Commission). Kinnock promised to incorporate most of the report's recommendations into his reform strategy, but shied away from those, such as the proposal for a Public Prosecutor's Office, that could prove too difficult for Member States to enact.

This was the background to the reform strategy unveiled in February 2000. The challenge was obvious. The Commission needs to introduce fewer but better legislative initiatives. Commissioners and senior officials need to develop a sense of responsibility and become more accountable for their actions. *Cabinets* need to be reigned in. Financial controls need to be tightened and financial management strengthened. Administrative procedures need to be improved. Most difficult of all, deeply entrenched attitudes and modes of behaviour have to be changed.

Most of these reforms are likely to be implemented, however slowly and painfully. Yet given its multinational, multicultural and multilingual character, and given also the nature of the EU system, the Commission will never conform to neat political and administrative models. For reasons of legitimacy, a rough balance of nationalities will always be important. For reasons of prestige and national advantage, Member States will always seek to influence staff policy and the implementation of EU legislation. For systemic reasons, the Commission can never become simply an executive body. Thus the Commission can be reformed, but there are limits to how much it can be transformed.

IV. The European Parliament

The EP enjoyed a less tumultuous year than the Commission, but was not impervious to change. This came mostly as a result of direct elections in June 1999, but was due also to fallout from the Commission resignation crisis. Internal reform in the EP in 1999 was limited largely to a contentious effort to implement a statute for MEPs, in accordance with a provision of the Amsterdam Treaty.

Direct Elections

The fifth direct elections to the EP took place on 10–13 June. For the fourth time, the turnout was lower than previously (down from 56.8 per cent in 1994 to 49.9 per cent in 1999). Although each of the main party groups had published manifestos advocating European solutions to European problems, the elections were fought almost exclusively along national lines, on national issues. The EP's heroic stand against the Commission, as it was portrayed in the media, failed to mobilize voters. To the extent that voters cared about institutional affairs, they seemed angered by the EP's highly publicized rejection, only a month before the elections, of a statute to standardize pay and reform allowance (see below).

Nevertheless, the result of the elections marked a watershed in the EP's history. For the first time since direct elections were held, the EPP became the largest group. So used had the PES become to being in the majority, that it had induced Mario Soares, the venerable former Prime Minister of Portugal, to stand for election by unofficially offering him the Presidency of the Parliament for the next two-and-a-half years. Even when the PES came in second (due largely to heavy losses in Britain and Germany), and the EPP put forward its own candidate, the PES presumed that it would win sufficient support in the EP to have Soares elected. Much to its surprise and Soares' annoyance, Nicole Fontaine, the EPP candidate, easily won the presidential election on the first round.

The presidential election signalled the breakdown of a long period of 'technical co-operation' between the PES and the EPP, during which time they divided the spoils of office between them and jointly managed parliamentary affairs. A rancorous dispute between the PES and EPP over censure of the Commission in January 1999 was the first manifestation of an imminent split. Over the years, many members of the EPP had come to resent the party's seemingly excessive deference to the PES, and pressed for a more assertive line. The group's spectacular election victory put such members, personified by Hans-Gert Pöttering, the new group leader, in the ascendant. Conversely, the disarray of the PES was symbolized by the ousting of its leader, Pauline Green. Ironically, the EPP consolidated its position in the newly elected EP by forming another alliance, this time with the much smaller Liberal group. Such a coalition may be better for the EP's reputation, however, than the one between the EPP and the PES, the EP's two giant groups.

The elections and their aftermath therefore resulted in a major shake-up in the distribution of senior leadership positions in the Parliament, especially of committee chairmanships. At the same time, the newly elected EP decided to reduce the number of committees and alter their functions to correspond more closely to the EU's post-Amsterdam profile.

The new relationship between the EPP and the PES presaged a more adversarial, ideologically driven approach to legislative decision-making in the EP, notably in the fields of social policy, employment and the environment. Nevertheless, differences between both groups, and the difficulty of future co-operation, should not be exaggerated. Ideological divisions are generally not as acute as they were in the past, and the EP's two largest groups often have a greater interest in enhancing the institution's power than in dividing along partisan lines. In any case, each group (but especially the EPP) will probably have to devote more time to formulating common positions among its heterogeneous national delegations than it will to squaring off against the other.

Parliamentary Reform

Apart from changes to the committee system and a corresponding staff reorganization, the EP did not undertake the kind of far-reaching reform in 1999 that the Commission and, to a lesser extent, the Council either initiated or accelerated. Instead, parliamentary reform revolved around efforts to introduce a statute to standardize MEPs' pay and conditions, in accordance with a provision of the Amsterdam Treaty (Art. 190 EC). In December 1998, in anticipation of the Amsterdam Treaty's implementation in mid-1999, the EP had adopted a draft statute (the Rothley Report). A Commission opinion, required under the Treaty, generally supported the EP's draft. The Council, by contrast, whose unanimous approval was necessary in order to enact the statute, unilaterally altered the EP's draft on 26 April. The Council was particularly perturbed about the question of taxation. Should MEPs be taxed at the 'Union' level (i.e. at the level applicable to EU civil servants) or at much higher national levels? Some national governments, notably the Scandinavian ones, insisted on national taxation of MEPs' salaries. The Council's compromise recommended the Union level, but included an option for national taxation at Member States' discretion. Not surprisingly, the EP had opted in its draft statute for the Union level only.

In a highly publicized vote on 5 May, the EP rejected the Council's proposed statute. At a time when the Commission had just resigned, the EP's action went down badly with a public inclined in any case to dismiss parliamentarians, and Euro-parliamentarians in particular, as pampered and irresponsible. The sight of MEPs voting down a seemingly generous package of pay and allowances inevitably engendered a negative reaction. The EP's explanation – that the Council had taken too long to act on the Rothley Report and had eventually done so in a high-handed way – did little to help the EP's image.

The EP's rejection of the Council's offer meant that the statute could not come into effect at the beginning of the new Parliament's mandate. Both sides revisited the issue in October 1999 amid mutual recriminations and accusations of bad faith. Nevertheless, the EP's position had softened somewhat because of expressions of public outrage during the election campaign. On the Council side, Finland pressed for a solution before the end of its Presidency. Despite some Council concessions on parts of the statute – but not on taxation – an agreement was not reached by the end of December.

V. The Council

Member States intensified their efforts in 1999 to reform the functioning of the Council, especially in view of enlargement. In a move that irritated many national governments, the EP weighed into the debate when it adopted a report on 11 February (the Bourlanges Report) calling for a radical overhaul of the Council's role, structures and operating procedures. Member States preferred to keep Council reform within the family. Their deliberations, conducted mostly in COREPER, were based on the so-called Trumpf–Piris report of March 1999. This laid the basis for 'An Effective Council for an Enlarged Union', a series of guidelines and operational recommendations approved by the European Council in Helsinki in December 1999.

The most significant of the proposed reforms – none of which would require treaty revision – included strengthening the co-ordinating role of the foreign ministers' General Affairs Council (GAC); reducing the number of Council formations to a maximum of 15; limiting the number of informal Council meetings to five per presidency; streamlining legislative procedures; and improving preparatory work at all levels. Although not at all as well publicized as the Prodi reformation, in many respects Council reform is more consequential for the successful functioning of the EU. The efficiency of an enlarging EU depends to a great extent on Member States' willingness to implement the changes outlined in the Helsinki-approved report.

The HOSG agreed at the Cologne summit on 3–4 June to appoint NATO's Secretary-General, Javier Solana, to be the first High Representative for the CFSP. Because the High Representative is also nominally the Secretary-General of the Council Secretariat, Solana's appointment necessitated the retirement of Jürgen Trumpf, then in that office. In a classic example of Franco–German collusion, Chancellor Schröder announced in Cologne that Pierre de Boissieu, France's Permanent Representative in Brussels, would become Deputy Secretary-General (effectively head) of the Council Secretariat. Unable to leave NATO until his successor was announced, Solana took up his new EU position on 18 October, when de Boissieu also took over as Deputy Secretary-General. Known as a tenacious defender of French interests and as an opponent of institutional openness, de Boissieu's tenure at the Secretariat promises to make one of the EU's least known but most important bodies even more interesting, although possibly more difficult, to observe.

Solana's arrival in Brussels, together with the emergence in 1999 of an incipient EU defence policy, heralded additional institutional changes. As stipulated in the Amsterdam Treaty's CFSP provisions, a Policy Planning and Early Warning Unit formally came into being when the Treaty was implemented (it is known simply as the Policy Unit). Steps towards the formulation of a CESDP led to the first meeting of EU foreign and defence ministers, on 15 November in Brussels. The new, post-Amsterdam CFSP troika also came into operation (in fact it has four members: the current and succeeding Council presidencies, the External Relations Commissioner and the CFSP High Representative).

Apart from these institutional reforms and innovations, the Council's rules of procedure were changed in order to facilitate implementation of the Amsterdam Treaty. Although the Commission and the EP also changed their rules of procedure, the Council's changes were more far-reaching because of the need to make practical arrangements for decision-making in areas in which not all Member States would participate, either because they chose not to avail themselves of closer co-operation, or because they had opt-outs. In the event, there was no recourse to closer co-operation in 1999.

Finally, language wars intensified in the Council in 1999. Once again, Spain and Germany were the most belligerent Member States. Germany spoiled the early weeks of Finland's Presidency by insisting on the use of German at informal Council meetings (where the use of French, English and the presidency language is the norm). Nobody challenged the use of all official languages in the legislative process, despite the increasing cost and complexity of interpretation and translation with each new accession. German and Spanish insistence on the use of their languages in less formal situations, however, indicates a growing emphasis on national identity and a growing push for national advantage in the EU, a development that has long been apparent in battles over EU appointments.

VI. Other Procedures, Institutions and Bodies

Comitology

The Commission had started the ball rolling for a new Council decision on EU implementing procedures (comitology) when it submitted a proposal in 1998. The Commission sought to simplify comitology's notoriously complicated procedures, make them more transparent, and introduce greater democratic accountability by strengthening the role of the EP. Politically, the Commission hoped to reduce interinstitutional conflict on comitology, notably between the Council and the Parliament, which had sparked a budgetary dispute and had occasionally resulted in Parliament's refusal to adopt certain pieces of legislation. Despite the sensitive nature of the issue, the new Council decision was adopted without much fuss in June 1999, having taken into account a Parliamentary opinion that did not substantially differ from the Commission's proposal. The Council agreed to involve the EP more fully in the implementation of acts adopted by codecision, to simplify procedures largely by dropping the variations of the management and regulatory committees, and to provide more public information on comitology. The decision still favours Council control over the Commission's executive authority, but should greatly defuse, if not entirely end, the interinstitutional conflict over comitology that has raged since the 1987 decision.

From UCLAF to OLAF

UCLAF, the Commission's short-lived anti-fraud office (it was established in 1998) was replaced in May 1999 by OLAF, the EU's independent anti-fraud office. An interinstitutional agreement (IIA) (between the Commission, Council and Parliament), signed on 25 May, set out the scope of and procedures for OLAF investigations, and the rights and obligations of persons and institutions subject to such investigations. A classic procedural wrangle between the Commission and the EP delayed the selection of OLAF's first director (perhaps because of the nature of the job, national governments seem not to have interfered in the selection process). Eventually, Franz-Hermann Bruener, then head of the anti-fraud unit in the Office of the High Representative in Bosnia, was appointed.

The Economic and Social Committee (ESC) and the Committee of the Regions (COR)

The Amsterdam Treaty extended the consultative roles of the ESC and the COR into additional policy areas. Buoyed by that development, the EU's two consultative bodies declared a truce in their relations, with the COR president attending for the first time a plenary session of the ESC (on 28 April). Later, the presidents of both bodies signed an agreement on administrative co-operation, and the ESC also moderated its recent animosity towards the EP. Although the ESC and the COR maintained an impressive output of reports and opinions, often meeting tight deadlines, the impact of their deliberations on EU legislation remained weak. A good case could probably be made for the abolition of both committees, although it would be politically incorrect to do so because each of them champions a cherished principle of EU governance (the social dialogue in the case of the ESC; subsidiarity in the case of the COR).

The European Investment Bank (EIB)

With the retirement of Sir Brian Unwin, the presidency of the EIB became a piece of the jigsaw puzzle of top-level EU positions painstakingly put together by national governments in 1999. Traditionally held by a citizen of one of the big Member States, for the first time in the EIB's history the presidency was made available to a small one. Belgium emerged triumphant, beating off a strong Portuguese challenge for the job. In deference to Portuguese sensitivities, the appointment of Philippe Maystadt, a former Belgian finance minister, was not announced until November 1999, after the Portuguese general election.

VII. Good Governance

The Commission resignation crisis was all about good governance, or the lack thereof. The Committee of Independent Experts' second report (September 1999) lambasted the Commission for a ' culture of secrecy', among other major failings. Based on his personal experience, the Ombudsman emphasized in his annual report for 1998 (published in April 1999) the need for greater transparency in the Commission. As in previous years, allegations of opacity were also levelled against the Council, particularly with regard to legislative decision-making. Transparency – already recognized as gravely inadequate at the EU level – therefore attracted considerable attention in 1999, not least because of a number of key rulings by the Court of First Instance and because of the institutions' obligations, under the terms of the Amsterdam Treaty, to become more open. In response, the Commission planned to introduce a proposal in January 2000 on general principles for access to Commission, Council and EP documents. The Council's new comitology decision should improve transparency in the key area of legislative implementation.

Perhaps because it was a year in which voters had an opportunity to participate in direct elections to the EP, relatively little was heard about the democratic deficit in 1999. The disappointing turnout in the elections demonstrated yet again that voters are either unconcerned about the deficit, or that they do not see direct elections as a solution to the problem. Greater transparency and accountability at the European level should help to erode the deficit (or at least the perception of it), although the Commission resignation crisis undoubtedly deepened public cynicism towards EU governance in general. Public reaction to the Commission's collapse, together with poor participation in the direct elections, suggest that the democratic deficit may be primarily an attitudinal rather than a structural problem.

In addition to its annual report on implementing the subsidiarity principle (presented to the COR in March 1999), the Commission presented a special report on subsidiarity (entitled 'Better Law-Making') to the European Council in December 1999. The Commission drafted its special report in a contradictory climate of continuing scepticism towards EU institutions, coupled with growing public support for EU action in areas such as food safety and JHA. Apart from statistical information about legislative proposals, the special report gave an interesting insight into the legislative process in general, and the little understood pre-proposal stage in particular. Thus the Commission complained that heavy 'legislative pressure' from other institutions impaired the effectiveness and applicability of the subsidiarity principle. However, a marked increase in the number of legislative proposals in 1999 was due largely to implementation of the *Agenda 2000* agreement.

VIII. Towards the IGC

The Commission resignation crisis hastened not only internal reform efforts but also preparations for the next IGC. Whereas in January 1999 the German Presidency speculated that the IGC might take place in 2001, in June 1999 the European Council decided that the IGC would begin and end in 2000, even though the first round of enlargement was not expected to happen for another three or four years. The timing of the IGC having been agreed upon, Member States remained divided on the agenda of the conference itself. Should the IGC be confined to the so-called Amsterdam leftovers – the size and composition of the Commission; the weighting of votes in the Council; and the scope of qualified majority voting (QMV) – or include additional institutional and policy issues? Lacking the political appetite for a broader agenda, and fearful of risking the conference's tight schedule, a majority of Member States initially insisted on sticking to the Amsterdam leftovers. While also aiming to complete the IGC by December 2000, a few Member States (notably the Benelux countries) pushed for a more ambitious agenda. In particular, they advocated a renegotiation of the Amsterdam Treaty's flexibility clauses, hoping to remove a Member State's ability to veto closer co-operation and/or to reduce the quorum of states necessary to participate in closer co-operation. Their rationale was that, as an agreement to extend QMV would be hard to reach, a relaxation of the flexibility rules was essential to avoid legislative paralysis.

The Commission and the EP supported calls for a broader agenda, although their views on the modalities of flexibility inevitably differed. Prodi used the impending IGC to try to strengthen his leadership in the Commission and to enhance the Commission's influence in the EU system. He may have gone too far in both respects. An 'orientation paper' by the former Belgian Prime Minister, Jean-Luc Dehaene, and two other eminent Europeans (Lord Simon, a former British Trade Secretary and Richard von Weizsäcker), requested by Prodi and presented on 18 October, went too far for most Member States and also for some Commissioners. Prodi then made a tactical retreat, although the Commission's report to the Presidency (10 November) and later official opinion on the IGC (26 January) were markedly more ambitious than the still officially undeclared positions of most Member States. The EP was less circumspect in its approach to the IGC (notably in its resolution of 18 November), and chided the Commission for failing to advocate more far-reaching reform. Such a divergence in positions – however slight – may have helped the Commission to emerge from under the shadow of the EP in the post-resignation period.

The Commission's and the EP's positions were, in any event, largely irrelevant to the IGC debate, over which Member States retained control. Thanks largely to a change of heart in France and Germany, Member State opinion began to swing by the end of the year towards a broader IGC agenda, at least as far as the inclusion of flexibility was concerned. Whereas in the mid-1990s, Franco–German ruminations on flexibility had scared the smaller members, in 1999 it was the smaller Member States who convinced France and Germany that revisiting flexibility could be advantageous for all, especially if the scope of QMV was not radically extended. The outcome of these deliberations was an agreement at the Helsinki summit to deal with the Amsterdam leftovers in the IGC, and to allow 'the incoming Presidency … [to] propose additional issues to be taken on the agenda of the Conference'.

Whether narrow or broad in its agenda, the IGC threatened to be a dry and dreary affair. At a time when the EU craved public support, an IGC about such arcane issues as weighting of votes, QMV, and triggering mechanisms for closer co-operation was bound to reinforce a negative image of Brussels. Hence the need for the EU to link the IGC to internal institutional reform, and to emphasize the relevance of ongoing treaty and other changes to such key principles as legitimacy, efficiency, responsibility, transparency and accountability. In that way 1999 may eventually be remembered not only as the year the Commission resigned, but also as the year that the EU began to turn itself around.

Journal of Common Market Studies

Volume 38, Annual Review
September 2000

The German Presidency of the Council: Continuity or Change in Germany's European Policy?

ANDREAS MAURER
University of Cologne

I. Introduction

Germany held the EU Presidency from January to June 1999. After 16 years of a Christian Democrat–Liberal coalition government, German ministers now came from a Red–Green coalition. During those 16 years, there had been three Intergovernmental Conferences, all of them marked by joint Franco–German and German–Italian initiatives, as well as a considerable personal input from Chancellor Helmut Kohl towards Economic and Monetary Union (EMU) and Political Union. In 1999, the Greens (Bündnis 90/ Die Grünen) – to which the Foreign Minister, the Minister for the Environment and the Minister for Health policy belong – had not only had no experience at all in running an EU presidency, they had never been in government at a federal level before, and only in a handful of cases had they been in government at Länder level. Given these internal circumstances, the 1999 EU Presidency was widely perceived as a test-case for measuring the 'Europability' of the Red–Green coalition.

Moreover, the EU, itself, was at a crossroads. Having brought the Amsterdam IGC to an end – albeit with limited success on institutional reform – and with the next – Nice 2000 – IGC already looming, the immediate task of major importance for the EU was the *Agenda 2000* package. *Agenda 2000* not only had major internal implications, it was also important for eastern enlargement and the World Trade Organization negotiations. Although the Austrian Presidency had achieved some progress (especially with regard to the structural funds[1]), the bulk of the negotiations were to be completed under the German Presidency.

Thirdly, the Presidency's start coincided with the launch of Monetary Union, uniting 11 EU Member States in one currency. German public opinion on EMU had been negative ever since the Heads of State or Government decided on it in Maastricht. Long-term studies, however, confirm a gradual increase of support for the single currency up to the beginning of 1999. In January 1999, for the first time, the number of supporters was higher than that of opponents.[2] This result is consistent with other national public opinion polls and – as regards the overall trend – with the data of *Eurobarometer*.

The German Presidency also faced unexpected challenges, not least the resignation of the entire Commission on 16 March, the war in Kosovo and the launch of NATO's air campaign on 24 March. In addition, the Amsterdam Treaty came into force, granting greater legislative powers to the European Parliament. The EP itself held its elections at the end of the German Presidency.

The performance of the German Presidency was closely scrutinized against a background of international fears that the stability of German European and foreign policy would be at risk for two major reasons. The first revolved around the figure of the Finance Minister, Oskar Lafontaine who, inspired by France's notion of a countervailing power to the ECB (*gouvernement économique*), set out an ambitious strategy for macroeconomic policy co-ordination to reduce unemployment. Lafontaine resigned dramatically on 11 March. As Lankowski has suggested, it eerily presaged a change of course that paralleled that undertaken under the Mitterrand government in 1983, when France was brought back into conformity with its neoliberal European environment.[3] The other uncertainty concerned the Greens as a party in government. A decade earlier, they had supported the dissolution of NATO and denounced any kind of EC/EU related security, military and defence policy. However, immediately after its election in September 1999, the German government was keen to assure its partners within EU and NATO of the 'continuity' in German European and foreign policy. Foreign Minister Joschka Fischer took over Helmut Kohl's 'mantra' that German interests and European interests were two sides of the same coin and, in line with the preceding government, the new one followed the path of further integration with respect to the Common Foreign and Security Policy (CFSP).[4]

---

[1] Commission (1998) 'Report to the European Council'. 8 December, 13621/98, Addendum 2.
[2] Allensbacher Berichte (1999) 'Euro im Portemonnaie hat keine Eile. Von Euro-Optimisten und Euro-Skeptikern'. Institut für Demoskopie Allensbach, No. 2, p. 3.
[3] Lankowski, C. (1999) 'The Red–Green Government and the European Union 1999'. AICGS online papers, p. 1.
[4] Korte, K-R. and Maurer, A. (2000) 'Soziopolitische Grundlagen der deutschen Europapolitik. Konturen der Kontinuität und des Wandels'. In Jopp, M., Schneider, H. and Schmalz, U. (eds) *Die neue deutsche Europapolitik* (Bonn: Europa Union Verlag).

II. Preferences and the Programme

Nonetheless, there were some clear differences in the Red–Green government's strategic ideas on the functional scope of European integration. In their key statements, the new government indicated that:

- Monetary Union was not seen as the successful conclusion to integration policy, but as a fresh starting point for further initiatives for the supranational design of social and environmental policy in Europe;
- the enlargement of the Union was viewed as both a moral-economic and a socio-political challenge including a stronger emphasis on civil rights;
- the central point of reference for the reform of the institutional and procedural bases of the EU's political system was not to be the subsidiarity principle as such, but the EU's ability to take action and shape global policies.

The new government also gave considerably more emphasis to the social dimension of European integration. The top priority was, and remains, the fight against unemployment.[5] In this context, the Presidency called not only for a European Employment Pact, that was as important as the Stability Pact within EMU, but also for flanking policies that involved co-ordinated economic, financial and social policy. Here the coalition agreement called for binding acts against fiscal, social and environmental dumping.

As the junior coalition partner, the Green Party had a different approach in a number of crucial areas, including co-operation in Justice and Home Affairs (JHA). Their call for deepening the field of EC asylum and migration policy and the adoption of an EU charter on fundamental rights was channelled through the parliamentary group in the Bundestag. The party also called for the introduction of an 'Eco-tax', to extend the EU's own resources as well as urging further institutional and procedural reforms. In this respect, the party supported the initiative of Belgium, France and Italy to undertake fundamental reforms before the next enlargement.[6]

The presidency programme, presented by Chancellor Gerhard Schröder in early 1999, reflected these new priorities for European policy-making:[7]

- combating unemployment at European level;
- closer co-operation to combat trans-frontier crime and in the areas of migration and refugee policy;

---

[5] Coalition agreement between the German Social Democratic Party and Alliance 90/ the Greens, Bonn, 20 October 1998, point XI.2.
[6] Statz, A. and Sterzing, C. (1999) 'Grüne Perspektiven auf die deutsche Ratspräsidentschaft'. *Integration*, 22. Jg. 1/99, p. 26 et seq.
[7] German Chancellor Gerhard Schröder's speech, 10 December 1998.

- enhancing the effectiveness of the Common Foreign and Security Policy;
- bringing *Agenda 2000* to a successful conclusion.

Other priorities were to 'combat unfair or damaging tax competition',[8] and reflecting the particular priorities of the junior coalition partner – drafting a list of civil rights, the harmonization of energy taxation, and using electricity from renewable energy sources.

III. Achievements

The main achievement of the Presidency was the successful outcome of the European Council in Berlin (24–26 March 1999) devoted to *Agenda 2000*, which established the financial framework designed to accommodate eastern enlargement by reforming the Common Agricultural Policy (CAP), adopting the financial perspective for 2000–06, and an overall agreement on reform of the structural funds. Continuity in German EU policy-making was visible with regard to the demand for a fairer sharing of the financial burden to the EU within the limits set by the EU's own resources of 1.27 per cent of EU GNP.[9] The Schröder government also proposed that those Member States entering the third phase of EMU should no longer be eligible for cohesion fund support and called for an end to the British rebate which contributed to the imbalance in Germany's 'net payer' position.[10] With regard to the *Agenda 2000* negotiations, the most significant difference from the former government was to be found in the most expensive EC policy area: the CAP. While the Kohl/Kinkel government had not shown any inclination to follow the Commission's proposals for CAP reform, the new government indicated its readiness to support the Commission and a fundamental shift from a price support system to direct payment to farmers. With the focus moving more towards balancing the 'excessive' net contributions of individual Member States instead of an absolute reduction of payments to the EU, negotiations concentrated on national co-financing of the CAP.

The Schröder/Fischer government faced the ambivalent legacy of its predecessor. The inconsistencies of the approach of the late Kohl government towards *Agenda 2000* had been a target of criticism both of the then Red–Green opposition in the German *Bundestag*, and of many EU Member States who felt that Germany's pro-enlargement stance was not compatible with claims for a reduction of net payments, a continuation of a high inflow of structural funds to Germany, and a no-reform attitude as far as the CAP was concerned. Against

---

[8] German Presidency Programme, point II.B.I.4.
[9] 'Bonn drückt bei Reformen aufs Tempo'. *Frankfurter Rundschau*, 8.12.1998.
[10] 'Bonn dringt auf EU-Beschäftigungspakt'. Süddeutsche *Zeitung*, 12–13.12.1998.

this background, the German government had to take into account the responsibilities of the EU Presidency at the cost of rigorously defending narrowly defined national interests. The German Presidency then merely followed a muddling-through strategy that accepted the impossibility of fundamental policy changes and deep budget cuts.

The new government also seems to have adopted a different approach towards the overall European integration process, with more long-term implications. As the Foreign Minister emphasized in his speech to the European Parliament, the German Presidency was determined to hold an Intergovernmental Conference before the entry of the 16th Member State.[11] 'The key question here is the Union's readiness to accept majority decisions in as many areas as possible. The new government advocates limiting the need for unanimity in the EU in the longer term to questions of fundamental importance such as treaty amendments'.[12] Consequently, the subsidiarity principle does not play such an important role for the Red–Green coalition. Hence, the Presidency programme simply called for a 'consistent and effective' application of the protocol on subsidiarity.[13] As Gerhard Schröder claimed, real subsidiarity manifests itself in its closeness to the citizens and not in a clear cut – constitution-like – list of competencies.[14] The fact that the new government suggested new initiatives for the harmonization of tax, environmental and social policy as well as Justice and Home Affairs at a European level, bears witness to its readiness to share the responsibility for European governance with the EU institutions and therefore implies a marked change in German European policy.

[11] Press statement by German Foreign Minister Joschka Fischer, Paris 20.1.1999.
[12] Press statement by German Foreign Minister Joschka Fischer, Strasbourg 12.1.1999.
[13] Presidency Programme of Germany, point II.A.I.
[14] German Chancellor Gerhard Schröder, Government Declaration of 10.12.1998, *Deutscher Bundestag*, Plenarprotokoll 14/14, p. 820.

© Blackwell Publishers Ltd 2000

Journal of Common Market Studies

Volume 38, Annual Review
September 2000

The Finnish Presidency*

ALEXANDER STUBB
Permanent Representation of Finland to the European Union

I. Inheriting a Heavy Agenda

At the beginning of its Presidency, every Member State claims that its stint in office coincides with one of the most challenging six-month periods in the history of the Union. Finland, which held its first Presidency in the second half of 1999, was no exception.[1] The last Presidency of the millennium had to manage a heavy agenda which included enlargement negotiations, preparations for the Intergovernmental Conference, an extraordinary European Council on Justice and Home Affairs, difficult subjects linked to external relations, important issues relating to the internal market, and work on both fundamental rights and defence.

It has been said that the Finnish Presidency was one the most thoroughly prepared presidencies in the history of the European Union. This statement is probably not far from the truth.[2] In many ways Finland had been preparing for

* During the Finnish Presidency the author worked as first secretary (Deputy Antici) at the Finnish Permanent Representation in Brussels. The author would like to thank Alec Aalto, David Galloway, Mark Gray, Kare Halonen, Reijo Kemppinen, Brent Nelsen, Jan Store, Helen Wallace, Jan Vapaavuori and the editors for their helpful comments. A special thanks is extended to Antti Satuli and Markku Keinänen, without whom the Finnish Presidency might have been rather different. The opinions presented in the article are strictly personal.

[1] For all documents relating to the Finnish Presidency, please refer to the Presidency home page «www.presidency.finland.fi»

[2] The Ministry of Finance allocated a special Presidency budget as early as March 1996. Before the beginning of the Presidency, some 900 civil servants had participated in various training programmes,

the Presidency ever since it became a member of the Union on 1 January 1995. Initial meetings about the Presidency were held in 1995 and the necessary institutions and working groups for its management were established in 1996–97. Decisions on the calendar for informal and formal Council meetings and the European Councils were taken as early as 1997. Linked to this, the preparations for the Presidency programme began in the spring of 1997 with outline proposals circulated within the administration and different ministries asked to indicate priorities. By the end of April 1999, the Prime Minister's office had hundreds of pages of priorities from which to choose.

II. Managing a Heavy Agenda

Thorough preparation is obviously important, but it is not the litmus test for a successful Presidency. The final verdict is always based on how the Presidency was run, what it achieved and how it was perceived.

The beginning of the Finnish Presidency was not easy because a political vacuum had been created in the EU. National elections, the resignation of the Santer Commission in March, the entry into force of the Amsterdam Treaty in May, the end of the Kosovo conflict and the elections of the European Parliament in June, all provided a difficult, testing background against which the Finns had to set out their objectives. Their main focus revolved around five 'classic' themes: (1) enlargement, (2) institutional questions, (3) justice and home affairs, (4) external relations, and (5) the internal market, including the information society.

(1) Enlargement. Under the Finnish Presidency, important steps were taken which laid the foundation for a Union which will be radically different from its predecessor in terms of both size and diversity. It took the historical step in Helsinki of confirming Turkey's status as a candidate state, with the aim of eventual membership. The negotiations with Cyprus, Hungary, Poland, the Czech Republic, Estonia and Slovenia were advanced. The Helsinki European Council also decided to open negotiations with six additional applicants – Latvia, Lithuania, Slovakia, Bulgaria, Romania and Malta.

(2) Institutional questions. The Finnish Presidency dealt with two important institutional questions linked to enlargement: the IGC and the so-called Trumpf-Piris report on Council reform. On the basis of the Cologne Conclusions, the Presidency prepared a report outlining the possible agenda of the IGC and taking stock of the different institutional options at hand. Its sugges-

---

ranging from language courses to negotiating simulations. The EU Secretariat was in charge of co-ordinating Finnish EU policy in general. Two extra bodies were established for the Presidency: the EU Presidency Secretariat in 1996 (in charge of technical preparations), and the Prime Minister's Presidency EU Unit in 1997 (in charge of overall co-ordintaion of the Presidency).

tions followed those of Cologne – i.e. reweighting of votes in the Council, the composition of the Commission, qualified majority voting and other institutional issues relating to enlargement and the implementation of the Amsterdam Treaty. However, the time was not ripe for finalising the agenda in Helsinki and it was left to the Portuguese Presidency, which was also given the option to propose additional issues for the IGC, to achieve agreement. The Council will be profoundly influenced by enlargement hence the efforts devoted to the so-called Trumpf-Piris report on Council reform. The final product was approved in Helsinki and contained 55 guidelines for reform and operational recommendations. The key recommendation is to reduce the number of Council compositions from 22 to 15.[3]

(3) Justice and Home Affairs. The Tampere European Council established political guidelines for Justice and Home Affairs by giving the new provisions of the Amsterdam Treaty both a political and a practical content. The content was defined through the 'Ten Milestones of Tampere', which contain a clear timetable for pursuing 'an area of freedom, security and justice'. The policy orientations include a call for a common asylum and migration policy, a common European asylum system, fair treatment of resident third country nationals and more efficient management of migration flows. The 'milestones' also call for measures to bring about better access to justice, mutual recognition of judicial decisions, greater convergence in civil law, and measures to step up police, judicial and administrative co-operation in the fight against organized and transnational crime.

(4) External relations.[4] The entry into force of the Amsterdam Treaty provided new scope for the further enhancement of the Union's common foreign and security policy. The most important issue was linked to the development of the Union's defence dimension. Work in this area was stimulated anew by the EU's poor performance in Bosnia and Kosovo. The Helsinki European Council made concrete decisions on the military capabilities and decision-making mechanisms for crisis management. It decided on a common European headline goal for a readily deployable military capability, new political and military bodies and structures within the Council and principles for consulting with non-European allies and NATO. Much of the push in this field came from the new High Representative/Secretary General of the Council, Javier Solana.

---

[3] In April 2000 the General Affairs Council reduced the Council composition to 16.
[4] The Finnish Presidency also achieved results and progressed in an array of external relations questions other than those mentioned above. These include the common strategies (Russia, Ukraine, Balkans, Mediterranean), the Western Balkans, TACIS, the Middle East, Indonesia, East Timor, Mercosur and Chile, Mexico, Congo, Pakistan, Myanmar and the EU–Africa summit.

(5) The internal market. Issues relating to the internal market form the bulk of the day-to-day work of the Presidency.[5] During the Finnish Presidency, the Council approved hundreds of regulations and directives in the first pillar. The key achievements were linked to decisions on the railway-package, electronic commerce and the information society. The key failures were the tax package and resale rights in arts, both due to British recalcitrance.

III. Assessing the Presidency

It is not the Presidency that makes the agenda – it is the agenda that makes the Presidency. Finland saw the Presidency as an investment which would bring dividends in its EU work for years to come and had therefore mobilized the whole administrative machinery with one aim – running a successful Presidency. It was institutionally orthodox and aimed at coherence and continuity. As a small Member State, with relatively light political luggage, Finland was able to take on the full role of the Presidency as a mediator, compromise seeker and neutral broker which did not push its national positions.[6] The focus was on the European, not the national agenda. Finland had prepared well, may have been lucky with its agenda, but it was able to exploit its luck to provide one of the most efficient procedural presidencies in recent years.

Despite the German language problem,[7] the Presidency got off to a flying start. The political vacuum surrounding the start of the Finnish Presidency meant that the Member States had to rely on the Presidency more than usual. The Presidency gave a good first impression by producing clear timetables in the working groups and COREPER for dealing with the IGC, defence, fundamental rights and the Trumpf-Piris report among other issues. The institutions and the Member States were left with the impression that the Finnish Presidency knew what it was doing. This created positive momentum for the rest of the Presidency.

The management of the day-to-day business of the Presidency was conducted from the Permanent Representation in Brussels, while the political leadership remained in Helsinki. The team work and good relationship between the Presidency and the Council Secretariat and the Commission also provided a solid foundation for the Presidency. The key was to establish a close

---

[5] Areas mentioned in the Presidency programme include employment, taxation, environment, information society and social policy consumer policy, industrial policy, energy policy, transport, agriculture and fisheries, research, technology and education, culture and audio-visual policy.
[6] A good example of this is that Finland made no national interventions in COREPER or the General Affairs Council.
[7] The German delegation boycotted the first informal ministerial meeting (and others) in Oulu because the Presidency based the language regime on a precedent which did not include German interpretation.

relationship between the chairman of the working group, the chairman of COREPER and the chairman of the Council.

The Finns were also procedurally innovative. The increased use of information technology (email, internet, mobile communications) improved the efficiency of the Presidency. Working group, COREPER and Council agendas were published on the internet and the Presidency home page was used as a tool for information distribution. The basic approach was pragmatic and transparent. Issues were well prepared, the working schedule was clear and documents were distributed on time. Media relations were managed with unforeseen transparency and efficiency. If the basic working framework is in order it is much easier to achieve results.

The Finnish experience highlights the importance of the Presidency as an institution. A well-managed Presidency is able to advance the European agenda. A Presidency is also very important domestically – it focuses the minds of politicians and national administrators on EU affairs. At the same time, extended media coverage brings EU issues to the public realm. Through enlargement, the role of the Presidency becomes increasingly important and difficult. For this reason the institutional debate on the future structure and management of the Presidency should continue.

Journal of Common Market Studies

Volume 38, Annual Review
September 2000

Internal Policy Developments*

HUSSEIN KASSIM
University of London

I. Introduction

The *Agenda 2000* package, agreed at the Berlin European Council in March, led to major reforms in finance, agriculture and the structural funds. The implementation of the Amsterdam Treaty, which came into force on 1 May, and the introduction of the single currency had an impact in several fields, while the installation of the Prodi Commission provided a further impetus to change.

II. Economic and Related Policies

Internal Market Developments

In February, the Commission reported significant progress in a number of areas in the operation and effectiveness of the single market. Its analysis of the implementation of the single market action plan, sanctioned by the European Council in June 1997, informed the new strategy presented by the Commission in October. The four objectives identified for the internal market in the period 2002–04 included: improving the quality of life of EU citizens; enhancing the

* For reasons of continuity and convenience, I have generally followed the format developed and used by John Redmond who has written on internal policy developments for the past six years. I should like to thank Andrew Jordan for advice on environmental developments, and Mark Walsh and Giuseppe Abbamonte for reading through the text in purely personal capacities. Any errors and all infelicities are, of course, entirely my own.

efficiency of the EU's product and capital markets; improving the business environment; and exploiting the achievements of the internal market in the global market. The programme was endorsed at the Helsinki European Council in December.

The Commission reported a significant improvement in implementation at the end of the year. Only 12.6 per cent of directives were overdue in November 1999, compared with 26.7 per cent in the same month in 1997. Moreover, ten Member States showed an implementation deficit of below 4 per cent, compared with two in 1997. Greece, Luxembourg, France, Portugal and Ireland were the countries with the poorest record, while Italy's progress – down from 7.6 to 3.9 per cent – was particularly notable. Although overall performance has improved, implementation is still slow, particularly concerning recent legislation (78 per cent of 1998 directives not implemented by all Member States and 95.7 per cent of 1999 directives). In addition, infringement activity remained high and the time taken to resolve disputes lengthy (40 per cent of cases opened in 1997–98 remained unclosed in November 1999). The worst offenders were Belgium, Germany, France, Italy and Spain, and most reasoned opinions concerned the freedom of movement of persons or goods, and the establishment or provision of services. A survey conducted by the Commission in September indicated that business confidence in the internal market remained high.

Other developments relating to the internal market included the following:

- In telecommunications, the Commission amended legislation to ensure that telecommunications networks and cable television networks owned by a single operator are separate legal entities. In June, the Council adopted a directive that makes non-member suppliers eligible for VAT by taxing services at the point of consumption rather than where the supplier is based.
- In October, the Council endorsed the Commission's approach to improving citizen awareness of mutual recognition, Member State enforcement and Commission handling of infringements.
- The Commission drew up recommendations for insurance, the coordination of social security, and a directive on electromagnetic compatibility, under the third phase of SLIM (Simpler Legislation for the Internal Market). It also reported positively on earlier phases of the initiative.
- The Commission implemented measures on public procurement relating to concession contracts, services exempted from the main directive, and a report on access to third country public procurement in water, energy, transport and telecommunications.

- Following the Green Paper on the Community patent, the Commission introduced measures to improve the patent system in the European Union. A Green Paper on counterfeiting and piracy was also produced.
- The Commission reported that few obstacles to the free movement of capital and payments were brought to its attention in 1999.
- The Commission's action plan for creating a more integrated market in financial services was endorsed by the Council in May. In November, the Commission produced an interim report and the Council put forward its conclusions on progress achieved.
- The Commission introduced proposals on pensions following its Green Paper.
- Initiatives taken with regard to direct taxation included the adoption of a report on business taxation and the creation of a high-level group to study the benefits of introducing a savings tax on EU residents.
- In June, the EP and Council adopted a directive on the mutual recognition of qualifications in craft, commerce and service sectors. At the end of the year, the Council agreed a common position on a proposal that aims to simplify the system for recognizing the professional qualifications of nurses, dentists, veterinary surgeons, midwives, pharmacists and doctors.

Duty-free sales for travel within the EU were abolished on 1 July. The Vienna Council in 1998 responded to concerns from the travel industry about the impact of the 1991 decision on abolition by asking the Commission to examine the likely effects on employment. However, support for postponement of the deadline fell short of the unanimity threshold required to overturn the earlier decision. In May the Council set the standard rate of VAT at 15 per cent until 31 December 2000, and five months later adopted a directive allowing Member States to reduce VAT rates on highly labour-intensive services from 1 January 2000 to 31 December 2002.

Economic and Monetary Union

Eleven Member States – Austria, Belgium, Finland, France, Germany, Ireland, Italy, Luxembourg, the Netherlands, Portugal and Spain – entered the final stage of Economic and Monetary Union when they adopted the euro as their official currency on 1 January. Accordingly, the Eurosystem – the European Central Bank and the national central banks of the 11 – has assumed exclusive responsibility for the single monetary policy and has set interest rates in line with the goal of price stability set out in the EC Treaty. In November, these were: 3 per cent for refinancing operations, 2 per cent for marginal lending, and a 4 per cent deposit rate.

As the 11 Member States share a common monetary policy and exchange rate, but retain responsibility for economic policy in other areas, economic policy co-ordination between the Member States has become extremely important. A system of continuous multilateral surveillance has been introduced to ensure that the policies pursued within the euro-zone and at the national level are consistent, together with formal mechanisms and less formal support. The broad economic policy guidelines of the Member States and the Community adopted in July are one of the most important instruments. Under Art. 99 (2) of the EC Treaty, the Commission forwarded to the Council in March the guidelines submitted by the Member States together with its country-specific recommendations. A draft recommendation was adopted by the Council in May, and adopted by the European Council in June. The strategy outlined in the first set of guidelines aims at high levels of growth and job creation and covers three areas:

- sound macroeconomic policies based on public finances managed in accordance with the Stability and Growth Pact, monetary policy aimed at maintaining price stability, and responsible behaviour on the part of the social partners;
- active policies to modernize labour markets to promote employability, entrepreneurship, adaptability and equal opportunities in line with the employment guidelines;
- reforms aimed at improving the functioning of goods, service and capital markets by exploiting the single market (see section on internal market developments).

The Stability and Growth Pact, designed to promote budgetary discipline, is a second mechanism. In accordance with the Pact, the Council adopted opinions on the stability programmes of Ireland and France (January), Italy and Portugal (February) and Belgium, German, Spain, France and Luxembourg (March). The convergence programmes of Sweden and the United Kingdom were examined in February. Excessive deficits are also subject to a procedure as laid down in Art. 104 of the EC Treaty. In December the Council repealed the 1994 decision on the existence of an excessive deficit in Greece, so that no Member State is now considered to be running such a deficit. In addition, the Commission supplied the Economic and Financial Committee – the successor to the Monetary Committee – the 'Euro-11' group and the Council with assessments of developments and prospects relating to inflation, exchange rates and national budgets throughout the year.

Institutionally, the ECB has established its authority inside and outside the European Union. Within the Community, it participates in Ecofin, the 'Euro-11' group, the Economic and Financial Committee, the Economic Policy

Committee and the macroeconomic dialogue. Outside, it takes part in meetings of the G-7, the G-10 and the OECD, and has a permanent observer at the IMF. The 'Euro-11' group – the political counterweight to the ECB – has grown increasingly important.

Arrangements for the next phase of Economic and Monetary Union were put in place during the year. The production of euro banknotes and coins was already underway, but it was decided that they should not be introduced into circulation earlier than the deadline – 1 January 2002 – originally envisaged.

Growth, Competitiveness and Employment

Major developments in employment policy followed the implementation of the Amsterdam Treaty. In February, the Council adopted the 1999 Guidelines for Employment, approved by the Vienna European Council, that are modelled on the four pillars outlined in Luxembourg in 1997. They include the promotion of employability, entrepreneurship, adaptability and equal opportunities. The guidelines provided the basis for the Member States' National Employment Plans (NEPs) for 1999. After examining the NEPs and the reports submitted by the Member States on the implementation of the 1998 action plans, and following the new Art. 128 of the EC Treaty, the Commission presented its draft report to the Council in September. Also, for the first time, the Commission submitted recommendations to each Member State in relation to the implementation of its employment policy. These centred on eight areas of action: tackling youth unemployment, preventing long-term unemployment, reforming tax and benefit systems, creating job opportunities in the service sector, reducing fiscal pressure on labour, modernizing the organization of work, tackling gender inequality in the labour market, and improving indicators and statistics. Three weeks after the EP had examined the draft report at the beginning of November, the Council adopted the joint report and endorsed the recommendations to the Member States, which were approved at the Helsinki summit the following month.

In September, the Commission submitted its proposal for employment guidelines for 2000. Agreed by the Council in November, they were approved by the Member States at the Helsinki European Council. The 2000 guidelines adopt the same structure as the 1999 plans.

At its meeting in Cologne in June 1999, the European Council adopted the European Employment Pact, as agreed in December 1998. The Pact brings together three categories of employment policy measures within the same framework:

- co-ordination of economic policy and the improvement of mutually supportive interaction between wage developments and monetary,

budget and fiscal policy through macroeconomic dialogue aimed at non-inflationary growth (Cologne process);
- further development of the co-ordinated employment strategy (Luxembourg process);
- comprehensive structural reform and modernization to improve the efficiency of the labour market and the markets in goods, services and capital (Cardiff process).

The Pact provides for a regular dialogue between the Council, the Commission, the European Central Bank and the social partners. The European Council attached particular priority to measures aimed at job creation.

Trans-European networks (TENs) experienced a mixed year. The total funds available were increased to EUR 4.6bn for the 2000–06 period under the terms of the new financial perspective (see below). In addition, reforms were introduced to make it easier for projects to draw on private capital with the expansion of possibilities for public–private partnerships. However, implementation remained disappointing. Only three of the 14 priority TENs transport projects – the Cork–Dublin–Belfast–Larne rail link, Malpensa airport, and the Øresund fixed link – were near completion, while five looked to be in trouble due either to lack of funding or uncertain scheduling.

Structural Funds and Regional Policy

Agreement within *Agenda 2000* placed regional policy on a new financial footing and in the case of the structural funds has been accompanied by a comprehensive overhaul. Of the EUR 213bn allocated to regional development, the structural funds will receive EUR 195bn over the period 2000–06. A series of reforms was introduced that closely followed the Commission's 1998 proposals and were guided by four principles: the concentration of aid, the clarification of responsibilities, simplification, and the stricter application of subsidiarity. The number of Community objectives has been reduced from seven to three and Commission initiatives from 13 to four.

- Objective 1, financed from the European Research and Development Fund (ERDF) the European Social Fund (ESF), the Financial Instrument for Fisheries Guidance (FIFG) and the European Agriculture Guidance and Guarantee Fund (EAGGF), covers regions where the level of development in terms of GDP per capita over the last three years is less than 75 per cent of the Community average. These regions – the home of nearly a fifth of the Union's population – will receive 69.7 per cent of the funds. The new threshold will be more strictly applied than previously.

- Objective 2 (ERDF, ESF and EAGGF) is directed at regions undergoing structural change. Coverage has been limited to 18 per cent of the Union's population, and up to one-third only of the areas currently eligible under Objectives 2 and 5b in each Member State will be eligible.
- Objective 3 (ESF) supports the adaptation and modernization of education, training and employment policies and systems.

The four initiatives are:

- INTERREG (EDRF) covering interregional, cross-border co-operation to encourage sustainable development;
- URBAN (ERDF) directed at the economic and social regeneration of cities to promote sustainable urban development;
- Leader (EAGGF Guidance Section) to support rural development;
- EQUAL (ESF) to promote new means of combating discrimination and inequality in the labour market.

The cohesion fund will receive EUR 18bn to be distributed as follows: Spain 62 per cent, Greece 17 per cent and Portugal 17 per cent. Ireland – the fourth cohesion country, which has enjoyed rising prosperity in recent years – will be able to spend up to EUR 557m between 2000 and 2003. If, thereafter, Ireland is no longer eligible because it has surpassed the ceiling – a country must have a GNP of less than 90 per cent of the EU average to qualify – the overall cohesion budget will be reduced.

The principal instrument governing the structural funds is Council Regulation (EC) No. 1260/1999, adopted by the Council on 21 June. As well as setting out the above, it provides for a clear definition of responsibilities, simplifies financial management, and gives regional and local authorities a greater role in defining policy. The implementing measures needed to launch the new programmes were adopted on 1 July. The guidelines on Community initiatives were issued in October.

Industrial and Competition Policies

The European Union continued to investigate ways in which the competitiveness of European enterprise could be improved. In April, the Council recommended that the scheme for benchmarking the competitiveness of European industry be extended to new sectors. Accordingly, the Commission set up a benchmarking working party with the Member States in November. In January, the Commission put forward a five-strand strategy outlining how European companies could respond effectively to globalization. These included: improving protection for intellectual property; developing venture capital; making greater use of human resources and entrepreneurship; taking advantage of the competitive advantages offered by the single market; and promoting fair rules at world level. The Commission also submitted a report on changes in European manufacturing, where it foresaw continuing restructuring. Following its 1998 report, the Commission continued its work on European standardization under the new approach. A website was created by European standards bodies to make access to information more readily available.

A number of sectors were the subject of more specific activities: a White Paper on Commerce was launched in January; a conference on the challenges facing forest-based and related industries was held in July; two programmes on steel were presented; recommendations on craft industries were implemented; and communications on chemicals, textiles, construction, engineering, maritime, aircraft and space industries, and defence-related industries were presented by the Commission during the course of the year.

The Commission continued to modernize Community competition rules. Particular attention was focused on the implementation of Arts. 81 and 82 (ex 85 and 86) governing, respectively, anti-competitive agreements between undertakings and the abuse of a dominant position. In its White Paper adopted in April, the Commission put forward a radical proposal for abolishing the system of notification and authorization. Instead of notifying the Commission of agreements between undertakings that fall within the scope of Art. 81 (1), but that may benefit from a block exemption under Art. 81 (3), commercial undertakings could have their applications heard before national courts or competent public authorities. This measure is intended to enable the Commission to deal more efficiently with a heavy caseload and avoid time delays that are costly to business. Fears have been expressed that Community-level rules may not be consistently applied across the territory of the Union by national authorities.

The Commission's efforts to build on the 1997 Green Paper on vertical competition came to a successful conclusion in 1999. Following authorization from the Council, two regulations were adopted in June: the first, a single exemption regulation for vertical restraints and the second a regulation under which not all vertical agreements need to be notified in advance to the Commission for the purpose of individual exemption. Both measures were adopted in June. The Commission completed its reforms in this area in December, when it adopted a regulation granting exemptions from the rules governing vertical restraints on competition to certain types of exclusive arrangement.

On state aids, efforts continued to simplify and strengthen the rules. In March, the Council adopted a regulation that clarified the procedural rules relating to Art. 88 (ex Art. 93) of the EC Treaty. Four months later, the Commission agreed new guidelines for state aid for rescuing firms in difficulty, identifying the conditions that state aid must meet to be compatible with the common market, and strengthening the 'one time, last time' principle. In November, the Commission set out the conditions under which a guarantee made by the state constitutes state aid. In addition, the Commission took specific action with respect to the synthetic fibres industry, coal, shipbuilding and agriculture. New ceilings for regional aid coverage were also decided.

The Commission dealt with a total of 387 new cases under Art. 81 and Art. 82 during the year, of which 162 were notifications, 149 complaints and 77 cases where the Commission acted on its own initiative. Notable decisions included the granting of exemptions to UK brewers and to beer distribution agreements in the UK. In cases concerning the CFO (for the sale of soccer World Cup 1998 tickets), British Airways (for commissions offered to travel agents by the airline), and airport operators in Finland and in Portugal, the Commission found that a dominant position had been abused. In state aid, the Commission received 812 notifications of new schemes or amendments to existing aid schemes and recorded 159 cases of unnotified aid schemes. In 563 cases, it took the decision not to object, and in 91 it initiated proceedings. Of these, 48 ended in a negative final decision and in three a conditional decision. The Commission received 292 notifications under the merger regulation. It took 270 decisions, only 20 of which went to the second stage. Eight of these were given conditional approval, in five the plan was abandoned, and in nine a decision deferred until 2000. In only one case – the acquisition of the package holiday company, First Choice Holidays, by a rival company, Airtours – was a merger banned. The merger between Exxon and Mobil, and BP Amoco and Atlantic Richfield, the merger of Denmark's two largest slaughterhouses, and the joint venture between British Telecommunications and AT&T in the UK market, were among the operations authorized.

Other Developments

In transport, the EU took a step towards harmonizing charges for the use of infrastructures with the adoption of the 'Eurovignette' directive in June which sets levels of tax that can be levied on heavy goods vehicles using motorways. The Commission was authorized to negotiate the necessary agreements with the US and Russia for developing the Galileo satellite navigation system. Initiatives were adopted on inter-modal transport and the interoperability of railway systems, and a report submitted on the single air services market.

The ratification of the Energy Charter Treaty and the protocol on energy efficiency by all Member States was finally completed when Ireland and France became signatories. In a second report on liberalization of the energy market, the Commission observed that progress had been highly satisfactory, especially in electricity. It did, however, express concern in reports in April and November, respectively, that the implementation of harmonization directives may not lead to single markets in electricity or gas, and identified the likely obstacles. In the context of the 1998 framework programme, agreement came in December on a new multi-annual programme to encourage energy efficiency (SAVE II). The main development in research was the launch of the fifth framework programme. In contrast to its predecessors, which were directed towards scientific and technological disciplines, the new programme called for research on 23 key socio-economic issues relating to four themes: quality of life and management of living resources; creating a user-friendly information society; promoting competitiveness and sustainable growth; and energy and sustainable development. The aim is to encourage research work that will benefit European citizens directly. In addition, a total of 31 countries, including applicants and neighbouring states, are associated with the programme. The ten specific programmes were formally adopted by the Council in January. Meanwhile, following the 1998 reform, the EU's Joint Research Centre were reorganized to enable them to provide an effective response to issues arising in environment, health and consumer protection. Thus, for example, it provided scientific support in relation to the dioxin crisis in Belgium.

In education, legislative developments included agreements on the second phase of the Leonardo da Vinci action programme (vocational training) in April and in December on the second phase of the Socrates programme (education) to strengthen European education at all levels. Also in April, the Council adopted the third phase of TEMPUS (the trans-European co-operation scheme for higher education) to continue higher education reform in eastern Europe. On 28 June, the Council adopted a common position on the proposal for a decision establishing the youth action programme for the period 2000–06.

In December, agreement was reached on 'Culture 2000', a single financing and programming instrument for cultural co-operation. This groups together within a single framework the Kaleidoscope programme (living arts), Raphael (cultural heritage) and Ariane (books and reading), and includes tests for the evaluation of actions provided under the instrument. In May, a decision was adopted on Community action for 'The European Capital of Culture' event for 2005–19, which established a new procedure for designating such 'Capitals'. The Commission presented a Community plan for combating doping in sport.

The Commission introduced its plans for audio-visual policy for 2000–05 in a communication in December. The MEDIA II programme assisted European professionals in the industry, and the Commission proposed a new MEDIA Plus programme to continue support from 2001–02.

The action programme in public health first proposed in 1993 was completed in 1999, when the EP and the Council adopted a series of measures to combat rare diseases, prevent injuries, and control pollution-related disease. Efforts to protect consumer health were focused on protection against dioxin contamination of foodstuffs, hormones in beef and transmissible spongiform encephalopathies. Various initiatives relating to tobacco were launched.

Developments in consumer policy included the provision of a legal base to enable the implementation of the 1999–2001 action plan adopted by the Commission in 1998. A directive providing a two-year guarantee for consumer goods after purchase was agreed by the EP and Council in May.

The Commission highlighted the importance of tourism to employment in a report presented in 1998. An estimated 9 million jobs in Europe are tourism related. A second communication examined the effectiveness of measures introduced since 1996 to combat child sex tourism and put forward new proposals.

Measures relating to the information society included initiatives on citizens' access, public sector information and a regulatory framework for telecommunications. Progress in internet use and electronic signatures was also reported. Particular attention was devoted to the year 2000 computer problem.

III. Finances

The issues of fraud and negotiations on a new interinstitutional agreement preoccupied the Union for much of 1999 (as Desmond Dinan reports above).

Practical measures taken in 1999 included the adoption of codes of conduct in March to govern the declaration by Commissioners of their financial interests, the recruitment of Commissioner *cabinets*, and the appointment of senior Commission staff. Also, a new Fraud Prevention Office, OLAF, was created in June. The new body will take over the functions of its predecessor, UCLAF, but has a broader remit, commands more substantial resources, and enjoys greater operational independence. Its activities are monitored by a Supervisory Committee of five independent persons, appointed by common accord of the Parliament, the Commission and the Council, thereby establishing its autonomy from the Commission. The Supervisory Committee was installed in July.

The annual report on the fight against fraud for 1998 was presented by the Commission in November. A total of 5,318 cases were investigated, about a fifth of which proved to be fraudulent. The Court of Auditors' report on the 1998 budget, submitted in November again found evidence of fraud, misspending and poor accounting.

A New Interinstitutional Agreement

A new financial perspective was agreed for the period 2000–06 as part of *Agenda 2000* and formed an integral part of the Interinstitutional Agreement

(IIA) signed in May. The new IIA succeeds the agreement covering 1993–99. The total for commitments will fall from EUR 92.03bn in 2000 to EUR 90.66bn in 2006, and for payments 89.6bn and 89.62bn respectively – a decline in terms of GNP from 1.13 per cent to 0.97 per cent. Complying with the original Commission proposal, the overall ceiling on own resources has been maintained at 1.27 per cent of GNP. The cost of enlargement will be covered by budgetary discipline and an expected increase in GNP. If the first wave of enlargement takes place in the middle of the period, the costs incurred will take the form of increased pre-accession aid and will be paid for by funds reserved for Community policy and below the overall own resources ceiling. The perspective makes a clear distinction between expenditure arising from the implementation of internal policies within the EU-15 and accession-related costs, and provides that the amounts available for accession do not exceed the own resources ceiling from 2002. Estimates of the expenditure for an enlarged Union of 21 Member States has been appended with figures indicating the adjustments necessary for the accession of each new Member State.

The new IIA also includes measures designed to improve the budgetary procedure. In particular, the conciliation procedure has been extended, and efforts made to resolve the problems that have previously arisen with respect to the classification of expenditure and the need for all budget items to have a legal basis. All relevant interinstitutional texts have been incorporated in the same framework. In addition, the agreement includes a flexibility instrument of EUR 200m a year which is available to finance one-off items where expenditure overshoots the ceiling of the financial perspective.

Agreement on the 'own resources' system avoided the more radical options outlined by the Commission in its report of October 1998. The maximum rate for VAT resources will be reduced from 1.0 to 0.75 per cent in 2002 and 0.5 per cent in 2004, and the percentage of traditional own resources retained by the Member States (as collection costs) increased from 10 to 25 per cent in 2001. These changes are accompanied by a corresponding increase in the proportion of the GNP resource. Some minor adjustments were made to the correction mechanism for the UK agreed at Fontainebleau in 1984, with the share paid by Germany, the Netherlands, Austria and Sweden reduced to a quarter.

The 2000 budget, adopted in December, was the first to be agreed within the new financial perspective. The Commission's original proposal foresaw a 4.4 per cent reduction in commitment appropriations (EUR 92.71bn) against 1999 and a payments increase of 4.7 per cent (EUR 89,584m) to cover spending arising from the structural funds, research and external action. The draft budget was set at 1.11 per cent of GNP and EUR 1,800m below the ceiling agreed at Berlin. The Council made only modest cuts (EUR 424m in commitment and

EUR 1,718m in payments). Reductions were made under most headings, except for external action (Heading 4), where the Council established an external reserve for Kosovo of EUR 500m in commitment and EUR 280m in payment appropriations by redeploying other funds within the heading. It proposed an increase in commitment appropriations of EUR 132m, including EUR 125m for the fisheries agreement with Morocco (see below). The cuts agreed by the Council were restored by the Parliament in its first reading. The main point of contention, however, concerned the method of funding the EU's operations in East Timor and Turkey, as well as Kosovo and the agreement with Morocco. The Parliament believed these expenditures should be in addition to planned external activities – a position that reflected the latter body's long-standing desire to persuade the Council to establish a flexibility instrument. The Parliament's draft budget used up virtually all payment appropriations, but excluded Kosovo, East Timor, Turkey and the agreement with Morocco, and held out the possibility that it might break the IIA and apply Art. 272 of the Treaty, which would permit it to increase total commitments by EUR 5bn or more. Following the Parliament's first reading, the Commission presented a letter of amendment, which proposed changes to expenditure on agriculture and fisheries to be made as part of the interinstitutional agreement, as well as two further proposals linked to the financing of the Anti-Fraud Office and the appropriation for Kosovo. With regard to the latter, the Commission proposed raising the appropriations ceiling for external action by drawing on unused rural development allocation and funds from the flexibility instrument.

The Council's second reading on 26 November was preceded by a conciliation meeting with the Parliament. The Council draft was far lower than Parliament's first reading. The main difference surrounded EU action on Kosovo. The Council argued that it was not yet possible to establish annual requirements, so any revision of the financial perspective would be premature. In its view, operations should be financed from redeployment within the heading, though some use might be made of the flexibility instrument. On other items, the Council sought to restore the levels decided at its first reading with regard to agriculture, except for dioxin, and structural funds, though it made few other changes to the amendments introduced by Parliament.

The Parliament adopted the 2000 budget at its second reading in mid-December, after tough negotiations that continued until the last minute. The disagreement on how to finance reconstruction in Kosovo and other Heading 4 priorities was finally resolved by an on overall compromise under which the whole EUR 200m allowed by the IIA would be drawn under the flexibility instrument and the question of revising the financial perspective was to be considered in the more general context of funding for the aid programme for the western Balkans over the period 2000–06. Under this compromise,

Parliament reduced the level of payment appropriations by EUR 1,900m compared to its first reading. The 2000 budget totals EUR 93.28bn in commitments – 3.5 per cent less than in 1999 – and EUR 89.39bn in appropriations for payments – an increase of 4.4 per cent.

The 1999 budget was subject to an unprecedented number of supplementary and amending budgets to cover the updating of forecasts, administrative expenditure, and the funding of reconstruction in Kosovo. On the revenue side, total own resources for 1999 came to EUR 86.44bn or 1.12 per cent of Community GNP. Unused appropriations were established provisionally at EUR 3,972m in commitments and EUR 6,953m in payments.

In May, the European Parliament took its final decision not to discharge the 1996 budget for reasons set out in December 1998 – and took note of the closure of the 1996 accounts only. Moreover, it decided not to discharge the 1997 budget on the grounds that the decision should await the new Commission's undertakings on reform and its response to the recommendations made by the Committee of Independent Experts.

VI. Agriculture and Fisheries

Agriculture

Agreement within *Agenda 2000* led to a number of reforms to the CAP under the slogan of preserving the European agricultural model. Continuing in the direction of the MacSharry reforms, guaranteed prices would be reduced, while direct support for farmers would be increased. Prices for cereals were cut by 15 per cent in two steps from 2000–01, for beef by 20 per cent in three steps, and for dairy products by 15 per cent from 2005–06. The rules governing wine were subject to a total overhaul. A new common market organization was introduced, which replaced 23 existing regulations. Reform of milk quotas involved a three-step increase of 1.5 per cent with five Member States – Greece, Spain, Ireland, Italy and the UK (Northern Ireland) – permitted to increase output from 2001, and a review of the regime is to take place in 2006.

The reform aimed at producing an integrated approach to agriculture, adding a commitment to rural development and the environment to the traditional concerns of the CAP. The aim of preserving the rural heritage, while at the same time enabling farmers to create alternative sources of income, was supported by measures to create a stronger agricultural and forestry sector, to make rural areas more competitive, and to encourage environmentally friendly agricultural methods. Member States were called upon to introduce systems to ensure the sustainability of agriculture. Expenditure on agriculture was set in the 2000 budget at EUR 40,994m, of which EUR 36,889m are intended for

Table 1: European Community Budget, 1999 and 2000, Appropriations for Commitment

Heading	1999 Budget (euro)	Budget 2000 (euro)	% Change 2000 over 1999
1. AGRICULTURE			
Agricultural expenditure (excluding rural development)	37 441 000 000	36 889 000 000	−1.5
Rural development and ancillary measures	2 619 050 000	4 104 900 000	56.7
TOTAL 1			
	40 060 050 000	40 993 900 000	2.3
2. STRUCTURAL OPERATIONS			
Objective 1	20 238 000 000	20 781 000 000	2.7
Objective 2	6 024 000 000	3 668 000 000	−39.1
Objective 3	3 104 000 000	3 505 000 000	12.9
Other structural measures (excluding objective 1)	1 860 975 000	161 000 000	−91.3
Community initiatives	4 256 000 000	1 743 000 000	−59.0
Innovative measures and technical assistance	395 250 000	161 000 000	−59.3
Cohesion fund	3 117 700 000	2 659 000 000	−14.7
EEA financial mechanism	5 000 000	p.m.	− 100.0
TOTAL 2			
	39 000 925 000	32 678 000 000	−16.2
3. INTERNAL POLICIES			
Research and technological development	3 450 000 000	3 630 000 000	5.2
Other agricultural operations	147 800 000	52 500 000	−64.5
Other regional operations	17 000 000	15 000 000	−11.8
Transport	21 200 000	20 500 000	−3.3
Other actions in the field of fisheries and the sea	49 925 000	45 550 000	−8.8
Education. vocational training and youth	441 700 000	481 500 000	9.0
Culture and audiovisual sector	95 700 000	111 500 000	16.5
Information and communication	107 600 000	104 000 000	−3.3
Social dimension and employment	127 490 000	144 615 000	13.4
Energy	40 580 000	36 800 000	−9.3
Euratom nuclear safeguards	16 400 000	16 700 000	1.8
Environment	178 450 000	157 700 000	−11.6
Consumer policy and health protection	23 850 000	22 500 000	−5.7
Aid for reconstruction	2 234 000	3 698 000	65.5
Internal market	150 745 000	145 445 000	−3.5
Industry	92 017 000	2 000 000	−97.8
Labour market and technological innovation	209 280 000	214 493 000	2.5
Statistical information	30 725 000	31 400 000	2.2
Trans-European networks	585 190 000	688 000 000	17.6
Co-operation in the fields of justice and home affairs	68 050 000	97 500 000	43.3
Fraud prevention and expenditure in support of internal policies	7 650 000	5 650 000	−26.1
TOTAL 3			
	5 863 586 000	6 027 051 000	2.8
4. EXTERNAL ACTION			
European Development Fund	n/a	n/a	
Food aid and support measures	505 000 000	463 406 000	−8.2
Humanitarian aid	360 850 000	472 590 000	31.0
Co-operation − Asia	438 500 000	446 284 000	2.0
Co-operation − in Latin America	314 050 000	335 914 000	7.0
Co-operation − southern Africa and South Africa	127 500 000	123 540 000	−3.1
Co-operation − the Mediterranean and the Middle East	1 094 000 000	1 142 923 000	4.5
European Bank for Reconstruction and Development	33 750 000	n/a	
Co-operation with the New Independent States and Mongolia	440 210 000	450 373 000	−100.0
Other Community operations for the CCEE, the NIS, Mongolia and the western Balkan countries	53 000 000	34 766 000	2.3
Co-operation with the Balkan countries	406 500 000	456 630 000	−34.4
Other co-operation measures	375 900 000	356 850 000	12.3
European initiatives for democracy and human rights	101 000 000	95 373 000	−5.1
International fisheries agreements	283 700 000	276 105 000	−5.6
External aspects of certain Community policies	111 530 000	103 316 000	−2.7
Common foreign and security policy	27 000 000	47 000 000	−7.4
TOTAL 4	4 672 490 000	4 805 070 000	74.1

Table 1: *(Contd)*

Heading	1999 Budget (euro)	Budget 2000 (euro)	% Change 2000 over 1999
5.ADMINISTRATION			
Commission (excluding pensions)	2 425 442 354	2 504 992 410	3.3
Other institutions (excluding pensions)	1 581 064 249	1 634 370 360	3.4
Pensions (all institutions)	497 556 000	564 311 000	13.4
TOTAL 5	4 504 062 603	4 703 673 770	4.4
6. RESERVES			
Monetary reserve	500 000 000	500 000 000	
Guarantee reserve (Chapter B0-23)	346 000 000	203 000 000	−41.3
Emergency aid reserve (Chapter B7-91)	346 000 000	203 000 000	−41.3
TOTAL 6	1 192 000 000	906 000 000	−24.0
7. PRE– ACCESSION AID			
Agriculture		529 000 000	
Pre-accession structural instrument		1 058 000 000	
Phare (applicant countries)	1 372 350 000	1 579 710 000	15.1
TOTAL 7	1 372 350 000	3 166 710 000	130.8
Total appropriations for commitments	96 665 463 603	93 280 404 770	−3.5
Total appropriations for payments	85 584 463 603	89 386 951 293	
Appropriations for payment as per cent of GNP	1.06	1.11	4.4

Sources: Commission (2000) *Report on General Activities of the European Union in 1999* (Luxembourg: CEC), Table 23; Commission (2000) *Bulletin of the European Union.* Bull-EU 12 (Luxembourg: CEC), Table 25.

Table 2: Budget Revenue

	1999	2000
Agricultural duties	1 187.3	1 102.2
Sugar and isoglucose levies	1 203.6	1 162.7
Customs duties	13 016.8	12 300.0
Own resources collection costs	−1 540.8	−1 456.5
VAT own resources	31 212.2	32 554.6
GNP-based own resources	37 010.7	43 050.8
Balance of VAT and GNP own resources from previous years	447.5	n/a
Budget balance from previous year	3 022.2	n/a
Other revenue	877.6	674.1
Total	86 437.1	89 387.9
Maximum assigned own resources (% GNP)	1.27	1.27
Own resources actually assigned (% GNP)	1.12	1.11

Source: Commission (2000) *General Report on the Activities of the European Union in 1999* (Luxembourg: CEC), Table 25.

market organizations and EUR 4,105m for rural development and accompanying measures.

With respect to the farm prices package for 1999–2000, the Commission largely followed the provisions for 1998–99. There were changes relating to sugar, arable crops, wine and seed, but these were relatively minor, and only Italy announced its intention to vote against the package in July.

The BSE saga seemed to have reached an end in November 1998, at least as far as the UK was concerned. In that month, the Commission imposed a ban on the export of bovines and bovine products from Portugal in response to reports of BSE. It also introduced measures to allow the gradual resumption of UK beef exports under the date-based export system (permitting only deboned beef from animals born after 1 August 1996 to be sold abroad). The date set for the lifting of the embargo was 1 August 1999. However, when the Commission presented a draft decision to the Standing Veterinary Committee, a number of Member States refused to comply with the Committee's decision to lift the ban. In particular, the French government, which claimed to be acting on advice from its National Food Agency (AFSAA) argued that British beef was not safe, but its opinion was rejected by the EU's Scientific Steering Committee. After the negotiations between the Commission, France and the UK to resolve the issue failed in November, the Commission initiated proceedings against Paris. Judging its response inadequate, the Commission addressed a reasoned opinion to France in December and allowed it until the end of the month to answer. Also relating to BSE, the ban on the export of Portuguese beef was extended to August 2000. Discussions on the introduction of a beef labelling scheme continued.

Dioxin poisoning and the WTO Millennium Round occupied the Commission and Council respectively for much of the year. The Commission took a number of measures to protect consumers from the contamination of food by dioxins, following the crisis in Belgium. With respect to the WTO talks in Seattle, it was agreed that the EU should defend the European agricultural model, while supporting the liberalization and expansion of trade in agricultural products.

Fisheries

In November, the Council adopted a regulation on the Financial Instrument for Fisheries Guidance. This major piece of legislation provides a framework for structural assistance in the sector, allowing restructuring without encouraging overfishing. Member States are responsible for monitoring fleet renewal and modernization, subject to the limits on capacity stipulated by the Multi-Annual Guidance programme. The use of public money permitted under the regulation divided the Member States, with the Netherlands and the UK voting against the final agreement.

Agreement was also reached – with Denmark voting against – on the common organization of the market in fishery and acquaculture products. The regulation seeks to ensure that the rules governing the market, including intervention mechanisms, contribute to the sustainability of fishing. Among the measures introduced are labelling requirements of fishery products for consumer retail and the strengthening of the role of producer organizations in the management of resources.

The level of total allowable catches (TACs) and national quotas were agreed at the last Council session of the year in December. Negotiations were characteristically difficult, with anchovies proving the most contentious issue, pitting France, who eventually voted against the final compromise, against Spain. The Commission once again proposed steep reductions (often between 25 and 40 per cent, but rising to 69 per cent in the case of cod in the Irish Sea) but most were offset by the Council in the final agreement. Guide prices for 2000 were also adopted.

Other measures included:

• Council authorization of a negotiating mandate to the Commission to agree a new EU fisheries agreement with Morocco – the most valuable to the Union;
• adoption by the Council of a harmonized list of serious infringements of rules of the Common Fisheries Policy (CFP);
• the regulation on the protection of juveniles was amended on three occasions;
• Commission adoption of proposals on the collection of data to support monitoring of the implementation of the CFP.

V. Social Policy

The Commission launched a number of the initiatives that it had outlined in its 1998 Social Action Programme, where it proposed to build on the commitments made in the Amsterdam Treaty to employment, equal opportunities, exclusion, anti-discrimination and public health. These included:

• a Commission communication, endorsed by the Council in December, on modernizing social protection;
• a series of measures to implement the new Art. 13 of the EC Treaty to combat discrimination on the grounds of sex, racial or ethnic origin, religion or belief, disability, age or sexual orientation;
• the creation of a European work organization in collaboration with

national bodies and the European Foundation for the Improvement of Living and Working Conditions to promote organizational innovation;
- measures to reinforce health and safety at work;
- a communication on the implications of population ageing;
- a Council resolution on equal opportunities for people with disabilities.

A major reform agreed within *Agenda 2000* saw the ESF become the main financial instrument for supporting the adaptation and modernization of policies and systems of education, training and employment. Within the Social Dialogue, the social partners – ETUC, UNICE and the European Centre of Enterprises with Public Participation – signed a framework agreement in March on fixed-term work, which the Council agreed in June to implement. Action in the social field as part of the pre-accession strategy continued.

With respect to implementation, the Commission reported that the transposition rate for European legislation in the social field increased from 90.5 per cent to 95.8 per cent. Nine Member States have transposed all or almost all directives, but Italy and Luxembourg have poor records.

VI. Environmental Policy

The incorporation of environmental considerations in policy in other sectors and climate change were the most important issues in 1999. The Amsterdam Treaty made environmental integration an explicit EU objective, following commitments first made at the Luxembourg European Council in 1997, and reinforced at Cardiff and Vienna in 1998. The Commission presented reports at Cologne in June and Helsinki in December. It found evidence of significant developments in agriculture, fisheries and transport, some progress in the internal market and industry, and little achievement in energy and development. The further action on this front called for by the Commission following its review of the fifth environmental action programme will be repeated in its proposal for the sixth environmental action programme which the Member States requested it to submit before the end of 2000.

The EU continued its efforts on climate change. Signing the Kyoto Protocol in 1998 represented a first step towards implementing the agreement reached at the Kyoto conference and the commitment to reduce six greenhouse gases by 2008–12. The EU had also signed the United Nations Framework Convention on Climate Change adopted at Buenos Aires (the fourth conference on climate change) in 1998. In 1999, it worked towards realizing its commitments internationally and internally. At the fifth conference on climate change held in Bonn in October–November, it participated in preparing the ground for implementing the action plan agreed at Buenos Aires. A deadline – 2002 – was set for the entry of the Protocol and draft negotiating texts on the Kyoto mechanisms (emissions trading, joint implementation, the clean development mechanism) and compliance system were agreed. However, participants remained divided on the levels of ceilings that should be set for the use of the mechanisms, and on the voluntary commitments of developing countries. Internally, as well as the pursuit of mainstream environmental considerations, the Commission was entrusted with the tasks of preparing an action plan to combat climate change and a Green Paper on the use of emissions trading within the EU (so-called 'flexibility mechanisms') to be submitted early in 2000. In addition, the Council amended a decision on mechanisms for monitoring emissions of CO_2 and other greenhouse gases, and adopted a common position on a proposal for a new regulation on ozone depletion.

Other measures relating to air quality and waste management included:

- legislation on emissions of volatile organic compounds, landfill waste, the shipment to non-OECD countries of non-hazardous waste, ambient air quality (limit values for sulphur dioxide, oxides of nitrogen, particulate matter, lead, benzene, carbon dioxide, and maximum levels on the sulphur content of liquid fuels), information for consumers on the fuel economy of passenger cars, and limits on pollutants from tractor diesel engines;
- an amendment of the directive on the packaging and labelling of dangerous substances to allow Austria and Sweden to apply their existing rules until 31 December 2000;
- Council common positions on Commission proposals on voluntary participation in the Community's eco-management and audit scheme (EMAS), the amendment of the release of genetically modified organisms, end-of-life vehicles, the incineration of waste, a framework directive for Community action in water policy, and monitoring CO_2 emissions from new cars;
- an agreement with Japanese and Korean car manufacturers to limit CO_2 car emissions;
- Council conclusions on chemical policy which should be based on the precautionary principle, sustainable development, environmental safety, and efficient functioning of the market;
- a Commission report on the implementation of the urban wastewater directive and the 16th report on quality of bathing water;
- Commission proposals on national emissions ceilings on chemicals ozone levels in ambient air;
- a Commission decision in December granted five Member States (Italy, Spain, Greece, Portugal and France, for its Overseas Departments) derogations of between one and five years from the Auto-Oil Directive.

However, agreement on further limiting emissions from large combustion plants could not be reached. Neither was there progress on the auto-oil programme, the energy ('carbon') tax, or elsewhere in bio-diversity.

The LIFE programme – the EU's financial instrument for the environment – funded 272 projects in 1999, including 94 nature conservation schemes, 157 demonstration projects by industries and local authorities to implement Community environmental policy, and 21 schemes to provide technical assistance to non-member countries in neighbouring regions. In October, the Council adopted a common position on the revision of LIFE for 2002–04 which affirmed the inclusion of a new third strand, LIFE-Third Countries, to co-fund technical assistance and environmental demonstration projects in third countries), alongside LIFE-Environment (incorporation of environmental concerns into industrial and land-planning activities) and LIFE-Nature (nature conservation). However, the Commission objected to the type of comitology committee (regulatory) chosen by the Council in two of the three areas, and invited the EP to introduce an amendment to this effect. No decision on the renewal of the instrument had been reached by the end of the year, when the existing instrument expired.

Implementation was once more a problem. In July, the Commission initiated proceedings against Belgium, Portugal, Spain, Italy, Greece, the Netherlands, Denmark, France and Ireland for failing to provide the environmental reports required under EU legislation concerning, variously, water, waste and the shipment of waste. In October, warnings were sent to three Member States that had not responded to Commission letters requesting environmental information: Ireland (failure to clarify Dublin Bay as a special protection area), Italy (failure to assess the impact of a landfill site in Trapani) and France (threats to wildlife at Mont St Michel).

References

Agence Europe bulletin, various issues, Brussels.

Commission of the European Communities (2000) *General Report on the Activities of the European Union* (Luxembourg: OOPEC).

Council of the European Union, Press Releases on the Council, various.

European Voice, various issues, Brussels.

Presidency Conclusions, Berlin European Council, 24–25 March 1999:
    – Cologne European Council, 3–4 June 1999
    – Tampere European Council, 15–16 October 1999
    – Helsinki European Council, 10–11 December 1999.

Journal of Common Market Studies

Volume 38, Annual Review
September 2000

Softer Euro, Stronger Europe*

ALISON COTTRELL
Painewebber International (UK)

From the moment it was launched, the new single currency failed to do what was expected of it, and age has not made it any the more conformist. Its brief ups and more protracted downs have not endeared the euro to those with a professional interest in commenting on or predicting its moves; hell hath no fury like an analyst scorned, and few expectations have been so thoroughly thwarted as those concerning the level of the euro.

With always helpful 20:20 hindsight, however, the surprise of last year was not that the euro declined, but that it had ever been expected to strengthen in the first place. EMU members' national currencies appreciated sharply in late 1998 on the widespread assumption that a strong economic recovery was on the cards in Europe, and a slowdown in the US, with the Russian crisis applying a further dampener to the US$. Come January 1999, therefore, the euro found itself launched from an extremely high starting point – just as the European recovery was failing to live up to expectations, and the US to live down to them. As the market reassessed the US economy, so the US currency began to recover and, like a cartoon character running off a cliff and looking down, the euro's descent was dramatic. Hopes of a reviving Japan, as 1999 progressed, only compounded its problems. Investors sold euros, rather than US$, to buy yen,

* Alison Cottrell is employed as Chief International Economist for PaineWebber International (U.K.) Ltd. The views expressed herein are her personal views and do not necessarily reflect the views of PaineWebber.

and patchy market liquidity meant that even small increases in selling pressure could sometimes produce a sharp drop in the euro's price.

But important as external circumstances were, they were not the entire euro story. Some factors were grown rather closer to home. Politicians and central bankers demonstrated all too effectively that careless words cost euros, the diverse range of opinions expressed on the currency's decline creating an unfortunate impression of disarray. Sporadic government forays into corporate interventionism, meanwhile, only helped remind investors that more capital was flowing out of Euroland than its governments appeared inclined to allow in. In a world where capital flows, not current account balances (unless of crisis proportions), drive currencies – where mergers matter more than manufactured goods to a currency's mood swings – this was not what euro investors wanted to hear.

The result of adding together a high initial exchange rate, an unexpectedly strong US economy, a reviving yen, careless comments from policy-makers, and disappointment over the pace of European structural reform, was a 13 per cent fall in the euro's trade weighted value rate through 1999, and an even sharper 15 per cent decline against the US$ alone.

If the euro's decline came as a surprise to analysts, it was no less so to Euroland corporations, but of a rather more welcome variety. Behind the fanfare of EMU's launch, business confidence in early 1999 was floundering under the weight of 1998's crippling DM-bloc appreciation and recently imploded Asian demand. As Asia stabilized and the euro retreated, export orders improved and sentiment began to revive. (This export lifeline was particularly important in Germany, where businesses had also to contend in early 1999 with Lafontaine-related fiscal uncertainty.) Stabilizing employment helped reinforce wobbling consumer confidence, and came to the rescue of many a government's budget arithmetic. If the 'right' level of a currency is judged by its consequences for the economy concerned, the euro began 1999 at the wrong level and improved from then on.

This is not to say that this progress was either smooth or straightforward; far from it, thanks in part to the very growth it was generating. Upward revisions to Euroland growth forecasts were, by autumn 1999, persuading the euro to stop flirting with US$ parity and aspire to higher things. Not, however, for long. While interest rate rises are generally considered currency-supportive, gratitude is a rare commodity in financial markets; and almost as soon as the ECB had delivered its November rate rise, the euro was back to its old habits.

Why such anaemia? Primarily, because whatever growth rabbits Euroland pulled out of its hat, the US had always a bigger economic surprise hidden up its sleeve. Investors' appetite for high-tech stocks meant ever more capital being sucked into the rationally exuberant US equity market; and against this background, Euroland's were not the only interest rates to be rising. The ECB's key interest rate began 1999 at 3.0 per cent, fell to 2.5 per cent in April, and ended the year back at 3.0 per cent; the US Federal Funds rate opened the year at 4.75 per cent but closed at 5.50 per cent.

Early 2000 brought little change in either transatlantic interest rate differentials or the euro's fortunes, though it did draw increasingly explicit expressions of euro concern from the ECB (with currency weakness cited as influential in the timing of interest rate moves). Such intensified growling left investors wary of a follow-up 'bite' in the form of central bank intervention to support the euro; and when, in early June, US economic data turned a little softer, already nervous markets were quick to scale back their expectations of how much US interest rate tightening was still to come. The euro rose as a consequence, and the ECB moved to reinforce this revival both with a 50bp interest rate rise at its first June meeting, and by putting Euroland finance ministers under still greater verbal pressure to pursue more ambitious, more visible and more credible fiscal and structural reforms.

The ECB has long highlighted the euro's 'potential upside'. During EMU's first year such comments tended, embarrassingly, to leave that upside even larger than they found it; but ongoing economic revival, combined with an investor-friendly shift in official Euroland attitudes towards taxation, takeovers and competition, suggest that the odds on some of this potential being realized are beginning to improve. True, Euroland will need to exhibit a substantial degree of get up and go, to persuade investors to run after it. Equally true, the euro's progress is likely to be anything but straightforward, given not only the probability of further shifts in perception regarding US economic prospects, but also such home-grown political hurdles as Denmark's EMU referendum. Nevertheless, when the ECB comes to blow out the candles on the currency's second birthday cake, it may well find itself wishing for a less, not more, upwardly mobile euro. For a non-conformist currency, nothing would be more predictable.

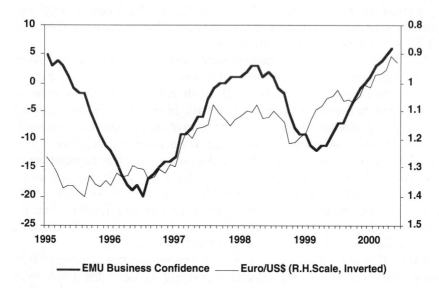

Figure 1: EMU Business Confidence and the Euro
Source: CEC.

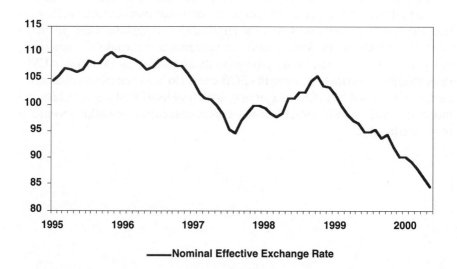

Figure 2: Euro Effective Exchange Rate (First Quarter 1999=100)
Source: ECB.

Journal of Common Market Studies

Volume 38, Annual Review
September 2000

Legal Developments*

NIGEL FOSTER
Cardiff Law School, University of Wales

I. Introduction

Following the Treaty of Amsterdam, the European Court of Justice (ECJ) has made proposals for amendment to its rules of procedure[1] and has undertaken a much more thorough review of the future of the judicial system of the European Union (EU).[2] The main suggestions for immediate reform are for a fast-track procedure for urgent cases, with some cases being dealt with by written proceedings only. The ECJ wants to be able to ask for clarifications from national courts in preliminary rulings and if an answer appears simple from past case law, to rule by simple order rather than full judgment. None of the proposals thus made actually seeks treaty amendment but until the power is transferred from the Member States, any proposed changes to the rules of procedure require the unanimous approval of the Member States in Council.[3]

Further treaty revision raises the prospect of further renumbering of treaty Articles.[4] The renumbering of the articles by the Treaty of Amsterdam has

---

* Senior Lecturer in Law, Cardiff Law School. With the Cardiff Law School funded undergraduate research assistance of Katherine Smith.

[1] See «http://europa.eu.int/cj/en/txts/propositions/txt5a.pdf», Court of Justice, Press Release No. 36/99, 28 May 1999 and also «http://www.curia.eu.int/en/txts/index.htm»

[2] «http://europa.eu.int/cj/en/txts/intergov/ave.pdf»

[3] See the present Rules of Procedure *OJ* 1991 L176/7 as amended to Decision 97/419 *OJ* 1997 L103/3.

[4] The IGC to agree institutional reforms commenced in Brussels on 14 February 2000. See *inter alia*, Commission Communication IP/99/826 of 10 November 1999. A proposal that the Treaty is split into two parts has already been taken on board by the Commission and there are numerous proposals for Treaty amendment. See «http://europa.eu.int/igc2000/index_en.htm»

already considerably complicated the discussion of EC law, particularly when considering cases which arose under the old numbering, as some cases, from commencement to final appeal, can take 13 years.[5] In an attempt to address this, the ECJ issued a policy statement in September 1999,[6] but whether this has helped is open to interpretation.[7] The possibility that the new system will be distorted by future treaty revisions becomes a disturbing new prospect.

Following reforms[8] of the jurisdiction of the Court of First Instance (CFI), the cases appearing before the Court of Justice at first instance now consist predominantly of preliminary ruling references under Art. 234 (ex 177), interspersed with Commission actions against Member States, the odd direct action and increasingly, appeals from the CFI. Despite the huge backlog of cases before the ECJ, time taken for cases to be heard has not increased. Average times,[9] with figures for both the ECJ and CFI taken together, are as follows: Art. 230 (ex 173) actions, 27 months; Art. 226 (ex 169) actions, 18 months; Art. 234 (ex 177) references, 24 months and Appeals, 32 months. Two developments in 1999 may help reduce times. On 17 May 1999, the CFI rules of procedure were amended to allow for single judge rulings in cases which hitherto had been assigned to a three judge chamber. This will apply only where there is no difficulty in the questions of law or fact raised, the case is of limited importance and there are no special circumstances.[10] Jurisdiction is limited to staff cases, actions under Arts. 230, 232, 235 and under the ECSC and EURATOM Treaties. Excluded are actions questioning the validity of treaty Articles or regulations or in respect of cases concerning competition law, state aid or the CAP, unless a previously decided case settles the matter.

Turning to the review of the cases dealt with by the ECJ and the CFI during 1999, the broad outline of previous reviews is maintained, except for a rearrangement to take account of the trend and incidence of case law; for example, intellectual property now has its own section.

---

[5] For example, the *Polypropylene* Cases 47, 51, 199–200, 227, 234–5, 245/92 and 5/93 *Commission* v. *Anic Partecipazioni SpA* and *Hercules Chemicals NV and others* v. *Commission,* Proceedings of the European Court of Justice 20/99, pp. 18–53, [1999] 5 CMLR 976–1166.

[6] Court of Justice Press Release No. 57/99 of 30 July 1999. Also reproduced in Proceedings of the European Court of Justice 21/99, p. 34.

[7] The Court's use in individual cases is not always consistent, e.g. see Case C-254/97 *Baxter* v. *Premier Ministre* Proceedings of the European Court of Justice 20/99, p. 7. Citation by the Court: Art. 52 (now, after amendment, Art. 43) and Art. 48 (ex Art. 58)! Whilst the system is described as a uniform system, it is the Court's system and it is not known whether the other institutions will also follow this or whether they too will have their own set of guidelines. Depending on the context, I will use, e.g., Art. 39 (ex 48) and Art. 48 (now 39).

[8] Decision 88/591 *OJ* 1988 L319/1, Decision 93/350 *OJ* 1993 L144/21, Decision 94/149 *OJ* 1994 L66/29.

[9] Based on looking at roughly 75 per cent of the cases decided in 1999. For the latest reported statistics which relate to 1998, see «http://www.curia.eu.int/en/pei/rapan.htm»

[10] See *OJ* 1999 L114/52 and L135/92. The first case, a staff case, was disposed of under this procedure on 28 October 1999. Case T-180/98, Proceedings of the Court of Justice, 28/99, p. 26.

II. The Development of the Competence and the Powers of the EU and its Institutions

External Competence

Article 40 of the EEC–Morocco Co-operation Agreement provides for the prohibition of discrimination in EC Member States against Moroccan workers who have lawfully settled and obtained employment. While the provision was held to have direct effects – which is, of course, important in securing individual rights – it does not, according to the ECJ,[11] have the effect of prohibiting the host Member State from refusing to extend the residence permit of a Moroccan migrant worker. Neither an analogy with the different terms of the EEC–Turkey Agreement nor with the position of nationals of the EU could be helpful in interpreting the EEC–Morocco Agreement. Article 40 is concerned with working conditions and not the rights of Member States to grant or refuse residence permits.[12] The ruling resembles the judicial thinking in respect of the public service proviso for the free movement of workers in that it applies to entry to the service in the first place but not to service and conditions of employment.[13]

Internal Competence

NSK Ltd v. *Commission*[14] involves a rare interpretation of a previous judgment, which is catered for under Art.102 of the Rules of Procedure of the Court of Justice and is instructive on the criteria for an application for an interpretation. This is admissible where it seeks clarification of the meaning of a specific point in question. Furthermore, interveners can submit an application, even where the applicant has not. In this case, the requirement in the previous judgment that the Commission pay the costs of the successful appeal, was interpreted to include the costs of the interveners who had been successful in their submissions.

Interinstitutional Relations

Legal base challenges by the EP continue.[15] Two regulations concerned with the protection of forests were adopted by the Council under Art. 43 (now 37)

---

[11] Case 416/96 *Nour Eddline El-Yassini* v. *Secretary of State for the Home Department* [1999] ECR I-1209, [1999] 2CMLR 32.
[12] For a fuller discussion of this case, see case note by Melis (1999) 36 CMLR, 1357–64, see Case 152/73 *Sotgui* v. *Deutsche Bundespost* [1974] ECR 153.
[13] See Case 152/73 *Sotgui* v. *Deutsche Bundespost* [1974] ECR 153.
[14] Case C-245 P-INT *NSK Ltd* v. *Commission* [1999] ECR I-1.
[15] Cases C-164-5/97 *EP* v. *Council* [1999] ECR I-1139 and see *Annual Review* 1997, p. 95 and *Annual Review*, 1998, p. 116. See also Cullen and Charlesworth (1999) 'Diplomacy by Other Means: The Use of Legal Base Litigation as a Political Strategy by the European Parliament and Member States'. 36 CMLR, 1243–70.

(the Common Agricultural Policy), which required the consultation of the EP only by the Council and not under Art. 130s (now 175) as contended by the EP. The regulations concerned the environment and required the use of the co-operation procedure. In accordance with previous case law, the ECJ held that while forests were connected with agriculture, the primary connection in this case was environmental protection and thus in order to uphold the democratic prerogatives of the EP, Art. 130s should have been used. Also in keeping with previous case law, the ECJ annulled the regulations but declared that they remain in force until replacement regulations were enacted under the correct legal base. Again, the Council and EP have contrived to waste a considerable amount of time, and European taxpayers' money has been spent on unneces-sary legal costs. There should be a procedure by which the legal base can be agreed as part of the legislative procedure before enactment, to save this unnecessary waste.

III. Development of the Principles of Primary EC Law

What may be regarded as primary EC law is now wider than it used to be. This section therefore accommodates the expansion in the policy areas of the EC and thus the jurisdiction of the ECJ.

Article 10 (ex Art. 5) The 'Good Faith' Clause

The ECJ has made it clear[16] that criminal liability does not arise from EC law; therefore improper use of European Social Fund money cannot be held to be a criminal offence under EC law. However, the ECJ stressed that Art. 10 (ex 5) nevertheless requires Member States to take all effective measures to control conduct adversely affecting the financial interests of the Community, includ-ing the imposition of criminal penalties, even if EC law envisages civil remedies only. If, under national law, similar conduct would be classified as criminal, the applicable penalties must equal national law penalties and be effective, proportionate and dissuasive.

Article 12 (ex Art. 6) Equality / No Discrimination

Once again equality of treatment focuses on national procedural law but, surprisingly, in *ED Srl* v. *Italo Fenocchio*,[17] the ECJ did not hold a rule of Italian national procedural law to be contrary to the fundamental freedoms of the Community, nor that it made the realization of fundamental rights more difficult and thus contrary to EC law. The law in question provided an *ex parte*

---

[16] Case C-186/98 *Nunes and de Matos* [1999] 2 CMLR 1403.
[17] Case C-412/97 *ED Srl* v. *Italo Fenocchio*, Proceedings of the European Court of Justice 18/99, p. 3.

summary procedure for the collection of debts but which was not applicable against debtors outside Italy. The ECJ held that this was not subject to the free movement of goods or services and that the procedural law, although clearly discriminatory did not, in its view, constitute a restriction on the freedom to make payments under Art. 56 (2) (ex 73b). It was thus lawful under Community law. This was not the view of the Advocate General, who had considered that the general prohibition of discrimination under Art. 6 (now 12) had been breached and whose opinion accords with the previous position of the ECJ.[18] This case therefore introduces an inconsistency with previous case law from which no firm assumptions can as yet be made. If followed up in future cases, it may be concluded that this indicates a shift in the willingness of the ECJ to consider whether elements of national procedural law stand in the way of rights under EC law.

Free Movement of Goods (Arts. 23–25 (ex 9–12) (Charges) and Art. 90 (ex 95) Taxation

France introduced a new tax on the supply of CB radio sets, none of which were produced in France.[19] While on the face of it, the tax appeared to be an acceptable, systematic and objective tax – levied on all products using the Hertzian radio spectrum in order to pay for the costs of its administration – evidence revealed that other forms of electronic equipment were not taxed on supply, but on sale. The alternative argument, that it was justified as a charge for the service of overseeing the spectrum, was also rejected as it did not provide a service to importers but only to users. Hence, the ECJ concluded that the charge was contrary to Arts. 9 and 12 (new 25). The tax was also incompatible for sets imported from non-EC Member States because it breached Art. 113 (new 133) as no new external tariff charges can be imposed unilaterally by a Member State.

Free Movement of Persons

Although the Treaty of Amsterdam added a new Title, Title VI,[20] to the EC Treaty concerned with immigration and the free movement of EU citizens, prior to this there was little provision regarding general rights of movement, and what there was[21] did not translate into an absolute right of free movement.

[18] See *Annual Review*, 1997, p. 96, in particular the case of *Hayes* v. *Kronenburger* [1997] ECR I-1711 and *Annual Review*, 1998, pp. 116–17. See also Biondi (1999) *The ECJ and Certain National Procedural Limitations: Not Such a Tough Relationship*, 36 CMLR, 1271–87.
[19] Case C-109/98 *CRT France International* v. *Directeur régional des impôts de Bourgogne* [1999] ECR I-2237.
[20] Title IV, Visas, Asylum, Immigration and other Policies Related to the Free Movement of Persons, Arts. 61–69.
[21] See Directive 90/364, *OJ*, 1990, L 180/26. General right of residence Directive 90/365, *OJ*, 1990, L 18028, the right of residence for employees and self-employed persons who have ceased their occupational activity. Directive 93/96 *OJ* 1993 L317/59, on the right of residence for students./

On re-entry to Holland, a Dutch national, *Florius Wijsenbeek*,[22] refused to show his passport, referring instead to the provisions of the EC Treaty, Arts. 7a and 8a (now 14 and 18) on the free movement of EU citizens as removing the requirement to do so. He was prosecuted and ordered either to pay a small fine or go to prison for one day. The ECJ held that, because Art. 7a (now 14) provides only that the Council may, rather than shall, adopt provisions to facilitate the objectives of the internal market, the provisions are not directly effective. The ECJ observed that, at the time of the events in question, there were no common rules on immigration or border controls, therefore, even if an unconditional right to movement was established, the Member States retain the right to carry out identity checks to determine whether the person entering the state is entitled to do so. Furthermore, Member States retain the right to impose penalties for breach of the obligation to be identified, provided that such penalties are proportionate and comparable to penalties for similar national infringements. The ECJ considered that imprisonment would create an obstacle to free movement of persons but that the fine of 65 Dutch guilder appeared to be acceptable.

Free Movement of Workers and Family (Art. 39 (ex 48))

In *Meeusen* v. *Beheer Groep*,[23] Mrs M was the daughter of a Belgian national, a director of a company established in the Netherlands. Her mother worked on a part-time basis for the company. All three continued to live in Belgium. Mrs M attended a higher education institution in Belgium but applied for and was initially granted study finance by the Dutch authorities, who subsequently overturned the decision on the grounds that her mother was not a migrant worker and was not resident in Holland. The ECJ, in keeping with past law,[24] held that, providing a person satisfy criteria to be a worker (services under direction of another for remuneration) and that the work was genuine and effective (not marginal or ancillary), they are to be regarded as a worker for the purposes of EC law. Marriage to the sole owner and director of the company did not, in the view of the ECJ, negate that conclusion. The mother was therefore a worker and as a dependent child of a worker, Mrs M was entitled under the equality of social advantages guaranteed by Art. 7 of Regulation 1612/68 to study finance under the same conditions as nationals. The ECJ also added that the father, as sole owner and director, was not to be regarded as a worker. However, as a self-employed person, under Art. 43 (ex 52) the same

---

[22] Case C-378/97 *Florius Wijsenbeek,* Proceedings of the Court of Justice 23/99, p. 31.

[23] Case C-337/97 *Meeusen* v. *Hoofdirectie van de Informatie Beheer Groep,* Proceedings of the European Court of Justice 16/99, p. 2.

[24] See Case 139/85 *Kempf* v. *Staats Secretaria van Justitie* [1986] ECR 1741, [1987] 1 CMLR 764 and Case 66/85 *Lawrie-Blum* v. *Land Baden-Württemberg* [1986] ECR 2121, [1987] 3 CMLR 389.

rights of the dependent child would also accrue. A residence requirement was therefore discriminatory.

Free Movement (Social Security Considerations)

In an application[25] for Income Support (a non-contributory social security benefit), it was held that the granting of the status of 'habitual residence' only on completion of an appreciable period of residence on the part of a UK national who had returned to the UK to seek work, was contrary to Art. 10 of Regulation 1408/71. The ECJ held that other circumstances can be employed to consider whether residence is habitual, such as the family situation, other personal circumstances and intentions, and not just length of residence.

Freedom of Establishment and Free Movement of Services (Arts. 43 and 55 (ex 52 and 66)); Company Law Art. 48 (ex Art. 58)

In a case which raises general matters of principle, the registration of a branch of a UK company in Denmark by Danish residents[26] cannot be prevented because it is suspected that it was done to avoid stricter capital requirements in Denmark. The UK principal company required lower share capital, which did not need to be paid up, but had never traded anywhere, and all its business was undertaken in Denmark by the Danish branch. The ECJ held that the refusal to register would be contrary to freedoms established under Arts. 52 and 59 (now 43 and 49) of the EC Treaty. Only if fraud or the attempted fraud of creditors or the authorities was established, would measures to restrict or hinder the freedom be possible and, in any event, such measures must meet the well-established requirements of Community law, that they be non-discriminatory, justified by imperative requirements in the general interest and proportionate. This appears to introduce the possibility of the 'Delaware company registration' factor as known in the USA.[27] But, as the ECJ pointed out, the place and country of registration will be known to Danish creditors who trade with the company and who may, as a result, be more cautious in their dealings. This implies that the ECJ has preferred the fundamental principle of the freedom of establishment over any possible considerations of consumer or creditor protection.

---

[25] Case C-90/97 *Robin Swaddling* v. *Adjudication Officer* [1999] ECR I-1075.

[26] Case C-212/97 *Centros Ltd* v. *Erhvervs- og Selskabsstyrelsen* [1999] ECR I-1459, [1999] 2 CMLR 551. See case note (2000) 37 CMLR, 147–55.

[27] The state with the most generous requirements for company registration and which attracts more registrations as a result. For a consideration of the Delaware registration factor in a different context, see Barnard (2000) *Social Dumping and the Race to the Bottom: Some Lessons for the European Union from Delaware?*, 25 EL Rev., p. 57.

Provision of Services

The provision of services includes the renting of boat moorings on the Austrian part of Lake Constance.[28] It was held by the ECJ that a prosecution for exceeding the quota of lettings for foreign residents was contrary to Art. 59 EC (now 49) because the quota was established for the economic protection of local owners. The argument by the *Vorarlberg* Authorities that the rents, which would necessarily be higher as a result of the removal of a protective quota, would drive away local boat owners, was not enough for the ECJ to overcome a fundamental freedom. The ECJ also held that the public policy proviso could not be relied upon to support economic aims.[29] One can have some sympathy for the local view, as now the highest bidder from anywhere in the EU will secure what is a scarce and finite resource, namely a mooring and thus the right to use Lake Constance. It is no wonder that some people are not happy about the kind of market that is being erected by the EU. It seems that a much more subtle approach in defending genuine local interests will have to be devised.

Previous case law established that the rights under free movement of services extends also to tourists as recipients of services[30] and which protect them from, *inter alia*, exclusion from national territories for minor offences. Greece automatically excluded for life an Italian national for a conviction for the personal use of a prohibited drug,[31] The public policy proviso which was employed to justify the ban is subject to Art. 3 of Directive 64/221 which requires that measures taken on the grounds of public policy must be based on personal conduct.[32] The ECJ had no difficulty in holding that the ban imposed without regard to personal circumstances would not meet the conditions required by the directive and was contrary to Community law.

Television Broadcasting

The extent to which television broadcasters can broadcast advertisements is clearly of the utmost importance to them as it affects their income. Directive 89/552[33] sought to regulate this but was considered not to have done so particularly clearly, hence the reason for the German case of *ARD* v. *Pro 7 et al*.[34] Under Art. 11 (1), adverts must normally be placed between programmes

---

[28] Case C-224/97 *Erich Ciola* v. *Land Vorarlberg* [1999] ECR I-2517, [1999] 2 CMLR 1220.
[29] See paras 16 and 17 of the judgment.
[30] Case 286/82, *Luisi* v. *Ministero del Tesauro* [1984] ECR 377, [1985] 3 CMLR 52.
[31] Case C-348/96 *D. Calfa* [1999] ECR I-11. See case note (1999) 24 EL Rev, pp. 621–6.
[32] Also confirming previous case law. Case 41/74 *Van Duyn* v. *H.O.* [1974] ECR 1337, [1975] 1 CMLR 1, Cases 115-116/81; *Adoui and Cornauille* v. *Belgian State* [1982] ECR 1665, [1982] 3 CMLR 631; and Case 67/74 *Bonsignore* v. *Oberstadtdirektor der Stadt Köln* [1975] ECR 297, [1975] 1 CMLR 472.
[33] *OJ* 1989 L298/23.
[34] Case C-6/98 *ARD* v. *Pro 7 Media AG, Sat 1 Satellitenfernsehen GmbH und Kabel 1 Fernsehen GmbH* [1999] 3 CMLR 769.

except for films and other longer broadcasts of more than 45 minutes, which may be interrupted once for each period of 45 minutes and a further interruption is allowed if the total broadcast time is longer than 1 hour 50 minutes.[35] Two interpretations of the Article were presented by the parties. The 'gross principle' allows the duration of the adverts themselves to be taken into account in calculating the length of time for the purposes of working out the permitted interruptions. Arguably if taken to the extreme, this would allow, every 45 minutes, 1 minute of film and 44 minutes of adverts, but it is unlikely that anyone would wish to tune in to a channel adopting this policy. The 'net principle' takes the simpler view that only the duration of the film broadcast should be calculated. The ECJ considered that Art. 11 (3) was ambiguous but that the purpose of Directive 89/552 was to ensure freedom to provide television broadcasting services and therefore any restrictions to what is a fundamental freedom must be expressed in clear terms. Where restrictions are not clear, they themselves must be subject to a restrictive interpretation. The ECJ held that Art. 11 (3) provides for the gross principle so that, in calculating the 45-minute period, adverts must be included. While that may be arguable, the ECJ did add that Art. 11 (3) in conjunction with Art. 3 (1) allows the Member States to prescribe the net principle providing such rules comply with other relevant provisions of Community law.

Intellectual Property[36]

In a judgment which is of clear importance to huge numbers of small traders in all branches of commerce, the German car manufacturer, BMW, and its Dutch subsidiary failed to prohibit the use of its trademark in an action against a small trader.[37] Similar to very many small-scale retailers and repairers who have concentrated their efforts and expertise on one particular brand or make of product, Mr Deenik specialized in the sale and repair of BMW cars and advertised himself as a 'BMW specialist'. BMW considered this to be an infringement of its trademark as protected by Directive 89/104.[38] The ECJ held that, although the use of the trademark in the circumstances was an unauthorized usage within the meaning of Art. 5 of the directive, such a use may be

---

[35] Article 11 (3) provides 'the transmission of audio-visual works such as feature films and films made for television (excluding series, serials, light entertainment programmes and documentaries), provided their programmed duration is more than 45 minutes, may be interrupted once for each complete period of 45 minutes. A further interruption is allowed if their programmed duration is at least 20 minutes longer than two or more complete periods of 45 minutes'.

[36] Intellectual property is a hard section to place within the scheme of things either within the Treaty or in this review as it is mentioned in connection with free movement of goods (Art. 30) and under property ownership under Art. 295, but legislation enacted concerning this topic has been based on both specific and general provisions of the Treaty including Arts. 57, 66, 100a and 235 (now 47, 55, 95 and 308).

[37] *Case Bayerische Motorenwerke AG and BMW Nederland BV* v. *Ronald Karen Deenik* [1999] ECR I-925, [1999] 1 CMLR 1099.

[38] *OJ* 1989 L40/1.

acceptable under Arts. 6 or 7 of the directive concerned with the limits and exhaustion of rights. The ECJ held that Art. 7 prevents BMW from prohibiting the use of its trademark by another person for the purpose of informing the public of the specialization in the sale of second-hand BMW cars. However, if the advertising suggested there was a commercial connection between the second-hand car garage and BMW, or that there was a special relationship between them, then BMW might be justified in its opposition to the use of the trademark. Turning to the advertising of the specialization in the repair of BMW cars, the ECJ held that this use merely identifies the goods for which a service is provided and that this expertise cannot be advertised without using the BMW mark. This was an acceptable use of the mark. This judgment must apply then to all examples of the sale and repair by independent traders of goods ranging from bicycles or cars to vacuum cleaners or washing machines, indeed any sale or repair of branded goods. This seems like common sense.

In *Sebago* v. *GB-Unic*,[39] the ECJ confirmed its judgment in *Silhouette*,[40] concerning the exhaustion of trademarks and parallel imports. Sebago has the trademarks in the Benelux for Sebago and Dockside shoes. GB-Unic imported genuine Sebago and Dockside shoes from outside the EEA. Sebago claimed infringement of trademark for the marketing of the goods without consent. In referring to the earlier case, the ECJ held there was no exhaustion of rights and that the trademark proprietor was entitled to enforce his rights against the retailer of the parallel imports coming from outside the EEA. As regards the exhaustion of the Community or now correctly, the EEA trademark, this applies only to each individual good which has been put on the EEA market with the consent of the trademark proprietor who can oppose imports of goods from outside the EEA market. The case has the effect of shifting the burden of proof on to retailers who sell designer goods to prove that the stock was not acquired as a parallel import from a non-EEA Member State. Furthermore, Member States are not permitted to recognize exhaustion of trademarks where the parallel imports are from countries outside the EEA.

Under Italian law, copyright protection lasted 30 years, whereas the Copyright Directive (93/98[41]) extended this to 50 years with the possibility, deliberately introduced into the directive, of reviving expired rights for the longer protection. This left a hiatus if the national protection expired before the entry into force of the directive (1 July 1995). Songs protected until 1992 were subsequently reissued by Butterfly Music after the copyright expired. Upon entry into force of the directive, the copyright was revived until 2012. The original producer (CEMED) sought to prevent further distribution by Butterfly

---

[39] Case C-173/98, *Sebago Inc., Ancienne Maison Dubois et Fils SA* v. *G-B Unic SA* [1999] 2 CMLR 1317.
[40] Case C-355/96 *Silhouette* v. *Hartlauer* [1998] ECR I-4799, [1998] 2 CMLR 953. See *Annual Review*, 1998, p. 119.
[41] *OJ* 1993 L248/15.

Music.[42] The ECJ held that the revival brought about by the directive was without prejudice to any acts of exploitation executed before 1 July 1995, but left it to Member States to lay down the necessary provisions to protect rights of third parties. The ECJ considered that the Member States have the discretion to regulate the intervening period provided that this did not inhibit the revived rights provided for by the directive. Italian law, which allowed third parties to exploit rights for a limited period, met this position according to the ECJ.

Free Movement of Capital (Art. 56 (2) (ex 73))

In *Trummer*,[43] Austrian legislation prohibited the creation of a mortgage in anything else but Austrian Schillings or fine gold. The validity of this provision in relation to the free movement of capital and whether mortgages were guarantees covered by Directive 88/361[44] were the issues raised by the Austrian Supreme Court in a reference to the ECJ. The ECJ held that a mortgage was another guarantee covered by the directive and to restrict its creation to the national currency of the Member State was a restriction on the free movement of currency contrary to old Art. 73b (now 56) of the Treaty.

Articles 85, 86 and 90 (Competition Law)

In a case which takes up where the *Kali & Salz* judgment (reviewed last year[45]) left off, *Gencor* v. *Commission*[46] confirms that the merger regulation is a suitable vehicle to prevent the creation of collective dominant positions to the detriment of competition in the EU. The CFI upheld the Commission Decision[47] to prohibit the proposed joint takeover by Gencor (RSA) and Lonrho (Eng.) of Implats (RSA) which together with Amplats Ltd would have created a dominant duopoly in the platinum and rhodium markets. The additionally important aspect of the extra-territorial jurisdiction of the Mergers Regulation[48] was also considered because the activities of all the companies were carried out in South Africa, and the South African competition authorities had already approved the proposed joint acquisition. Nevertheless, the CFI held that Art. 1 of the regulation applies to all concentrations with a Community dimension and that sales of the products in the EU were sufficient to constitute substantial operations and thus justify the Commission intervention.[49]

---

[42] Case C-60/98 *Butterfly Music* v. *CEMED* [2000] 1 CMLR 587.
[43] Case C-222/97 *Manfred Trummer and Peter Mayer* [1999] ECR I-1661.
[44] *OJ* 1988 L178/5.
[45] Joined cases C-68/94 *France* v. *Commission* and C-30/95 *Société Commerciale des Potasses et de l'Azote (SCPA)* v. *Commission* [1998] ECR I-1375, [1998] 4 CMLR 829. See *Annual Review* 1998, p. 122.
[46] T-102/96 [1999] 4 CMLR 971.
[47] Commission Decision 97/26/EC of 24 April 1996, *OJ* 1997 L11/30.
[48] Regulation 4064/89, *OJ* 1990 L257/14.
[49] This involved judgment cannot be done justice in a review of this nature, however, it has been in (1999) 24 EL Rev pp. 638–52.

The ECJ heard a series of appeals[50] arising from the Commission Polypropylene Decision[51] in a judgment which is more notable for the delay in final hearing than for the development of Community law. In the first case, the Commission appealed against the decision of the CFI partially to annul its decision and to reduce the fine. All the cases involved appeals against fines and judgments of the CFI upholding the Commission decision. The appeals took a notable 7 years and 2 months. In part this was because the undertakings had originally lodged their applications before the ECJ in 1986, before being referred in 1989 to the CFI once it had been set up. The actions all concentrate on the procedure adopted by the Commission. Points brought forward by the parties which had not been previously brought before the CFI were all dismissed by the ECJ as inadmissible, as were requests to review the finding of fact by the CFI, as beyond an appeal jurisdiction. In the first case, the concept of undertaking determined by the CFI was held to be incorrect and, as a consequence, the reduction in the fine was confirmed. In all other cases, the pleas were dismissed. For the most part, it had proved a serious waste of time.

Equal Pay and Sex Equality (Art.141 (ex 119) and Related Directives)

Seymour-Smith and Perez[52] concerns the minimum qualification period for unfair dismissal in the UK. Two female employees, who had been made redundant after 15 months, claimed that the two-year eligibility requirement for unfair dismissal was indirectly discriminatory to women because more women than men were affected by the rule.[53] The case reached the House of Lords in the UK before reference to the ECJ, which held that redundancy compensation equals pay for the purposes of Art. 141 (119), as do the conditions determining whether an employee can obtain compensation for unfair dismissal. The crux of the issue at hand was whether the two-year rule itself was less favourable to women. Although it was shown in the case that, statistically, a lower percentage of women than men were able to satisfy the rule, both the High Court and the ECJ were of the view that this alone was not enough to demonstrate a disproportionate effect. In order for that to be satisfied, the percentages of women and men not able to satisfy the condition

[50] Cases 47, 51, 199–200, 227, 234–5, 245/92 and 5/93, *Commission* v. *Anic Partecipazioni SpA* and *Hercules Chemicals NV and others* v. *Commission* [1999] 5 CMLR 976–1166, Proceedings of the European Court of Justice 20/99, pp. 18–53.
[51] Commission Decision 86/398 of 23 April 1986, *OJ* 1986 L230/1.
[52] Case C-167/93, *R.* v. *Secretary of State for Employment, ex parte Seymour-Smith and Perez* [1999] ECR I-623. The case was dismissed by industrial tribunal, but the Court of Appeal held the rule was disproportionate and not objectively justified. See *The Times,* 3 August 1995 and case note (2000) 37 CMLR 157–65.
[53] N.B. the law has now been amended by the Labour government and reduced to one year by Statutory Instrument 1999 No. 1436: The Unfair Dismissal and Statement of Reasons for Dismissal (Variation of Qualifying Period) Order 1999 made on 23 May 1999 and entered into force 1 June 1999 which amended the Employment Rights Act 1996.

had to be compared to the overall proportions of women and men in the workforce. The ECJ was of the view that, as 77.4 per cent of men and 68.9 per cent of women fulfilled the rule, this did not show a considerable difference. Since further information was not to hand in the case, the ECJ held that this was a matter for the national court to determine, but used the terms that a *considerably* smaller percentage of women would be required to avoid short-term phenomena. Even if that were the case, the Member State might still be able to demonstrate that the rule reflects a legitimate aim of its social policy unrelated to any discrimination based on sex and proportionate to achieving its aims. Careful attention to the presentation of statistics is required in such cases.[54]

A woman who cooked for the Commando Regiment of the Royal Artillery was prevented from cooking for the Royal Marines without it constituting unlawful discrimination. Article 2 (2) of Directive 76/207[55] provides that Member States may exclude from the principle of equal treatment occupational activities in which, by reason of their nature or the context in which they are carried out, the sex of the worker constitutes a determining factor. In *Sirdar* v. *The Army Board*,[56] Mrs Sirdar was made redundant for economic reasons from her post as chef for the Commando Regiment of the Royal Artillery, but was offered a post as chef for the Royal Marines. However, she was then informed that she was ineligible because of their policy of excluding women from their regiment on the public security ground that her presence was incompatible with the requirement of interoperability, that is, the need for every marine, regardless of specialization, to be capable of fighting in a commando unit. The ECJ accepted that the organization of Royal Marines differed fundamentally from other units in the British Army, being a small force in the first line of attack. It was established and accepted that chefs are also required to serve as front line commandos and that all members are engaged and trained for that purpose without exception. The ECJ held, therefore, that the competent authorities were entitled to exclude women providing the decision was proportionate.[57]

The case of *Abdoulaye* v. *Renault*[58] might be interpreted as one of positive discrimination in action. Additional or guaranteed payments for females on maternity leave, over and above those paid to males on paternity leave, were recognized by the ECJ as acceptable. This was because of the occupational

---

[54] The case was finally rejected by the House of Lords after a 10-year history, see *The Times,* 18 February 2000.
[55] *OJ* 1976 L39/40.
[56] Case C-273/97 *Angela Sirdar* v. *The Army Board, Secretary of State for Defence* [1999] 3 CMLR 559.
[57] In a forthcoming case also concerning the employment of women in the armed forces, it was held that not all army units could lawfully exclude women, see Case C-285/98 *Kreil* v. *Germany, The Times,* 22 February 2000.
[58] Case C-38/98 *Abdoulaye* v. *Renault,* Proceedings of the European Court of Justice 22/99, p. 27.

disadvantages suffered by women during their absence and was held not to be discriminatory.

Directive 79/7[59] was the basis for the claim by Mr Taylor that he had been discriminated against because he had been refused a winter fuel payment provided for under the UK Social Fund Winter Fuel Payment Regulations 1998,[60] whereas women of the same age received the additional £20 payment. He argued that Art. 3 (1)(a) applied so that statutory schemes to protect against old age were to be implemented without discrimination. The UK government argued that because the payments were necessarily linked to the determination of the statutory age of pensions payments, it was excused the application of Community law. The ECJ dismissed this and upheld the claim by Mr Taylor. The further argument that the payment was to help people in need was also rejected as it was paid to all elderly persons without reference to their financial position but on the basis of age. Therefore, the ECJ concluded, it was designed to help protect against the risk of old age. There was no necessary link of the protection against old age with the pensionable ages of men and women, hence it was unlawful discrimination on the part of the UK.[61]

In a case in which women were excluded from payment of a Christmas bonus while on maternity leave,[62] the ECJ held that a bonus is payable under Art. 141 (ex 119) but that it did not fall within the concept of payment under Art. 11 (2)(b) of the Pregnancy Directive 92/85[63] which seeks to ensure that workers on maternity leave are provided with an adequate allowance. The ECJ also considered Clause 2 (6) of the Annex to the Parental Leave Directive 96/34,[64] which provides that employment rights acquired or in the process of being acquired, are maintained until the end of parental leave. Two interpretations were put forward as to what the bonus might constitute: (1) it was an exceptional allowance and as such outside all Community law provisions; or (2) the bonus was retroactive pay for work performed. In the latter case, the view of the ECJ was that the refusal of the employer to pay this, even if reduced proportionately the time actually worked, places workers on leave at a disadvantage and constitutes discrimination contrary to Art. 141 since females are more likely to be on parenting leave than men. The ECJ was also of the view that the period on leave under the legal protection of EC directives must also be taken into account because, if it were not, it would discriminate against a female who would otherwise have been working. The ECJ summarily dismissed the view that the bonus was an incentive for future work and loyalty

[59] *OJ* 1979 L6/24.
[60] Case C-382/98 *R* v. *Secretary of State for Social Security ex parte John Taylor* [2000] 1 CMLR 873, *The Times,* 25 January 2000.
[61] See the *Guardian,* 17 December 1999 for general comments about the ruling.
[62] Case C-333/97 *Susanne Lewen* v. *Lothar Denda,* [2000] 2 CMLR 38.
[63] *OJ* 1992 L348/1.
[64] *OJ* 1996 L145/9.

rather than past activities, although quite what difference this would make, if any, is questionable, as it, too, would have to be paid without discrimination.

Worker Protection

The case of *Allen et al.*[65] is worth mentioning briefly because it appears to extend the scope of Directive 77/187,[66] which was designed to safeguard employees' rights in the event of transfers of undertakings, businesses or parts of businesses. The ECJ held that the directive also applies to a transfer between two subsidiary companies in the same group. The fact that the companies in question have the same ownership, the same management, the same premises and are engaged in the same work makes no difference in this regard.

Environment

The World Wildlife Fund (*WWF*[67]) contested the approval of improvements to an airport at Bozen in South Tyrol, because the environmental impact assessment procedure envisaged by Directive 85/337 was not undertaken by the authorities. The ECJ held that Member States could not exclude certain classes of project from assessment, but could exclude individual projects provided an alternative assessment was carried out. However, it was for the national courts to review that alternative assessment to see if it complied with the requirements of the directive. It would not satisfy the requirements of the directive if it failed to include public participation, as in this development. It was further held that the directive has direct effects and it is for the national courts to set aside decisions allowing developments to continue which have not been subject to an environmental assessment according to the directive. The decision reached by the ECJ may well provide support for environmentalists objecting to proposed development in that they can insist on their direct rights before national courts to ensure that environmental impact assessments are carried out in accordance with the provisions of the directive.

IV. Enforcement and Effectiveness of Community Law

Individual Enforcement

The failure by Austria to implement the Package Tour Directive[68] in time, led to loss by individuals[69] who had won holidays but who were required personally to pay airport taxes and low occupancy supplements. The Package

[65] Case C-234/98 *G.C. Allen et al.* [2000] 3 CMLR 1, *The Times,* 10 December 1999.
[66] *OJ* 1977 L61/27.
[67] World Wildlife Fund. Case C-435/97 *WWF* v. *Autonome Provinz Bozen* [2000] 1 CMLR 149, *The Times,* 12 October 1999.
[68] Directive 90/314, *OJ* 1994 L158/59.
[69] Case C-140/97 *Rechberger, Greindl, Hofmeister et al.* v. *Republic of Austria* [2000] 2 CMLR 1.

Tour Directive is applicable even if holidays are won in a competition or given away. The travel organizer concerned went bankrupt and the individuals sued the Austrian state instead. The ECJ held Austria could be made liable, even if there was imprudent action by the travel organizer and provided that a breach of superior rule of law for the protection of an individual and a causal link can be established.

An appeal to the ECJ by the Commission[70] against a decision of the CFI reviewed in 1997[71] concerned the finding by the CFI that a previous judgment of the ECJ, which had partially annulled Commission-imposed fines on certain wood pulp companies, had consequences for third parties not a party to the previous ECJ judgment. This effect is sometimes referred to as *ergo omnes* (thus applicable to all). The CFI had held that the Commission should have taken account of that judgment and refunded fines paid by the parties in the present proceedings who had not contested the original decision of the Commission. The consequences of a Community Court judgment were considered by the ECJ, which held that the Community legal order only allows judgments to be given on the subject matter in the case before it and which apply only to the parties bringing the action. It cannot apply to persons who were not party to the proceedings and with regard to whom the judgment cannot have decided anything whatever. Old Art. 176 (now 233) requires the institutions to take measures to comply with judgements, in this case the annulment of the original decision, but is not so wide as to mean that the Commission must, at the request of interested parties, re-examine decisions allegedly affected by the same irregularity. To ensure legal certainty, a decision becomes definitive, if not challenged within time under Art. 173 (now 230). Furthermore, Art. 173 does not allow a person to sue in the name of another. The ECJ thus overturned the 1997 CFI decision and gave final judgment in the matter, dismissing the application for annulment of the decision.

A particularly interesting feature of the case is the terminology employed by the ECJ and its discussion of previous case law. These increasingly resemble a common law system of precedent, rather than a civil law system, on which the Community legal order was originally based. Paragraph 54 of the Court's judgment makes specific reference to the *ratio descidendi* of a judgment: 'Furthermore, although the authority *erga omnes* exerted by an annulling judgment of a court of the Community judicature ... attaches to both the operative part and the *ratio descidendi* of the judgment ... '. The ECJ also carefully distinguished past cases relied on by the applicants in paragraphs 64–70, again as if to suggest a system of precedent operates in the Community legal order.

[70] Case C-310/97 P *Commission* v. *AssiDomän Kraft Products AB et al.* [1999] 5 CMLR 1253.
[71] Case T-225/95 *AssiDomän Kraft Products AB et al.* v. *Commission* [1997] ECR II-1185, See *Annual Review* 1997, p. 104.

V. Protection of Individual Rights

General Principles of Law and Fundamental Rights

In a case concerned with the protection of water and land from nitrate pollution, a group of farmers[72] challenged the measures undertaken by the UK authorities in fulfilling the requirements of Directive 91/676[73] and indirectly, the validity of the directive itself. The action in question was the designation of rivers which could be affected by nitrate pollution and areas of land draining into those rivers vulnerable to nitrates. The authorities could then issue orders restricting the use of nitrates on that land. The farmers objected to the designation on the grounds that the burden of the cost of the measures would fall on them. The ECJ held that the directive allowed Member States to apportion costs on those who pollute and not just to the farmers most affected by the land designation. The farmers also claimed their right to property was being infringed, but the ECJ held that the right to property was recognized in the EC legal order but was not an absolute right and must be reviewed in the light of its social function. The exercise of the right could be restricted, providing the restriction corresponded to an objective of general interest and that is was not disproportionate. Hence a restriction on the use of nitrate fertilizers would be acceptable as the general objectives of public health and environmental protection were being supported.

Consumer Protection

Directive 85/577,[74] the so-called doorstep-selling directive, was intended to protect consumers who had entered into contracts such as doorstep sales, by allowing them a cooling-off period during which they can decide not to continue with the contract without penalty. A second directive (the time-share Directive 94/47[75]) was enacted to provide protection to consumers entering into property time-share deals. The interpretation by the ECJ[76] has extended the protection of these directives. Mr S concluded a time-share contract but rather than confirming it, decided to rescind it. He was pursued by the time-share company for damages. The first and most important decision was that despite the exception in Art. 3 (2) of Directive 85/577 that it did not apply to contracts relating to immovable property, the ECJ concluded that time-share contracts are contracts of value over and above the cost of the immovable property therefore, they were not to be included in the exception in Art. 3 (2).

---

[72] Case C-293/97 *R* v. *Secretary of State for the Environment and Minister for Agriculture, Fisheries and Food ex parte Metson and others* [1999] ECR I-2603.
[73] *OJ* 1991 L375/1.
[74] *OJ* 1985 L372/31.
[75] *OJ* 1994, L280/83.
[76] Case C-423/97 *Travel Vac* v. *Manuel Sanchis* [1999] ECR I-2195.

Secondly, the ECJ was unable to conclude that contracts entered into at a special excursion laid on by the trader for consumers is one which was not contemplated by the doorstep-selling directive. As such then, the requirement for the consumer to compensate would be in breach of Art. 5 (2). This shows that the doorstep selling directive does apply to property time-share contracts.

Individual Rights of Redress against Community Institutions (including the Transparency Decisions)

Following on from a case reviewed last year[77] in which a Commission decision not to release documents was annulled by the CFI, Interporc[78] continued to request certain documents from the Commission but again met with refusal. This time the Commission justified its actions on different grounds. It cited the public interest exception of court proceedings concerning the use of the same documents as Interporc were using in another action to annul a Commission decision.[79] The CFI held this ground applies solely for the purposes of specific court proceedings and not documents previously drawn up in connection with a purely administrative matter, although any documents not authored by the Commission could be withheld. The ECJ has ruled here to prevent the Commission from using as an excuse to withhold documents, the ground of Court proceedings where the documents were not drawn up specifically for the case in hand, thus providing some support for the principle of freedom of information in the EC legal order.

Judicial Review (including the Locus Standi *of the Non-privileged Applicants under Art. 173 EC)*

Ecroyd Holdings v. *Commission*[80] is further fallout from the milk quota cases and in particular the *Mulder* cases,[81] which resulted in a large number of successful applications to annul Commission milk quota regulations and subsequently to obtain damages. The Commission was held to have failed to comply with a judgment of the ECJ. Ecroyd Holdings had previously obtained a judgment before the ECJ which had annulled part of a regulation denying them a special reference milk quota. Following this up, they asked the Commission twice what it would do to comply with the judgment. The Commission had advised the ministry in the UK that, as it had issued a new

---

[77] The case now known as *Interporc*/T-124/96 [1998] ECR II-231, [1998] 2 CMLR 82, see *Annual Review* 1998/1999, p. 129.
[78] Case T-92/98 *Interporc Im- und Export GmbH* v. *Commission* [2000] 1 CMLR 181.
[79] Case T-50/96 [1998] ECR II-3773, [1999] 1 CMLR 99 but itself now the subject of an appeal by the Commission in Case C-417/98 P.
[80] Case T-220/97 *H & R Ecroyd Holdings Ltd* v. *Commission* [1999] 2 CMLR 1361.
[81] Case 120/86 *Mulder* v. *Minister van Landbouw en Visserij* [1988] ECR 2321 and Cases C-104/89 and 37/90 *Mulder et al.* v. *Council and Commission* [1992] ECR I-3061.

correcting regulation, it need do nothing more. Milk producers could apply to the appropriate national ministry for a quota, which, the Commission had emphasized, the ministry was not obliged to grant. The CFI held that, just as an institution is obliged to comply with a judgment under Art. 233 (ex 176), so by analogy is an institution obliged to correct the position following the declaration of invalidity following a preliminary ruling. As a consequence, the Commission was obliged not just to replace the invalid regulation with another, it was also obliged to determine whether the original measure had caused any damage which was required to be made good. The CFI held that the Commission was therefore wrong in concluding it need do no more. The ECJ had previously suggested the Commission should have initiated action with a view to compensating the applicant. The CFI concluded that the conditions for non-contractual liability of the Community had already been fulfilled as evidenced by the earlier judgment in favour of Ecroyd, i.e. the breach of a superior rule of law for the protection of an individual. Hence the Commission failed in is obligation to comply with a judgment of the ECJ and the decision not to take further action was annulled.

Actions under Art. 232 (ex 175): Failure to Act

In *UPS Europe* v. *Commission*, [82] UPS secured a rare victory in an action to challenge a failure to act on the part of the Commission. In 1994, UPS notified the Commission alleging anti-competitive practices on the part of Deutsche Post contrary to EC law (Arts. 86, 90, 92 and 93 (now 82, 86, 87 and 88)). Although the Commission had undertaken investigations, it had not adopted a final decision regarding the complaints but had decided to investigate further under Art. 90 (now 86) only. Twice in correspondence, UPS referred to Art. 175 (now 232) and, in August 1998, UPS brought an action. The CFI held that the Commission's decision on the complaint must be adopted within a reasonable time according to the circumstances of the case. The CFI held that when the Commission received the formal request under Art. 175 (now 232), it should either have proceeded against the subject of the complaint or have adopted a definitive decision to reject the complaint. It should not have recommenced its investigation. It had not acted at all in respect of the complaint regarding Art. 86 (now 82), therefore the CFI held that the Commission had failed to act. The result goes further than previous case law,[83] which decided that the Commission need only define its position. This time the Commission must either accept the complaint or reject it definitively. If it rejects it, this action may then be challenged under Art. 230 (ex 173).

---

[82] Case T-127/98 U*PS Europe SA* v. *Commission* [2000] 4 CMLR 94.
[83] Case 191/82 *Fediol* v. *Commission* [1983] ECR 2913.

VI. Overall Evaluation and Conclusion

It was not a dynamic year in the development of EC case law. Free movement of goods was notable for its lack of significant cases, interinstitutional disputes rumbled on, whereas intellectual property provided a rich trawl of cases and again the area of sex discrimination has provided the most scope for judicial pronouncement.

Whilst not a theme by any means, a couple of cases highlight a generally felt concern about the degree to which the EU is establishing a kind of 'Fortress Europe'[84] position in the world, and indeed, sometimes in the face of the interests of some of its inhabitants. The Sebago judgment, for example, supports the maintenance of commercial interests rather than the interests of the EU consumer, while the *Calfa* case shows that the Community legal order has little regard for local interests when the big picture and a fundamental freedom is involved. The *Gencor* ruling may also be seen in this light. Then again, the various individual rights which have been upheld by the Court of Justice in the cases above, especially in the areas of free movement of persons and sex discrimination, may be more than enough to counterbalance any such observations.

Selected References

Cardiff University of Wales European Access «http://www.cf.ac.uk/uwcc/liby/edc/euracc/»

Case Law of the ECJ can be found at «http://europa.eu.int/jurisp/cgi-bin/form.pl?lang=en»

European Court of Justice Home Page «http://europa.eu.int/cj/en/index.htm»

Legislation in force at «http://europa.eu.int/eur-lex/en/lif/index.html»

Official Journal for legislation at «http://europa.eu.int/eur-lex/en/oj/index.html»

Proceedings of the ECJ for 1999 can be found at «http//www.curia.eu.int/en/act/index99.htm» and press releases on the most recent cases can be found at «http://www.curia.eu.int/en/cp/aff/index.htm»

---

[84] Follow the link here for some of the emerging mass of information concerned with Fortress Europe «http://www.iatelier.com/medira/current1.htm»

Journal of Common Market Studies

Volume 38, Annual Review
September 2000

External Policy Developments

DAVID ALLEN

and

MICHAEL SMITH
Loughborough University

I. General Themes

Introduction

Although events in Kosovo in the first part of the year emphasized the problems still facing the EU, some commentators saw the December 1999 Helsinki European Council as indicative of significant progress in the EU's search for a coherent and effective external role. Optimists might argue that, at Helsinki, the EU significantly amended and improved its enlargement strategy, resolved its differences with Turkey and accorded it candidate status, took a major step forward towards the establishment of a Common European Security and Defence Policy (CESDP) and, at last, proposed an acceptable response to the situation in Chechnya. Pessimists, on the other hand, might view the expanded enlargement decisions as merely a hasty adjustment to the bankruptcy of the 1997 Luxembourg scheme, might feel that the problems with Turkey's application had been postponed rather than solved, and might worry that the defence plans were over-ambitious with the potential to create yet another capability–expectations gap rather than a substantive advance. Certainly a great deal happened in 1999, but it remains to be seen whether these events will stimulate a more coherent and effective EU external stance.

There were a number of significant changes in the way that the EU organizes itself for external relations. Contrary to expectations, the new

European Commission led by Romano Prodi, did not allocate one of the two Vice-Presidential posts to an external relations supremo. Instead, as before, four Commissioners were appointed with external relations responsibilities, albeit with functional rather than geographical portfolios. Clearly *primus inter pares* amongst the four was to be Chris Patten (UK), who was given the External Relations portfolio – the key foreign policy co-ordinating job which also includes responsibility for the CFSP and the management of the Commission's external services. Pascal Lamy (France) received the Trade portfolio, Günter Verheugen (Germany), was put in charge of a new Enlargement portfolio, while Poul Nielson (Denmark) took responsibility for Development and Humanitarian Aid.

The Treaty of Amsterdam, which came into effect in May, provided for a number of changes affecting the foreign policy role of the Council. Most significantly, the Cologne European Council agreed that Javier Solana, then Secretary-General of NATO, would become the new Secretary-General of the Council and thus the High Representative for foreign and security policy (Mr CFSP or M. PESC depending on one's linguistic preference). Later in the year, Solana was also appointed as Secretary-General of WEU in order to preside over its incorporation into the EU. The Policy Planning and Early Warning Unit was established within the Council Secretariat and, under the direction of its first head, Christoph Heusgen, became known more simply as the Policy Unit.

The Helsinki Conclusions also anticipate a further strengthening of the Council and its machinery with the participation of defence ministers for the first time, the establishment of a new Political and Security Committee and a Military Committee and the enhancement of the Planning Unit with a military staff. Inevitably, towards the end of the year there was speculation in Brussels as to the potential for foreign policy rivalry between the Commission and the Council and, in particular, between Chris Patten and Javier Solana as they sought to develop and consolidate their new roles.

During 1999 the Commission adopted a major report on the development of its External Service which, among other things, called for a better interchange between Member State diplomats and Commission staff and proposed a further devolution of responsibilities for managing aid from Brussels to the delegations overseas. No new delegations were opened by the Commission in 1999, and it thus maintained its representation in 125 countries and five international organizations. Following the acceptance of Monaco for the first time, there are now 166 foreign missions accredited to the European Communities.

© Blackwell Publishers Ltd 2000

Foreign and Security Policy

The most significant development of the CFSP in 1999 came in the defence sphere and this is dealt with fully in John Roper's keynote article. The appointment of Javier Solana and the post-Amsterdam and post-Helsinki institutional developments noted above added further weight to the process of 'Brusselsization' that we have discussed in previous editions of the *Review*.

During 1999, the EU adopted 12 joint actions and defined 22 common positions as well as issuing 108 declarations. Under the provisions of the Amsterdam Treaty the first two common strategies, towards Russia (Cologne European Council) and the Ukraine (Helsinki European Council), were adopted. The joint actions included nine on the western Balkans (one relating to the Former Republic of Yugoslavia (FRY), three to Kosovo, one to Albania, one to Bosnia and three to the Stability Pact for south eastern Europe), two on the Middle East peace process and one on Russia. The common positions related to the western Balkans (five), Libya (two), Asia (five) and Africa (four). As part of a growing involvement in global security matters, the EU sought, via a common position, to promote ratification of the Comprehensive Nuclear Test-Ban Treaty (which was then rejected by the US Senate) and to enhance nuclear non-proliferation by financing a secure communication system for members of the Nuclear Suppliers Group. The EU also adopted a common position establishing verification criteria for the Biological and Toxin Weapons Convention. The Commission's claim to a role in the implementation of CFSP decisions was further enhanced by the EC's contribution of EUR 30m towards efforts to combat anti-personnel mines. The trend towards benchmarking as a means of policy co-ordination in the EU was illustrated by the Council's adoption of its first annual report on the working of the EU code of conduct for arms exports as well as its updating of the controls on dual-use goods.

The most significant event of the year was undoubtedly the NATO-led intervention in Kosovo. Under the circumstances, the EU-15 managed to maintain a remarkable solidarity despite the particular concerns of certain Member States. Although the US dominated the military action (even here providing further stimulus to an EU determination to improve its future capacity to use military force), it was EU negotiators, in particular from Germany and Finland, who played a significant role in the diplomatic endgame, especially when it came to persuading Russia to exert pressure on President Milosevic. Furthermore, it was the EU, under the Council Presidency of a Germany anxious to focus on civilian rather than military solutions, which followed up the ceasefire with extravagant plans for a stability pact for south eastern Europe built around the ultimate prospect of EU membership for the states of the region.

Developments in the western Balkans throughout the rest of the year tended to highlight the continuing need for the EU to be aware of the dangers of incoherence and lack of co-ordination in its external activities. The Helsinki Conclusions, for instance, called for a single regulatory framework for financial assistance to the region but it is notable that during 1999 the EU had no fewer than four envoys in the area – Bodo Hombach, the Special Representative responsible for co-ordinating the stability pact, Panagiotis Roumeliotis, the Special Representative for the 'Royaumont' process, Felipe Gonzalez, the Special Representative for the FRY, and Wolfgang Petritsch, Special Envoy for Kosovo (until July) and then High Representative for Bosnia (replacing Carlos Westendorp).

Elsewhere in the world, the EU sought to develop further its role in the defence of human rights and fundamental freedoms, mainly by issuing declarations but also by offering its services as a mediator and facilitator of dialogue between conflicting parties, as well as by providing humanitarian aid. The EU published its first annual report on the global human rights situation, sent electoral observers to East Timor, Indonesia and Nigeria, and allocated EUR 94m to a European initiative for democracy and the protection of human rights. Among its initiatives were pressure on Turkey to ensure that the Kurdish leader, Abdullah Ocalan, received a fair trial, pressure on the FRY to halt its actions in Kosovo and to maintain a peaceful dialogue with Montenegro, support for Libya following the handing over of the two Lockerbie bombing suspects, support for the Sharm-el-Sheik memorandum between Israel and the Palestine Authority, and encouragement to Russia to seek peaceful solutions to the situation in both Dagestan and Chechnya. The EU also sought to persuade Indonesia to revoke its annexation of East Timor, and several EU Member States, including the UK, France and Portugal, participated in the international peacekeeping force that was sent to East Timor in September. The EU is now actively considering admitting East Timor to the Lomé Convention once it becomes independent of UN interim administration. The EU chastised a number of governments for their continued use of the death penalty (China, Cuba, Uganda and, for the first time, the United States). Elsewhere in Asia, Africa and Latin America, the EU drew attention to a host of human rights abuses, electoral irregularities and military coups and sought to encourage a variety of forms of corrective action – a definitive list can be found in the European Commission's *1999 General Report on the Activities of the European Union* (point 634 and points 644–57).

External Trade and the Common Commercial Policy

While EU trade policy concerns during 1998 had been dominated by external crises in Asia and elsewhere, the central focus in 1999 was on the implications for trade of the crisis in the European Commission. These related to the ways in which it constrained EU policy formation during the spring and summer, and because it led to the restructuring of the Commission following the appointment of Romano Prodi. The transition from Sir Leon Brittan to Pascal Lamy, and the establishment of a Directorate-General focused specifically on foreign trade, was bound to have effects not only on the style but also on the substance of policy-making. Whatever the structure within which policy was framed and executed, there were also some dominant features of the external landscape to which European officials had to pay attention.

The key external feature in trade was the preparation for, and then the mounting of the Seattle ministerial meeting, putatively to launch the 'Millennium Round' of negotiations in the World Trade Organization. The Commission, and Sir Leon in particular, clearly saw this as an opportunity to build on the gains made since the end of the Uruguay Round in 1993–94, and on the potential for EU leadership both in agenda-setting and in the negotiations themselves. However, before serious attention could be paid to the negotiations, there was the matter of the installation of a new Secretary-General for the WTO to succeed Renato Ruggiero. Ruggiero's appointment had led to considerable tensions between the EU and the US, and it was anticipated that something similar might happen in 1999. In this case, there was the complicating factor that the Council of Ministers was itself split between support for a Thai candidate and the New Zealander, Mike Moore. Although the Council was eventually able to give its broad support to the Thai (Supachai), this did not tip the balance at WTO level; instead, several months of wrangling led to a split appointment, with Moore taking over for the first half of the term. At least it could be said that there was no crisis in EU–US relations over the appointment.

The 'Millennium Round' itself led to no such compromise. From the outset, it was clear that the EU's policy was partly defensive (for example, on agriculture and cultural issues) and partly assertive (as on matters concerning developing countries and the link between labour standards and trade). Apart from these sectoral issues, there was also a basic disagreement between the EU and the US over the scope of any round that might take place: the EU wanted a comprehensive set of negotiations (thereby giving the possibility of trade-offs and package deals), whereas the US wanted targeted negotiations on areas such as agriculture and the environment (giving the EU no place to hide on some of the most sensitive areas). The negotiating directives were developed by trade ministers from May onwards, and the Commission published a detailed paper on the agenda for Seattle at the end of June. EU policy was also actively pursued within the framework of the Quad Group (the EU, the US, Canada and Japan) at its meeting in May. It was apparent that the EU drive for a broad negotiating round had general support from both other members of the Quad and countries in many regions, but also that the opposition of the US was potentially fatal. The EU and the US clashed during the year not only in the WTO context but also in other arenas such as the OECD, and, as autumn wore on, there was an increasing suspicion that American policy would lead to a 'rigged' agenda reflecting their preferences.

In this context, it was inevitable that the intensification of preparations for Seattle would lead to escalating tensions. While there were still disagreements between EU Member States as late as October, these paled into insignificance beside the gathering storm as delegates tried to agree an overall agenda during November. In essence, the EU stood accused of sacrificing the potential for wide-ranging gains by its defensiveness over agriculture – a defensiveness which reflected in part the difficulties that had been experienced in agreeing *Agenda 2000* earlier in the year, and thus the basis for the EU's negotiating position. At the same time, the US clearly wanted to 'steer' the agenda on to ground in which it was interested, and where the EU was sensitive. As it turned out, the 'battle of Seattle' both inside and outside the conference hall was universally perceived to be a failure, and attention turned in December to the allocation of blame. This was not before a minor though acute crisis in the Council of Ministers, when it was discovered that Pascal Lamy had agreed in Seattle to a US proposal for a working group on biotechnology; a proposal that had been specifically opposed by the Member States.

Compared to this sound and fury, other commercial policy matters were relatively subdued during 1999. The EU was an active user of the WTO's dispute procedures, taking the initiative in the setting up of nine panel investigations, whilst it was also made a major target for dispute actions by the USA (see below). It remained an energetic player in anti-dumping and anti-subsidy measures, initiating 26 new anti-dumping proceedings during the year and instigating new anti-subsidy proceedings in half a dozen cases. Because of the range and intensity of its trading relations across the global system, the EU is bound to be both an active initiator of such proceedings and a recipient of attention from other actors. A further example of the ways in which the EU's involvement creates a continuing demand for policy is that of competition policy measures, which often spill beyond the boundaries of the Union itself, as in, for example, the case of strategic alliances between airlines. During 1999, a number of these cases continued to attract the attention of the Commission.

Whilst not strictly a matter of commercial policy, the EU's international representation saw important developments and tensions in 1999. Specifically, the inauguration of the euro in January 1999 created a position in which the EU's representation in a number of international financial bodies could be questioned. Two particular examples were the Group of Seven industrial countries (G-7), and the International Monetary Fund. In both cases, it was the Americans who raised the question whether 'Euroland' should continue to be represented by Member States or in some other fashion. While the EU would have welcomed additional representation, it was unwilling to give up any of its existing seats in such bodies, and the argument rumbled on through the year. Eventually a compromise was reached in the G-7, to the effect that national central bank governors in the G-7 finance meetings could be replaced by ECB officials; but the deal also excluded the relevant Commissioner from anything more than a watching brief, a situation to which acting Commissioner Yves Thibault de Silguy reacted angrily.

Development Co-operation Policy and Humanitarian Aid

The downfall of the Santer Commission was partly bought about by charges of scandal and incompetence relating to the EU's development and humanitarian aid programmes. In addition to an adverse report from the Court of Auditors which concentrated on the need to reform the management of EU policies in this area, the Commission was also forced to respond to a further series of criticisms from a group of Member States led by the United Kingdom. This group drew attention to the fact that EU aid was increasingly being targeted towards the EU's near neighbours in south eastern Europe, the Middle East and North Africa at the expense of the very poorest states in the world. Whereas in 1987, 75 per cent of EU aid was sent to the very poorest states with a per capita annual income of less than $750, by 1997 this figure had fallen to just below 50 per cent of total EU aid. Member States demanded that this situation be rectified so that by 2006 at least 70 per cent of EU aid would once again be sent to the very poorest states in the world. Criticisms were also aimed at the way that the Commission was organized, with four Commissioners and their respective Directorates-General having various geographical development responsibilities and a fifth Commissioner overseeing the European Community Humanitarian Office (ECHO). Prodi has gone a long way towards rectifying this situation with the appointment of just one Commissioner (Poul Nielson) in sole charge of all development policy and the work of ECHO.

Most of 1999 was taken up with a long negotiation between the EU and the African, Caribbean and Pacific (ACP) countries to renew the Lomé Convention which was due to expire at the end of February 2000. As we reported last year, the EU was keen to apply political conditionality to any new agreement and to move the relationship from one characterized by trade preferences granted by the EU to the ACP to one of free trade built around the concept of Regional Economic Partnership Agreements. After four rounds of negotiations, a compromise agreement was eventually reached in December 1999. In return for the EU extending its system of preferences for another eight years (provided the WTO grants the required waiver), the ACP states have agreed to begin trade liberalization talks in 2002 with a view eventually of liberalizing trade (by 2008), and concluding the regional free trade economic agreements sought by the EU. The ACP states also readily agreed to the application of conditions relating to respect for human rights, democratic principles and the rule of law but resisted for some time attempts by the EU to impose 'good governance' conditions, feeling that these represented an unacceptable EU intrusion into their domestic affairs. In the end, a compromise was reached around the acceptance of a package of anti-corruption measures. For its part, the EU has effectively offered a EUR 22.8bn development aid package for the next five years. This latest tranche of the European development fund will consist of EUR 13.8bn of new money plus an estimated EUR 9bn of unspent funds from previous programmes. The negotiations were significantly influenced by Member State demands for reform of EU development policies, by the scandals associated with the EU's own examples of 'bad governance' and, in the end, by the failure of the opening round of WTO talks in Seattle.

The EU also made a major contribution towards attempts by the International Monetary Fund and the World Bank to do something about Third World debt. In November, the Council agreed to allocate EUR 1bn towards this objective, with EUR 550m destined to wipe out debt owed to the EU, EUR 150m for rapid relief and EUR 350m for the World Bank Trust Fund. In 1999, the EU also extended EUR 500m in food aid, EUR 200m to development projects run by non-governmental organizations and EUR 800m in humanitarian aid through ECHO. A large proportion of the ECHO money went to the western Balkans (EUR 447m, of which EUR 378m went to Kosovo). Of the other major recipients, Turkey received EUR 30m in earthquake relief, EUR 64m went to the Former Soviet States, EUR 15m to East Timor, EUR 139m to the ACP states (EUR 74m to the Great Lakes region) and EUR 16m to the victims of Hurricane Mitch.

II. Regional Themes

The European Economic Area and EFTA

Given the evolution of relations with the EEA and EFTA during previous years (see appropriate *Annual Reviews*), it was perhaps to be expected that 1999 would be a quiet year. Very little of substance or drama affected relations with EEA countries; the Nordic partners were concerned at one stage about the implications for them of changes to the EU's regime on duty free products, and efforts were made to maintain the special arrangements pertaining in the Baltic and between Sweden, Denmark and Norway. The incorporation of parts of the

Schengen *acquis* on free movement into the Community framework, which had been part of the Amsterdam Treaty, was also a concern for Norway and Iceland, although the implications were not clear by the end of 1999. The other major focus of attention in this area was Switzerland. The agreements of late 1998 on the range of bilateral contacts between the EU and Switzerland had apparently resolved one of the major continuing 'legacies' from the failed Swiss attempt to join the Union in the early 1990s. During 1999, the focus was on the ratification of these deals, and (for the Swiss) on the further implications of EMU. The first part of the year saw a positive atmosphere in which even the prospect of a new membership application could be contemplated; but in October, Swiss elections saw a pronounced swing to the right and to anti-EU parties. As always, there were strong regional variations here, with the western (and French speaking) parts of the country significantly more in favour of EU membership, but it appeared that the prospect of membership was now a receding one.

Western Balkans

The conflict over Kosovo in the first half of 1999 saw the EU somewhat sidelined by the NATO (and US) dominated military operation. However, as in Bosnia, it was clear that the EU was destined to play a major role in the provision of humanitarian aid and eventually in reconstruction and rehabilitation. During the NATO military campaign, the EU maintained an impressive solidarity despite the doubts of several Member States and the difficult domestic situations that they faced. The German Presidency in particular sought to broker peace and to involve the Russians, who had been rather overlooked by those running the NATO operation. Germany also sought to develop a long-term strategy for the region which built on but essentially replaced earlier efforts by the Commission to encourage regional co-operation in the Balkans (a number of former Yugoslav states objected to being encouraged to work with one another for fear that this might imply a revival of the old Yugoslavia). The result was the proposal for an EU-led Stability Pact for south eastern Europe (the western Balkans), which envisaged the gradual negotiation of Stability and Association Agreements (similar to Europe Agreements) which were designed to pave the way for the integration of the Balkan states into the Euro-Atlantic area – in practice this would mean eventual membership of the EU and NATO. At a stroke, therefore, EU enlargement strategy, which had previously excluded the western Balkans, was fundamentally altered. In pursuit of these objectives, the EU organized and paid for a summit meeting in Sarajevo in July to discuss plans for the Pact and, in association with the World Bank, two donors' conferences for Kosovo in July and November. It became clear in the second half of the year that only the

Former Yugoslav Republic of Macedonia was in a position to begin negotiation on a Stability and Association Agreement. The Commission was of the opinion that this was not the case with Croatia, Bosnia, Albania or, more obviously, the FRY. For their part, the Bosnians were prepared to wait but they clearly saw the Stability Pact as a 'Europeanization' of the Dayton Peace Plan providing an eventual exit from the area for the United States.

The Stability Pact was, of course, to be a long-term measure. In the short term the EU did all it could to encourage the peace talks at Rambouillet before the bombing began, provided substantial humanitarian aid to Kosovo and the neighbouring states during and immediately after the conflict, and accepted responsibility for the reconstruction of Kosovo under the overall control of the UN civil administration. During the conflict the EU had also toughened its sanctions against the FRY by banning the sale of oil and petroleum, extending the list of FRY officials covered by its visa ban, freezing funds held by FRY officials abroad and banning all flights between the EU and the FRY. The EU's problem, which became more acute once the fighting was over, was to try to devise ways of hurting Serbia, and in particular those who supported Milosevic, without inflicting further misery on the inhabitants of Montenegro and Kosovo (both still part of the FRY). As 1999 drew to a close, it became clear that the sanctions were hitting ordinary people in the FRY and that they were in danger of becoming counter-productive – serving to strengthen the Milosevic regime rather than weaken it. In November, an operation known as 'Energy for Democracy', whereby the EU planned to deliver much-needed oil to two Serbian towns – Nils and Pirot – controlled by anti-Milosevic opposition parties, failed because of the ease with which the FRY government authorities forced the tankers carrying the oil to abandon their mission.

Similarly, when the EU chose to fly a group of FRY opposition politicians to Luxembourg as part of an 'encouragement' exercise, problems arose when the question of handing over suspected war criminals was raised. The opposition politicians had to explain to their EU hosts that such a pledge would be regarded as treason back in Yugoslavia and would serve to undermine rather than enhance their popular following.

Financing these new responsibilities also presented the EU with some short- and longer-term problems. It was estimated, for instance, that the long-term reconstruction of Kosovo (and eventually the rest of the FRY) was likely to rise above the $5bn already spent in Bosnia since 1995. This led the EU Member States into conflict with the European Parliament when they planned to provide short-term finance for Kosovo within established budgetary parameters. This was to be done by drawing on unspent funds from other programmes and by cutting 10 per cent off MEDA and TACIS aid and 20 per cent from funds earmarked for humanitarian aid elsewhere. In the longer term, the Member

States are clearly reluctant to adjust the third budgetary perspective (2000–06) that they so painfully negotiated earlier in the year.

By the end of the year, the EU was therefore involved in a number of ways in the western Balkans. Earlier, Commission President Romano Prodi had acknowledged that the EU's efforts could easily 'get buried in a complex web of competing structures'. Moreover, in addition to the four EU Special Representatives already mentioned, there are also the UN Mission for Kosovo under the overall direction of Bernard Kouchner, Special Representative of the UN Secretary-General, and the G-7 high level group for economic co-ordination. It certainly seems that in the year 2000 the western Balkans will continue to present the EU with formidable financial, policy and organizational challenges. Furthermore, as part of the effort to upgrade the EU's military role, the Eurocorps is due to take operational control of KFOR for a six-month period in 2000. All this should prove an excellent test of EU co-ordination and coherence and in particular of the ability of Solana, Patten and Verheugen to work together in the EU's common cause.

Russia and the Soviet Successor States

The EU's relationship with Russia in 1999 was inevitably affected by events in both Kosovo and Chechnya. The Russians felt that the provisions for political dialogue within the Partnership and Co-operation Agreement had not been used properly with regard to the military intervention in Kosovo, and the EU was eventually moved (at the Helsinki European Council) to discuss action against Russia if it did not moderate its relentless attacks on Chechnya. In December, the EU agreed that it would consider suspending some aspects (not trade!) of the Partnership Agreement, reviewing the implementation of the common strategy agreed at the Cologne European Council and redirecting TACIS funds towards humanitarian aid. Disquiet about Russian actions towards Chechnya disrupted the plans of the Finnish Presidency to give the 'northern dimension' of the EU further stimulation. Most EU Member States decided not to send their foreign ministers to a November meeting in Helsinki involving the EU, Russia, Norway and the other Baltic States, but it now seems likely that this aspect of the EU's external stance will be taken up once again by the Swedish Presidency in 2001.

Nevertheless the EU and Russia did manage to hold two summit meetings in Moscow (February) and Helsinki (October), Javier Solana making his debut for the EU at the latter. The Russians have begun to worry about the trade diversion effects of further EU enlargement, while the EU seems keen to use the common strategy to integrate Russia further into the European economic and political area. In 1999, the EU once again provided significant food aid to

Russia; EU food was sold at local market prices and the revenue used to bolster Russia's ailing pension funds further.

A second common strategy was agreed towards Ukraine at the Helsinki European Council. As before, the EU is concerned to use the enhanced links to maintain pressure on Ukraine to decommission the remaining nuclear facilities at Chernobyl – a concern that also impacts on its relationship with Lithuania, whose two Ignalina reactors are of similar design to those at Chernobyl. The EU also faces the dilemma of trying to prevent Ukraine from moving back towards Russia as Belarus has done, without actually offering the prospect of EU membership. With Lithuania, EU membership is clearly a bargaining 'carrot', but the problem with the Ignalina reactors is that they provide 80 per cent of Lithuania's energy requirements and they indirectly employ some 30,000 workers, most of whom are Russian.

The five EU ambassadors (UK, Germany, France, Italy and Greece) who were recalled to their capitals in June 1998 after being turned out of their residences by President Lukashenko, returned to Minsk in January. This was not well received by opposition parties in Belarus who saw it as a climb-down on the part of the EU (the US ambassador did not return), even though the sanctions imposed by the EU in 1998 remained in place at the end of 1999. In July, Partnership and Co-operation Agreements with six former Soviet States (Armenia, Azerbaijan, Georgia, Kazakhstan, Kyrgyzstan and Uzbekistan) entered into force. In 1999 the EU extended EUR 462m in TACIS grants to the region, but fears were expressed during the year that the 2000 allocation would be significantly reduced by the need to find new money for Kosovo.

The Mediterranean and the Middle East

The most important development in EU relations with the region was undoubtedly the decision by the Helsinki European Council to accord full candidate status to Turkey. This reversed the conclusions of the Luxembourg European Council of 1997 which had rejected Turkey's application. The change in Turkey's status was made possible by an improvement in the Turkish–Greek relationship following their mutual assistance to one another when faced with catastrophic earthquakes, and by willingness of both Sweden and Germany to drop their human rights objections for the time being. Turkey's position was also clearly advanced by the enormous support it enjoys from the United States and by its important position within NATO – EU attempts to consolidate its defence arrangements are dependent on the support of the non-EU European members of NATO.

The German Presidency organized a third meeting of foreign ministers of the Euro–Mediterranean Conference in Stuttgart in April, despite fears that the breakdown of the Middle East peace process would disrupt this meeting as it had in the past. Prior to the meeting, the EU had made strenuous and successful efforts to persuade Yasser Arafat not to declare a Palestinian state (as the Oslo accords allowed him to do) on 4 May, while EU Middle East envoy Manuel Moratinos worked hard to improve EU–Israel relations by advising against excluding Israel from EU R&D programmes and by proposing the establishment of an EU–Israel forum to improve mutual understanding. The change of government in Israel and the resultant relaunching of the peace process was welcomed by the EU which continues to provide the bulk (54 per cent) of economic assistance to the Palestinian territories.

Libya was invited to attend the Euro–Mediterranean Conference as a 'guest of the Presidency' and, in September, the EU lifted all its remaining sanctions against Libya with the exception of the arms embargo. Libya has now been invited to become a full member of the Barcelona process which in 1999 provided the framework for the granting of EUR 905m of MEDA aid.

The EU has now agreed new Association Agreements with eight of its current 12 partners in the Barcelona process. Negotiations with Egypt were still in progress at the end of 1999. Following an EU troika visit to Algiers in November, it was agreed that those with Algeria would resume. Negotiations with Morocco to replace the current fishing agreement, worth EUR150m per annum to Morocco, were still in progress when the agreement ran out at the end of the year.

Africa

In October, the EU finally concluded its long drawn out negotiations with South Africa and the resulting trade, co-operation and development agreement came into effect at the end of the year. The agreement proved hard to negotiate because it was seen by the EU, and the watching world, as setting an important precedent for the future development of EU trade relationships. The deal is a good one for protectionist EU agricultural interests, excluding as it does over 300 'sensitive' products. But the agreement, concluded at the Berlin European Council, begins a process which over a 12-year period should see the liberalization of 95 per cent of South African exports to the EU and 86 per cent of EU exports to South Africa. Throughout 1999, the 'Club Med' group of EU Member States (France, Spain, Italy, Greece and Portugal) had been much criticized for their determination to force South Africa to stop using names like sherry and port to describe their products. These, along with some 150 other generic terms such as 'grappa' and 'grand cru', will be gradually given up by the South Africans in exchange for a duty-free quota of 32 million litres of South African wine. Despite the bad faith that the squabbling over relatively minor matters generated on both sides, the EU still gave aid to South Africa totalling EUR 127m in 1999.

Although, during 1999, the EU threatened to suspend Lomé concessions to three African countries (Niger, Guinea-Bissau and Comoros) because of human rights and democratic violations, it was also able to act positively in the case of Nigeria. After financing a team of observers to the Nigerian elections, the EU lifted all its sanctions and has promised to restore some EUR 500m in aid once the transition from military to civilian rule is completed. Throughout the year, EU special envoy to the Great Lakes Region, Aldo Ajello, continued his shuttle diplomacy between the Great Lakes capitals trying, as yet unsuccessfully, to get the warring parties to agree to the peace proposals advanced by the Southern African Development Commission. Mindful of the fact that Africa can still be portrayed as the 'forgotten continent', the EU went ahead with plans to hold an EU–Africa summit in April 2000 under the Portuguese Presidency. Inevitably there were disagreements about representation and agenda items for such a meeting that involved some 65 states, but is clear that the EU has a real interest in giving its various involvements in Africa a new coherence.

Asia

Events in 1998 had been dominated by the financial crisis afflicting several of the 'tiger economies', and the echoes of this continued during 1999. Some of the aftermath was economic, with the need for continued attention to financial imbalances and to the trade problems created by violent swings in currency values. As such, these posed intriguing problems for the introduction of the euro and its take-up by Asian financial institutions (relatively low in most cases), and for the preparation of the WTO's 'Millennium Round' (where there was a fair measure of support for the EU position from governments in the Asia-Pacific region especially). As in previous years, the focus of activity was primarily on Asia-Pacific, although 1999 did see an increase in concern over the 'nuclearization' of South Asia and the signature of a new co-operation agreement with Bangladesh. Other concerns in the realm of 'high politics' included the crisis over East Timor (see above).

The most developed institutional framework for relations between Europe and Asia is to be found in the EU's links with the Association of Southeast Asian Nations (ASEAN) and then in the wider grouping, the Asia–Europe Meeting (ASEM). Relations with ASEAN have been tense for several years because of the presence in the organization of Burma, whose human rights record is the subject of EU sanctions and protests. This tension was responsible for the postponement of successive ministerial meetings up to 1999, and a further postponement took place in March 1999. Significantly, though, this was not symbolic of a complete freeze in relations and a formula was eventually found which allowed a high-level meeting (the EU–ASEAN Joint

© Blackwell Publishers Ltd 2000

Co-operation Committee) to take place during late May in Bangkok. At this meeting, Vietnam was welcomed as part of the dialogue, and proposals were made to introduce Cambodia and Laos. A group of officials representing the EU troika visited Rangoon, the Burmese capital, during July, with a view to exploring the basis for a dialogue.

Alongside this, the ASEM process provided a kind of 'by-pass', whereby meetings between the EU and its ten partners were a further opportunity to deal with matters of concern in the EU–ASEAN arena. The ASEM process itself generated a continuing flow of meetings during 1999, including those of finance ministers (in January), trade ministers (in October), and economics ministers (in November). It could be argued that in this way the balance between the EU–ASEAN relationship and the broader ASEM process was shifting to the advantage of the latter, but this would be to ignore the broader security implications of meetings such as those of the ASEAN Regional Forum and the Post-Ministerial Conference, which took place in July.

The major bilateral concern for the EU in Asia remained China, particularly in the context of trade relations and the moves towards Chinese entry into the WTO. Given that such entry has to be agreed by all WTO members, and particularly by the major trading economies, the EU clearly has a central role to play. Sir Leon Brittan visited Beijing in April, and talk was of the EU being at the 'head of the queue' of those who had to agree Chinese membership. The reality was, of course, that the EU's agreement was linked very closely to that of the US and, in many respects, the US held the initiative. The Chinese could also play the US off against the EU, and during May this is effectively what happened; a Chinese–US understanding after Premier Zhu Rong-Ji's visit to Washington was then used in talks with Brittan in which the Chinese apparently started to back-track on concessions already offered. The bombing of the Chinese Embassy in Belgrade during the Kosovo operation in the spring effectively set any substantive talks back by around six months. The EU–China talks finally resumed in October, though with little apparent prospect of agreement before the Seattle WTO meeting. However, in late November, the US pulled off a trade diplomacy coup by agreeing on a very wide-ranging set of provisions which led to US support for Chinese membership of the WTO. The Commission responded by underlining the need for EU–China as well as US–China agreement, and for concessions to be offered to the Union as well as to Washington. The chaotic state of WTO negotiations after the Seattle meeting, and the growth of hostility to China in the US Congress, meant that by the end of the year there was still a good deal of uncertainty in the air.

In terms of EU aid activities, financial and technical co-operation commitments to Asia during 1999 amounted to EUR 301.7m, with the prime focus on education, health, job creation and rural development. Economic co-operation commitments totalled EUR 28.2m. There was continued support for uprooted peoples in the region, and EUR 30.4m was committed in this respect. Finally, EUR 14.7m was committed for rehabilitation and reconstruction in Asia during the year.

Latin America

Relations between the EU and Latin American countries entered a new phase in 1999, with a wide range of negotiations directed towards multilateral, interregional and bilateral developments (and, some said, towards 'by-passing the USA'). At the multilateral level, the most prominent step was the first summit of Heads of State or Government of the countries of Latin America, the Caribbean and the EU, which took place in Rio de Janeiro on 28–29 June. The resulting declaration set out 55 priorities for action, as well as a number of broad principles for the conduct of relations in the political, economic and social spheres. Many of the issues discussed also tied in to broader international concerns, such as the global financial crisis which affected Brazil in particular, the need for consolidation or reform of international financial institutions, the forthcoming WTO negotiations, and the possibilities for co-operation in a range of international fora and organizations. In the margins of the conference, meetings were held of existing EU–Latin American dialogues, with the Andean Group and with the Mercosur countries (Argentina, Brazil, Paraguay and Uruguay) and Chile. During the year, meetings were also held with the San José Group (the 15th of its kind) and with the Rio Group.

The links between the EU and the Mercosur countries and Chile were consolidated by the entry into force of the interregional framework co-operation agreement on 1 July. The aim was to take this further by negotiating an ambitious trade agreement with a broadly free trade outcome, but by the spring it was clear that the formation of an EU mandate for the negotiations faced important difficulties in the Council of Ministers. Essentially, the difficulties revolved around agriculture, an area encompassing the bulk of Mercosur exports to the EU. Not surprisingly, a number of Member States were opposed to sweeping tariff concessions on agricultural products, among them France, Italy and Ireland, and this opposition effectively stalled the Council discussions. Efforts to resolve the impasse continued, and a watered-down mandate was agreed in the middle of June. As a result, the proposed launch of fully blown free trade negotiations gave way to a more modest effort in which commitments were conspicuously free of any target dates either for agreement or for implementation. Indeed, it was obvious as the year wore on that the free trade aim was likely to be replaced by a woollier and less focused 'liberalization' agenda from the EU. Unsurprisingly, when the negotiations were finally opened at the working group level in December, there was considerable bitterness on the side of Mercosur, as well as an atmosphere generally soured by the failure of the WTO meeting in Seattle.

Progress was more substantial and ground-breaking in the major bilateral negotiations of the year, those with Mexico. Here again, the initial aim had been to conclude a wide-ranging free trade agreement, and this time there was less of an 'agricultural dimension' to complicate matters. By April 1999, talks were in their fifth round, and significant progress had been made towards an agreement estimated to cover EUR 12bn of trade. There was still a lack of agreement on the rates at which industrial tariffs would be dismantled between the partners (essentially the EU wanted Mexico to eliminate tariffs on industrial goods within three years, so that the EU was almost on a par with Mexico's partners in the North American Free Trade Area). This remained a sticking point through much of the year, but by November there were signs of a movement towards agreement. The eventual agreement was signed in late November, after the resolution of last-minute problems with Spain over citrus fruits, but remained an outline free trade agreement rather than a set of detailed commitments in all areas. Subject to ratification by the Mexican Senate and the 15 EU Member States, it will be implemented from mid-2000.

In the area of development co-operation, financial and technical co-operation with Latin American countries totalled EUR 42m in 1999. Economic co-operation amounted to EUR 62.4m. The sum of EUR 21.2m was committed to the multi-annual programme of aid to uprooted people, and support for rehabilitation and reconstruction programmes totalled EUR 82.9m. As a consequence of the damage caused by Hurricane Mitch, the EU set aside EUR 250m for those worst affected (in El Salvador, Guatemala, Honduras and Nicaragua) over a four-year period.

The United States, Japan and Other Industrial Countries

European Union relations with the United States became ever more intense during the 1990s, and increasingly surrounded by an institutional framework. The key bilateral political events in this framework are the six-monthly EU–US summits, held alternately in Washington and the European presidency capital. During 1999, the two summits were held in Bonn (21 June) and Washington (17 December). Not surprisingly in view of the action in Kosovo, and in light of the EU's moves towards more extensive security and defence co-ordination, there was a decided emphasis on security issues at the Bonn summit, with discussion of crisis management and defence policy issues (see elsewhere in this *Review*). But there was also agreement on the establishment of an 'early warning system' to give advance notice of issues on which trade conflicts might take place and to allow for consultation. The Washington summit was not unnaturally focused more on trade in the aftermath of the

Seattle WTO meeting and its collapse. A notable feature of the summit agendas was the lack of preoccupation with issues such as the Helms–Burton Act or the Iran–Libya Solidarity Act, which had caused immense trouble during the late 1990s with their emphasis on the politicization of economic activities.

Alongside the 'summit diplomacy' of Bonn and Washington, there was an ever-increasing range of dialogues involving both government officials and private groupings: thus, the Transatlantic Business Dialogue (TABD) held its 5th Annual Conference in October, and was active in attempting to shape policies towards the WTO in both Washington and Brussels. As well as the established TABD, the Transatlantic Legislative Dialogue between the European Parliament and the House of Representatives was initiated, and by mid-1999 it had been joined by the Transatlantic Environmental Dialogue, which held its first meeting in Brussels during May.

This proliferation of collaboration did not, of course, mean that there were no disputes between the EU and the US. In fact, EU–US trade relations in 1999 were some of the most continuously contentious in recent memory. In the early part of the year, pride of place was held by the dispute over the EU's banana regime, which was declared illegal by the WTO. This led the US to impose sanctions on a wide range of EU exports, including a selection of luxury goods such as Roquefort cheese, designed to cause pain in France especially. After initially pushing for sanctions to the value of $540m, the US had to settle for $200m, and for the exclusion of certain items from their list (sometimes in response to pleas from EU Member States, as from the British over cashmere sweaters). Meanwhile, the EU was working on further amendments to the banana regime, and by the end of the year had produced a number of possible models for future development, none of which stood out as acceptable to all parties. Alongside this acrimonious dispute went another food-related issue: that of hormone-treated beef, on which the EU had imposed an import ban for reasons connected with public health. Here again, the EU's procrastination in responding to calls for a lifting of the ban led to US demands for sanctions (this time in company with Canada) This was countered by suggestions that all US beef (and indeed other meats) might be prohibited from entering the EU because of doubts about the monitoring of hormones even in apparently hormone-free beef. Although this dispute was to a degree defused by the end of the year, it was only one of a range of continuing conflicts involving everything from aircraft 'hush kits' to EU steel exports to 'electronic commerce' that continued to reflect the intense 'competitive interdependence' of the two sides of the Atlantic. By the end of the year, another two major issues were rearing their heads: first, the EU had been successful in getting a WTO judgment against the US device of 'Foreign Sales Corporations' which Brussels sees as a means of subsidizing US companies operating in Europe;

second, the US had threatened countries applying for EU membership with sanctions if they did not immediately adopt the EU's regime on imports from non-EU countries (this as a reflection of the US view that the 'Europe Agreements' gave unfair benefits in the form of market access to the EU in candidate countries). At the same time, the EU remained the single largest destination for US foreign direct investment, and the economic interpenetration of the two partners was ever more intense. No clearer example could be found of the link between intense interdependence and intense economic competition.

The EU's relations with Japan were largely quiet during 1999, a measure of the extent to which earlier economic frictions had declined because of the varying economic fortunes of the two partners, and because of the increasing 'transplantation' of industrial production from Japan to the EU. Indeed, the EU–Japan summit held in Bonn during May saw a good deal of agreement not only on bilateral issues but also on the forthcoming WTO negotiations. There was also a convergence of views between Japan and some EU Member States on the necessity for a 'managed currencies' regime in the aftermath of the introduction of the euro, and a broad agreement on how to deal with the changing position of North Korea. The major bilateral *casus belli* of the early 1990s, the level of imports of Japanese automobiles, was largely a non-issue by 1999, when the quota agreement which had been negotiated in the early 1990s was to expire. A significant preoccupation for the EU was the continuing struggle to enhance market access in Japan and to encourage domestic deregulation there. Something of the same was true for EU relations with South Korea, on which the Commission produced a communication welcomed by the Council in July, although in this case there were some specific issues to pursue arising from the Korean government's actions in the wake of the Asian financial crisis, which had produced symptoms of growing protectionism. Even here, though, the picture was not as simple as it might seem: in July, it was reported that Daewoo was taking increasing advantage of market access to the EU by exporting a growing number of its cars produced in Poland. Relations with Korea also inevitably linked with the development of the situation between North and South Korea, in which the EU is implicated most formally through its membership of the Korean Peninsular Energy Development Organization (KEDO) and through its status as the largest donor of humanitarian assistance. By the end of 1999, there were intriguing signs that the 'freeze' in North–South Korean relations might be easing.

EU relations with Canada, Australia and New Zealand have, in varying degrees, undergone the type of institutionalization already noted in respect of the EU–US relationship. The greatest similarities can be found between EU–US and EU–Canada relations, where there are regular summits (held in 1999 on 17 June and 16 December), a political dialogue (which met on 1 March and 2 September) and – new in 1999 – a European Union–Canada Business Round Table, paralleling the Transatlantic Business Dialogue. Apart from the spin-off from EU–US disputes, which saw Canada also seeking sanctions against the EU in respect of threats to their beef exports, EU–Canada relations in 1999 were calm; only late in the year did the previously acrimonious issue of fisheries come to the surface again, and then with no dramatic effect. The EU and Australia operate within the context of a Joint Declaration concluded in 1997, and held their annual meeting in Brussels on 21 May; there were also two political dialogue meetings, on 2 February in Bonn and 25 July in Singapore (the latter alongside ASEAN meetings). With New Zealand, there was a political dialogue meeting on 4 May in Strasbourg, and another in Singapore on 27 July. The major event in EU–New Zealand relations during 1999 was the signature of the Joint Declaration at the Strasbourg meeting. This establishes a framework for relations modelled on that between the EU and Australia, and outlines a wide range of areas for collaboration.

Journal of Common Market Studies
Volume 38, Annual Review
September 2000

Enlarging Europe

JULIE SMITH
University of Cambridge

I. Introduction

A decade after the collapse of communism in central and eastern Europe, the former German Democratic Republic remained the only formerly communist state to have joined the European Union.[1] Ten more, along with Cyprus, Malta, and Turkey, had applied to join, while several others, ranging from Ukraine to Kazakhstan had expressed their desire to become EU Members at some future date. 1999 saw considerable progress in moves towards EU enlargement: in March, Member States agreed on *Agenda 2000*, including a budget designed to cover enlargement beginning in 2002; six more candidate states were allowed to open membership negotiations; and Turkey's candidature was formally recognized. Nevertheless, for the candidate countries the enlargement process remained frustratingly slow.

Enlargement entails reform on the part of candidate states. Each is required to meet the so-called 'Copenhagen criteria' which include democratic credentials, functioning market economics, the ability to compete economically within the EU, respect for human rights and the rule of law, and the administrative capacity to enact and implement the *acquis communautaire* in its entirety. Of the 12 countries recognized as candidates at the Luxembourg summit in December 1997, six – Cyprus, the Czech Republic, Estonia,

---

[1] For a lengthier discussion of enlargement issues, see Smith (2000).

Hungary, Poland and Slovenia – were deemed at that stage to have made sufficient progress towards meeting the criteria to start accession negotiations in March 1998.

During 1999, the 'screening procedures' were completed and the six 'first wave' countries drew up negotiating positions on most issues. These countries made apparently rapid progress in the negotiations; each opened and provisionally closed between 10 and 15 of the 31 'chapters' of the *acquis* (they will finally be closed only when all the conditions are agreed to have been fulfilled). However, these chapters related largely to technical, non-sensitive issues on which agreement could be reached relatively easily. Although by spring 2000 all six had provisionally closed the chapter on foreign and security policy, negotiations on agriculture were only just beginning, with the issue of free movement of people still to be tackled.

The other five candidates, which the Commission had not felt to be ready to start full-blown accession negotiations – Bulgaria, Latvia, Lithuania, Romania, and Slovakia – began the 'screening process' in April 1998, with bilateral screening continuing through 1999. Following a change of government, Malta, whose application had been on hold for domestic reasons, also began the screening process. Some of these countries had made significant progress towards meeting the Copenhagen criteria. Latvia and, following Meciar's loss of power, Slovakia were doing particularly well, while Lithuania also seemed on a steady course. Thus there was considerable optimism in 1999 that they might be allowed to begin accession negotiations.

Bulgaria and Romania had also made progress, but might not have been in 1999 had it not been for the war in Kosovo. As candidates for NATO as well as EU membership, they played a constructive role in the NATO campaign which, alongside a desire to create peace and stability in the Balkans, contributed to agreement that they, too, could start negotiations. This was, perhaps, precipitated by Prime Minister Blair's visits to Bulgaria and Romania in May 1999 when he talked of their future membership.

The 'Helsinki Six' began formal negotiations in March 2000. In allowing the 'second wave' states to begin accession negotiations (conditionally in the cases of Romania and Bulgaria), the Helsinki Council adopted a 'regatta' approach to integration. In theory, the 12 candidates start from the same point and accession will depend on how quickly individual countries are able to complete the negotiations. Inevitably the 'Luxembourg Six' retain a significant advantage, given that they began negotiations two years earlier although, in principle, any of the Helsinki Six could catch up and even overtake some of the others. Malta, in particular, was well placed to catch up, although the possibility of a further change in government after the 2003 general elections there, means that its prospects remain uncertain. Latvia and Slovakia, too, appear to be moving up fairly fast.

A second major policy change at Helsinki was the decision to accept Turkey as a candidate country. This was a highly symbolic political decision. Turkey still fell far short of the Copenhagen criteria, but there was a widely-held belief that the Turkish government should be given some incentives to undertake further reform. Coupled with an improvement in Greco–Turkish relations, this led to the slightly anomalous decision to recognize Turkey as a candidate, but not to open negotiations or even start the screening process with it.

II. Preparing the EU for Enlargement

It is not only the candidate states that need to undertake reforms for successful enlargement to occur; the EU itself also needs to reform, particularly in the areas of the Common Agricultural Policy and its institutional arrangements. Progress on agricultural reform continued to be slow in 1999, despite agreement on *Agenda 2000* and the financial perspective for 2000–06 that was intended to provide sufficient funds for the EU to enlarge in 2002.[2] Since the agreement reached in Berlin in March 2000 only envisaged the budget increasing by 10 per cent, while the size of the population could be expected to rise by a third, there was considerable concern that the agreement would offer adequate funds.[3] Moreover, there was very little change to the CAP either, with France still unwilling to countenance any significant reforms. Thus, by the end of 1999, it seemed that candidates might face two equally unpalatable options: to delay entry pending further reform or greater convergence of their economies with those in the EU; or joining relatively soon, but accept long transitional periods before they would be entitled to the benefits of membership in agriculture.

By contrast, in 1999, the EU did make some progress on the institutional reforms necessary to ensure that an enlarged Union would be an effective Union. Three main issues that had been fudged at Maastricht and again at Amsterdam – the number of members of the Commission, weighting of votes in the Council, and the scope of qualified majority voting in the Council – the so-called 'Amsterdam leftovers' needed to be addressed prior to enlargement. The European Council meeting in Cologne in June 1999 asked the Finnish Presidency to produce a report at the Helsinki summit taking the views of the Commission, Parliament and Member States into consideration. This report,

---

[2] For a detailed discussion of the *Agenda 2000* proposals and an early assessment of the Berlin summit, see Galloway (1999).
[3] Question by Lord Lamont of Lerwick to Minister of State for Europe, Keith Vaz, Evidence by the Minister of State, Foreign and Commonwealth Office, on the Helsinki European Council (Select Committee on the European Union, House of Lords, Session 1999–2000, 3rd Report), p. 2.

duly presented in December, indicated considerable convergence on the idea of one Commissioner per Member State. There was less agreement concerning the other two issues, however, and lengthy discussions are likely during the Intergovernmental Conference (IGC) which the Helsinki summit requested should tackle these issues.

An IGC was formally opened on 14 February 2000, with most states favouring a short and focused meeting. The expectation was that reforms would be agreed under the French Presidency in the second half of 2000, culminating with a Treaty of Nice in December 2000 that would pave the way for the candidates to negotiate the institutional chapter of the *acquis*. This would be a major step forward on the part of the EU. However, the need to ratify both the Treaty that emerges from the IGC and the accession treaties for the candidates means that enlargement remains some way off. The candidates may have committed themselves to be ready to join by 31 December 2002; in practice, enlargement before 2004–05 remains unlikely.

References

Smith, J. (2000) *An Ever Larger Europe?* Briefing Paper 14 RIIA, May.

Galloway, D. (1999) 'Keynote Article: *Agenda 2000* – Packaging the Deal'. *The European Union Annual Review 1998/1999*, pp. 9–35.

Journal of Common Market Studies

Volume 38, Annual Review
September 2000

Justice and Home Affairs

JÖRG MONAR
University of Leicester

I. Introduction

1999 will enter the annals of EU Justice and Home Affairs (JHA) as year one of the 'area of freedom, security and justice' (AFSJ). After most of the issues of the incorporation of the Schengen *acquis* had been settled, on 1 May, with the entry into force of the Treaty of Amsterdam, the AFSJ became formally part of the fundamental treaty objectives of the EU. Its political significance was further enhanced by the fact that the Heads of State or Government met in October in Tampere for the first ever European Council focusing on JHA matters. While leaving a number of problems unresolved, the summit defined a number of principles and objectives, which went significantly beyond the pre-Amsterdam approach. Yet progress was also achieved below the lofty level of the European Council. During the year both Council and Commission decided on a major overhaul and expansion of their working structures, which demonstrated the increasing importance given to JHA. In the individual JHA areas several measures and initiatives were adopted along the lines of the 1998 Vienna Action Plan.

JÖRG MONAR

II. Developments in Individual Policy Areas

Asylum and Immigration

The Union's move towards a more comprehensive and 'cross-pillar' approach to asylum and immigration, which had started in 1998, continued. The new High Level Working Group on Asylum and Immigration was given a formal mandate on 25 January to work on an integrated strategy towards main countries of origin and transit for asylum-seekers and immigrants. In the following weeks it drew up 'action plans' for five main countries of origin and transit – Afghanistan and the neighbouring region, Iraq, Morocco, Somalia and Sri Lanka – which contain operational proposals for co-operation with the countries concerned in three integrated domains of action: foreign policy, development and economic assistance as well as concrete measures in the fields of asylum and immigration. The five action plans – which were endorsed by the Council in October 1999 – make use of a mixed set of instruments such as support for democratization and the rule of law, social and economic development, alleviation of poverty, support of conflict prevention and co-operation with the United Nations High Commission for Refugees (UNHCR) to reduce the number of asylum applications in the EU Member States (Council documents 11424/99, 11425/99, 11426/99, 11427/99 and 11428/99). The European Parliament gave broad support to the Council's new comprehensive approach in a resolution adopted on 13 April, but it emphasized the need to maintain a careful distinction between asylum as a fundamental right and migration as a primarily economic issue (*OJ* C 219/73 of 30.7.1999).

As a result of the events in Kosovo, several Member States had to cope with large numbers of refugees and asylum-seekers from March onwards. An obligatory system of burden-sharing proved again impossible to attain. Yet on 26 April the Council adopted a Joint Action on practical support in relation to the reception and voluntary repatriation of refugees, displaced persons and asylum-seekers (1999/290/JHA) which, for the first time, allowed EC funding of measures in areas such as the improvement of reception infrastructures, legal assistance and counselling services, basic standards of living conditions and the provision of information to the public in order to facilitate acceptance. The Joint Action also opened the possibility of supporting projects aimed at facilitating the voluntary return of refugees through information on the situation in the country of origin, training and education, and the financing of repatriation costs. Although targeted at smaller projects only, and providing funding only up to 80 per cent of total costs, the Joint Action can be regarded as a first step towards financial burden-sharing in the sphere of asylum and immigration policy through the EC budget.

The European Commission went a step further on the issue of burden-sharing when, on 14 December, it adopted a proposal for a Council Decision on the establishment of a European Refugee Fund aimed at striking a balance between the Member States' efforts to receive refugees and displaced persons (*COM*(1999) 686). According to the Commission's proposal, the fund should, firstly, support action at the national level as regards conditions for reception of refugees and displaced persons through actions on infrastructure, services for accommodation, supply of material aid and social assistance. Secondly, it should facilitate integration into the society of residence through social assistance in areas such as housing, and means of subsistence and healthcare. Thirdly, it should support voluntary repatriation through information and advice on the situation in the country of origin, vocational training and help in resettlement. The Commission's proposal was partly based on the same principles as the Joint Action of 26 April, but was innovative in that it provided, for the first time, for the establishment of a dedicated fund with a five-year financial framework organized on the same principles of decentralized implementation which apply to the structural funds. Taking into account the reluctance of some Member States to use the EC budget as an instrument of burden-sharing, the Commission proposed an initial budget of only EUR 26m plus EUR 10m as a reserve) for the year 2000. Arguably, this amount would make no great difference to those Member States faced with a major influx of refugees. Yet the creation of the fund would be tantamount to the establishment of a more permanent mechanism of solidarity whose financial volume could be substantially increased – with possible support by the European Parliament – from one year to the next.

Signs increased during the year that the Union was moving towards a more realistic discussion of immigration issues. In the context of the Third Pillar, discussions had largely been based on the principle of 'zero immigration'. Yet most of the Member States have never fully implemented that policy. Special regimes for immigration from certain third countries, the dependence of certain branches of industry on immigrant workers and humanitarian considerations (such as on family reunification) have ensured that the EU, despite assertions to the contrary, is *de facto* an area of immigration. After a first acknowledgement of the need for harmonization of the conditions for admission and residence by the Tampere European Council (see below), the Commission took a first step towards an EU policy on legal immigration by proposing on 1 December a directive on the right to family reunification (*COM*(1999) 638). In its justification of the proposal, the Commission not only described family reunification as a necessary way of making a success of the integration of third-country nationals residing lawfully in the Member States, but also hinted at the need for the Member States to allow for legal immigration in order to offset the effects of demographic factors such as the ageing of the population with their impact on welfare protection and the funding of pension schemes. The Commission proposed to grant third-country nationals residing lawfully in the territory of the Member States a harmonized right to family reunification, based on a number of provisions of existing Community law regulating the family reunification of EU citizens who exercise their right to free movement. A number of restrictive criteria would apply (on 'adequate accommodation' and 'stable and adequate resources', for instance) but family members authorized to enter and reside in a Member State would be entitled to a range of social rights, such as full access to all levels of education and access to employment. If accepted, the proposed directive would go some way to reduce the still considerable differences in treatment of family members of third-country nationals and EU nationals which have often been criticized by human rights groups. After a first discussion in the JHA Council on 2 December, a rapid decision on the Commission proposal seemed unlikely: there were objections to the inclusion of unmarried partners and disagreements over several criteria and social rights.

In the battle against illegal immigration, on 29 April the Council adopted a recommendation aimed at improving the detection of false or falsified documents in the visa departments of both domestic authorities and representations abroad (*OJ* C 140/1 of 20.5.1999). This text reflects the growing concerns in the EU about the increasing sophistication of criminal groups in the falsification of visas for the purpose of illegal immigration. The recommendation provides for several levels of training and technical provision for detection purposes depending on a national evaluation of risk during the visa procedure. At the same time, the Council also adopted a resolution on an early warning system on illegal immigration and facilitator networks in the framework of the existing CIREFI co-operation. It provides for the direct exchange of information between central national authorities on illegal immigration phenomena requiring immediate counter-measures such as perceptible changes in routes and methods, concentrations of specific nationalities, new types of large-scale document forgery or large-scale facilitation, i.e. for groups of over 40 people (Council documents 7965/99 and 8204/99). It is intended to make all the central and eastern European countries participate in this early warning system because it is through their territory that much of the illegal immigration takes place. The Council was also able on 2 December to agree on the future wording of readmission clauses to be inserted into agreements with third countries (Council Document 12134/99).

Another year passed by without the adoption of the long prepared Eurodac system for the electronic fingerprinting of asylum-seekers. Originally proposed as a Third Pillar Convention, the Commission reintroduced it as a proposal for an EC regulation on 26 May (*COM*(1999) 260). Yet in December there was still controversy over the territorial scope and the European Parliament still needed to be reconsulted on changes made to the provisions on implementation.

Police Co-operation and the Fight against Organized Crime

On 1 July, Europol finally became fully operational after all remaining protocols had been ratified by the Member States. This had been preceded by a decision of the Council on 29 April to extend the mandate of Europol to include the fight against forgery of money and means of payment (*OJ* C 149/ 16 of 28.5.1999), which was partly motivated by concerns over the protection of the euro against counterfeiting. Europol's final coming of age was slightly overshadowed, however, by a resolution of the European Parliament adopted on 13 April which severely criticized the absence of more comprehensive information and consultation of the Parliament on Europol matters (*OJ* C 219/ 102 of 30.7.1999). The Parliament rightly pointed to the limited effectiveness of control of Europol by national parliaments and called on the Council to establish a number of special procedures to better inform and consult both itself and the national parliaments on Europol's activities and development. Europol's rapid growth – staff numbers grew to over 300 during the year – make it likely that, sooner or later, the question of its funding out of the EC budget will arise, which would give some leverage to the European Parliament.

The tasks of Europol also include providing support to 'route-policing' projects of the Member States. On 27 May the Council adopted a resolution on combating international crime with fuller coverage of the routes used (*OJ* C 162/1 of 9.6.1999). The recommendation provides for co-ordinated policing projects on overland, waterway or air routes particularly used by specific forms of cross-border crime, which involve deploying forces, methods and equipment. The primary purposes of such projects are to achieve optimum results in both the prevention and detection of offences, improvements in the co-ordination of joint police action and communication, and obtaining additional intelligence on criminal behaviour and methods. In the interest of improving route strategies, the Member States may undertake joint evaluations and inform the other Member States of the results. No provision was made, however, for Europol to initiate such route-policing projects, which would, in principle, have been possible on the basis of Art. 30(2)(a) TEU.

The 1997 action plan against organized crime had also provided for measures in the fight against high-tech crime. In line with this objective, on 27 May the Council adopted a common position on the negotiations relating to the Draft Convention on Cyber Crime held in the Council of Europe (*OJ* L 142/ 1 of 5.6.1999). The Member States undertook to support the inclusion in the

Convention of provisions facilitating the effective investigation and prosecution of criminal offences against the confidentiality, integrity and availability of computer data, with a particular emphasis also on content-related offences such as child pornography. Building on its positive experiences with special national contact points, the common position also suggested the setting of 24-hour law enforcement points of contact in order to facilitate swift co-operation on computer-related offences. The Member States also declared themselves willing, subject to constitutional principles and certain safeguards, to accept the possibility of trans-border computer searches in emergency situations. In view of the increasing dependency of European economies, administrations and societies on computer data and networks, and therefore their vulnerability, this common position can be no more than a first step in addressing the rapidly growing security risks posed by organized crime in this area.

Action against Drugs

1999 saw the completion of the second (1995–99) EU Action Plan to Combat Drugs. Its integrated approach aimed at reducing both demand and supply in combination with increased international co-operation. Intra-EU co-ordination was on the whole seen as a success, although the lack of more comprehensive funding for EU action had been frequently criticized. On 26 May the Commission proposed a new action plan for the years 2000–04 (*COM*(1999) 239), whose objectives were approved by the European Parliament in November and by the Council in December. In its communication on the action plan, the Commission identified a number of new challenges for EU action. It pointed, in particular, to the growing appeal of synthetic drugs (of which the EU is a major production region) among young people, increasing urban delinquency linked to the sale of illicit drugs and the need to ensure adequate participation of the candidate countries in EU structures and programmes in preparation for enlargement. The new action plan provides for five domains of action with the following main targets.

In the area of information, the European Monitoring Centre for Drugs and Drug Addiction (EMCDDA) in Lisbon will have the task, besides the regular collection, analysis and dissemination of data, of improving data comparison methods, extending the implementation of common indicators among Member States, expanding the scientific evaluation of demand reduction activities, and engaging in more co-operation with international bodies and non-EU countries. The EMCCDA will also have to analyse the implications of the drugs phenomenon for producer, consumer and transit countries, including money laundering, which should help the EU to develop integrated strategies for co-operation with third countries. As regards *action on demand reduction,* the action plan recommends, *inter alia,* further studies and pilot projects on the early identification of changed drug-use trends and the valuation of the impact of preventive actions, the adoption of a more proactive approach for the prevention and reduction of associated health risks and the development of training programmes in the prevention of drug dependence with a particular emphasis on integration mechanisms able to ensure community-based measures. Further action is also envisaged in the areas of education and public awareness campaigns. *Action on reduction of illicit trafficking* focuses on the control of chemical precursors diversion within the EU and in third countries, the fight against money laundering, increased co-operation between police, customs and judicial authorities, the prevention of the use of new communication systems (especially the internet) for drug abuse, production and trafficking and increased international co-operation. As regards *action at the international level,* the action plan builds on the principle of integrating EU objectives in the fight against drugs more effectively into the broader objectives of EU external relations. This includes a fuller use of EC instruments such as development, technical and financial assistance and the Generalized System of Preferences. On the latter, the Commission came out in favour of continuing the special commercial arrangements in support of efforts to reduce illicit crop production. Finally, the action plan aims at an improved intra-EU co-ordination, in particular in the context of the Horizontal Drugs Group set up by COREPER, and the Common Foreign and Security Policy Council Working Group on Drugs (CODRO).

The 2000–04 action plan provides a number of useful guidelines for EU action against drugs, especially in the areas of demand reduction and international co-operation, but the Treaty of Amsterdam has given the EU no new 'hard' competencies to implement the plan. The new Treaty has not singled out drugs as a major 'health scourge' in Art. 152(1) TEC, and Community action can only 'complement' the actions of the Member States in this field. Nor is there any longer a specific legal base for action in the fight against drug trafficking in what remains of the old Third Pillar. All this will not help with the implementation of the action plan and is likely to limit the possibilities of EC funding. One also misses in the action plan, apart from their envisaged participation in the EMCCD, more comprehensive proposals on the preparation of the applicant countries.

In spite of these limitations, the Commission demonstrated its intention to use fully existing treaty provisions. Based on a risk assessment provided by the EMCDDA, the Commission, on 23 June, proposed for the first time a Council decision on making a new synthetic drug (the amphetamine derivative 4-MTA) subject to control measures and criminal penalties. This decision was adopted by the Council on 13 September and provided for appropriate control and legislative measures to be taken by the Member States within three months (*OJ* L 244/1 of 16.9.1999).

Effective international co-operation remained a crucial element of EU action. In April the first meeting took place of experts in the context of the new co-operation framework with the Latin American and Caribbean countries. The Commission expressed its hope that this framework would contribute to both better targeting of aid and reinforcement of interregional co-operation between Latin America and the Caribbean.

Judicial Co-operation

In the area of judicial co-operation, EU activities focused partially on the consolidation of the EU's legal *acquis*. In the sphere of civil law, as had been expected, the Commission introduced several proposals on the reintroduction of Third Pillar instruments as Community legal instruments following the communitarization of civil law co-operation by the Treaty of Amsterdam. In this context, the first negative effects of Amsterdam 'flexibility' in this area became apparent. The United Kingdom and Ireland notified their wish to take part in both the proposed directive on the service of judicial and extra-judicial documents in civil and commercial matters (*COM*(1999) 219, reproducing the content of the 1997 Convention) and the proposed regulation on jurisdiction and the recognition and enforcement of judgments in matrimonial matters (*COM*(1999) 220, reproducing the substance of the 1998 Convention). Denmark, however – on the basis of its Amsterdam opt-out protocol – requested a separate international agreement between the EC and itself on both of these legal acts. On 14 July the Commission also introduced a proposal for a regulation on jurisdiction and the recognition and enforcement of judgments in civil and commercial matters which was based on the progress achieved on the parallel revision of the Brussels and Lugano Conventions (*COM*(1999) 348). By the end of the year the United Kingdom had 'opted in', but Ireland and Denmark had not yet fully clarified their position. Germany and Finland exercised, again for the first time, a Member State's new right of initiative under Art. 67(1) TEC by introducing a draft resolution on 28 May on jurisdiction over and enforcement of insolvency proceedings (*OJ* C 221/8 of 3.8.1999). The United Kingdom and Ireland declared a wish to 'opt in', but Denmark insisted again on a separate international agreement.

Responding to the concern about the protection of the euro against counterfeiting, the Council adopted a resolution on 28 May on penal sanctions against counterfeiting and the falsification of euro banknotes and coins (*OJ* C 171/1 of 18.6.1999). The resolution established the provisions of the 1929 International Convention for the Suppression of Counterfeiting Currency (to which not all Member States have yet acceded) as a common minimum standard for the protection of the euro. It also provided, *inter alia*, that the Member States should impose 'effective and appropriate penal sanctions', which may lead to extradition and calls for adequate measures to ensure effective prosecution.

Judicial co-operation, as it had emerged in the context of the Third Pillar had largely concentrated on issues of mutual legal assistance, recognition and enforcement. The situation and the rights of victims of crime had been largely left aside. In a communication on 'Crime victims in the European Union' (*COM*(1999) 349) adopted on 14 July, the Commission argued that European citizens who have become victims of crime should be provided not only with legal protection, but also with assistance at every stage of the criminal procedure, irrespective of their location. Pointing to the increasing cross-border mobility of European citizens, it suggested a range of measures aimed at helping those falling victim to a crime in a Member State other than their own, before they arrive at the compensation stage. The measures proposed included common standards on the accessibility of material, medical, psycho-logical and social assistance services, the availability of contact persons in court to assist victims on procedural matters, improvements in the possibility of foreign victims to participate adequately in a procedure, assistance to victims in debt collection of damages from the offender and the facilitation, through co-operation between the Member States, of applications for state compensation. The Commission made no concrete legislative proposals and some of its ideas met immediate resistance in some national ministries, who did not relish the prospect of having to adapt national crime victim support schemes to common EU standards. Yet the Commission's reflections built upon the reference to victims' rights which had been included in the 1998 Vienna Action Plan. They were also fully in line with some of the ideas that the French Minister of Justice, Elisabeth Guigou, had been putting forward since the autumn of 1998 on the substance of a 'European judicial area', which would guarantee citizens better access to justice and to the enforcement of their rights. The issue of victims' rights could well become a test-case on the extent to which the AFSJ is really becoming an 'area for citizens' and not only for governments, courts and law enforcement officers.

III. Post-Amsterdam Adaptations: Schengen and New Institutional Working Structures

Although negotiations on the necessary adaptations to the Amsterdam Treaty reforms had already started in the autumn of 1997, several key issues could only be settled in the months before and after the entry into force of the new Treaty. This was the case, in particular, for the unresolved questions relating to the incorporation of the Schengen *acquis* and the reform of the working structures of Council and Commission.

Schengen: The Incorporation and the Agreement with Iceland and Norway

With the entry into force of the Treaty of Amsterdam on 1 May, the Schengen system ceased to exist as a separate structure outside the EU framework. On the institutional side, this was a fairly straightforward affair: the Schengen Executive Committee met for the last time on 27–28 April and was then formally replaced by the EU Justice and Home Affairs Council. A number of other bodies and working groups of the Schengen system were either merged with existing EU bodies or were transferred into the EU Council structure. The only major difficulty was the transfer of 59 members of the personnel of the former Schengen Secretariat to the Secretariat-General of the EU Council where it was met by strike action from EU officials protesting against what they saw as a violation of EU staff statutes and procedures. In what the trade unions termed 'Schengengate', France opposed the incorporation of the Schengen staff as well because it felt that their numbers (which included no French personnel) exceeded real needs and because of the absence of 'aptitude tests'.

On the legal side, the difficult negotiations over the appropriate legal bases under the EC and/or EU treaties continued even beyond the deadline of 1 May. Spanish reservations on the status of Gibraltar caused delays even in the final stages. It was only on 20 May that the Council was finally able to adopt both a decision concerning the definition of the Schengen *acquis* (*OJ* L 176/1 of 10.7.1999) and a decision determining the legal basis for each of the provisions of the *acquis* (*OJ* L 176/17 of 10.7.1999). Yet the latter remained incomplete because the Schengen members had failed to reach agreement on the legal basis for the Schengen Information System (SIS). While some of the Schengen countries took the view that the SIS was primarily an instrument of police co-operation and therefore required a legal basis under Title VI TEU, others saw it as an instrument primarily related to the free movement of persons with relevance to asylum and immigration issues which would require a legal basis under Title IV TEC. As a result of the failure to reach agreement, the provisions on the SIS were provisionally based on Title VI TEU. The Netherlands and Belgium, however, took the unusual step of adding a formal statement to the decision of 20 May on their position that the SIS should instead be based on an EC legal basis. The issue, which also has implications for the role of the Commission and the future possibility of majority voting on the SIS, still had not been resolved by the end of the year. The European Parliament added a further note of dissatisfaction by sharply criticizing the fact that it had not been consulted on the incorporation of Schengen. It is, indeed, difficult to avoid the view that the Member States have done little to reduce the democratic deficit in EU Justice and Home Affairs by incorporating hundreds of pages of binding legal texts in the EC/EU *acquis* without formal consultation of the Parliament.

As a result of the incorporation of Schengen into the EU, the association of Iceland and Norway with the Schengen group – made necessary because of the 1957 Nordic Passport Union and, more practically, because of the largely uncontrolled 1,650 kilometres of land border between Norway and Sweden – had to be put on a new legal basis. Since the EU insisted on complete institutional autonomy as regards the further development of the Schengen *acquis,* the solution agreed was that Norway and Iceland would content themselves with 'decision-shaping' instead of 'decision-making'. Yet the agreement providing for the association of Iceland and Norway with the Schengen *acquis* (*OJ* No. L 176/36 of 10.7.1999), which was concluded on 18 May 1999 and took the place of the first agreement between the Schengen members and Iceland and Norway, in fact left little room for future 'decision-shaping' by the associated countries. By virtue of Art. 2 of the agreement, Iceland and Norway were placed under an obligation to implement and apply most of the operational parts of the Schengen *acquis*, yet their opportunity to influence EU decision-making is limited to the possibility that they may 'explain' the problems they may encounter and 'express' themselves on any questions of concern to the Mixed Committee set up under the agreement. Art. 8(1) provides, however, that the adoption of acts or measures amending or building upon the Schengen *acquis* 'shall be reserved to the competent institutions of the European Union'. Should Iceland or Norway decide not to accept the content of an EU act or measure building upon Schengen or should they fail to make a notification of the fulfilment of their constitutional requirements within a period of six months, the agreement will be considered to be terminated (Art. 8(4)). One can hardly envisage a more one-sided type of agreement or – if one looks at it from the EU–Schengen side – a more successful extension of the Schengen regime to two non-EU countries whose position is only marginally stronger than that of an 'observer'.

On 20 May the UK government requested participation in substantial parts of the Schengen *acquis* relating to police and judicial co-operation in criminal matters, narcotic drugs and the SIS without, however, changing its position on the border control and free movement of persons related elements of the Schengen system (House of Lords, 2000). Ireland indicated that it would submit a request along the same lines 'shortly'. The Commission delivered a favourable opinion on the British request on 20 July (*SEC*(1999) 1198) but at the end of the year the necessary Council decision was still blocked by the reluctance of the Spanish government to recognize Gibraltar as competent authorities. Spain was obviously using this issue as a political lever in order to put pressure on the British position on Gibraltar. This case illustrates how easily 'flexibility' arrangements can be (ab)used as an instrument of exclusion for political purposes which have nothing to do with the actual subject matter.

The Reform of the Working Structures of Council and Commission

It had always been clear that with the communitarization of a major part of the areas of Justice and Home Affairs, the Council working structures would need substantial change. One inevitable effect of the Amsterdam reforms was the limitation of the remit of the former 'K.4 Committee' (now Article 36 Committee) to the few areas still covered by the Third Pillar (Title VI TEU). One may also have expected that, as a result of communitarization, the working structures of the areas now falling under Title IV TEC, would be organized in accordance with the usual three-level system (working groups–COREPER–Council) existing in other areas of EC policy-making. It was easy enough to agree on the abolition of the former Third Pillar Steering Groups. They had already ceased to meet during the second half of 1997. Yet several Member States insisted on retaining a special co-ordinating body for matters of asylum, immigration and external border controls. When the new working structures of the Council were drawn up during April and May, it was decided that this co-ordinating body should take the form of a 'strategic committee' working directly under the authority of COREPER. This solution – which was mainly due to the unwillingness of several national ministries to see certain supervisory and co-ordinating powers transferred to the permanent representatives – leaves the newly communitarized areas of asylum and immigration with a similar four-level structure as the remaining intergovernmental areas falling within the remit of the Article 36 Committee (see Figure 1). A further intergovernmental feature in the revised working structure of the Council is the fact that the working parties dealing with the functioning of the SIS have all been included in the police and customs co-operation part of the working structure in spite of the SIS functions in the communitarized areas of external border controls, asylum and immigration. Equally noteworthy is that the working party on customs co-operation remains within the Third Pillar working structure, although customs co-operation has been transferred to new Title X TEC. Some Member States took the view that this area was so closely related to police co-operation it should remain in the context of the Title VI TEU working structures. Within the First Pillar working structure, the decision to upgrade the working party on civil law co-operation to a 'Committee on Civil Law' matters reflected the Union's increased agenda and legislative possibilities in this area.

Because of the Commission's extended right of initiative and the communitarization of the areas now under Title IV, the case for reform of the

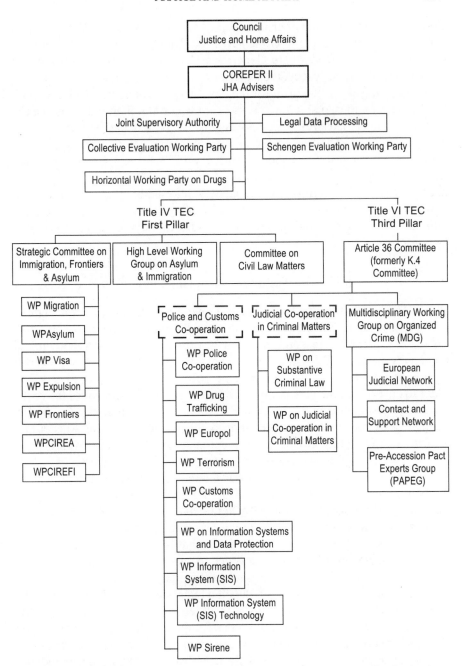

Figure 1: New Working Structure of the Council of the European Union in the Area of Justice and Home Affairs (After Information Provided by the Secretariat-General of the Council of the EU).

Commission's until then rather small Task Force for Justice and Home Affairs was also evident. In September the new Prodi Commission took the decision to establish a new Directorate-General for Justice and Home Affairs to be headed by Adrian Fortescue, the experienced Head of the old Task Force. By the end of the year, a blueprint for the new DG had emerged which provided for the creation of two directorates, one for the communitarized areas and the co-ordination of measures in the fight against drugs, and one for the remaining areas under Title VI and external relations (including enlargement questions). Special units for resources and information will be directly attached to the Director-General. While the creation of the new JHA DG was certainly a necessary step, the Commission's capacity to play a more proactive role in the build-up of the AFSJ will, to a considerable extent, also depend on the numbers, the expertise and the resources with which the new DG is going to be equipped.

IV. The Tampere European Council

By October 1998, the Heads of State or Government had in principle agreed to hold a special European Council on JHA matters under the Finnish Presidency of 1999. In some national governments the relatively limited objectives of the 1998 Vienna Action Plan confirmed the view that powerful signals and guidelines from the supreme political level would be needed in order to ensure that the new treaty objective of the establishment of the AFSJ would not just be a new label attached to the old Third Pillar system. By the beginning of the year it seemed, indeed, fairly clear that the Amsterdam reforms were meeting considerable scepticism in many national ministries which preferred a 'business as usual' approach to EU JHA matters.

Preparations for the special European Council started early. In a joint letter to their colleagues of 18 March 1999, the German Chancellor, Gerhard Schröder, and the Finnish Prime Minister, Paavo Lipponen, emphasized their view that the aims of bringing the Union closer to its citizens and developing the new AFSJ were closely interrelated, and that 'significant political results' should be achieved at Tampere in order to meet the expectations of their citizens. As a result of this letter, a tour of capitals was organized in April, which explored – on the basis of a detailed questionnaire and extensive talks with ministers and senior officials – the Member States' views about the central issues which should be put on the Tampere agenda. As a result of the tour, the governments were able to agree in April that the agenda should be focused on asylum and immigration, the establishment of a European judicial area and the fight against cross-border crime.

The preparatory work and the summit itself, which was held on 15–16 October in the Finnish city of Tampere, revealed a considerable degree of consensus on the part of the Heads of State or Government on the need to make active use of the new possibilities created by the Amsterdam Treaty and to develop the AFSJ. Yet there were also a number of diverging national priorities and some disagreement over questions of substance which are likely to remain on the EU's agenda for some years to come. The following were of particular importance:

- The German government – concerned about Germany's position as a 'frontline' state as regards asylum and immigration pressure and refugee movements – aimed at substantial progress towards a single asylum and migration policy which would involve a system of burden-sharing among the Member States. This was supported among others by Austria and Italy, but met the resistance of some Member States less exposed to asylum and immigration problems, such as Denmark, Ireland and the UK which preferred a less communitarian approach without obligatory burden-sharing mechanisms.
- The French government was particularly keen on the establishment of a 'European judicial area' with common minimum standards and rules on European citizens' access to justice, cross-border litigation and enforcement of judgments. This objective – which tied in well with the Jospin government's efforts to reform the French judicial system – would have involved a considerable degree of approximation and – ultimately – the harmonization of national laws. The British government, however, took the view that mutual recognition of judicial standards and judgments would be preferable to approximation and harmonization because it would take less time and require far less change to existing national legislation.

The decisions adopted by the Tampere European Council (Council Document SN 200/99) were largely related to the three priority areas agreed on earlier in the year.

1. The Development of a Common EU Asylum and Migration Policy: During the 1990s EU action in this sphere had largely concentrated on reducing the number of asylum applicants and immigrants by restrictive control, adjudication and returning procedures. This 'Fortress Europe' approach had been criticized by human rights groups and the UNHCR. The Tampere summit agreed on a more comprehensive strategy which combines preventive measures outside the EU, with a greater emphasis on common standards and minimum rights for asylum seekers and immigrants. On the external side, a green light was given to the use of EU external economic and political instruments for the purpose of co-operating with countries of origin in order to reduce asylum and immigration pressures. On the internal side, agreement was reached on the establishment of a Common European Asylum System which provides for common standards for the examination of asylum applications, minimum conditions of reception for asylum-seekers and the approximation of rules on refugee status. This should be accompanied by a more active EU policy on the integration of legally resident third-country nationals aimed at improving their rights and legal status, and measures against racism and xenophobia. However, more ambitious proposals aimed at creating a 'single' asylum policy with the harmonization of basic national rules failed. Germany struggled in vain to secure an agreement on a comprehensive automatic system of burden-sharing in situations of mass influx of refugees. In spite of the recognition that freedom within the EU acts as a powerful draw to people in other countries, and a reference to the aim of an 'open' European Union, the main emphasis of the Presidency Conclusions in the sphere of migration policy was again on restrictive measures such as improving controls, legislation against trafficking in human beings, the promotion of voluntary return and the use of readmission clauses.

2. The 'European Area of Justice': Access to Justice and Mutual Recognition of Judicial Decisions: The complexity, cost and, often enough, also the inefficiency of litigation, which involves individuals or businesses from different EU countries, remains one of the most glaring deficits of over 40 years of economic integration within the internal market. At Tampere, the HOSG agreed on a number of measures which should enhance both access to justice and the mutual recognition of judgments in cases of cross-border litigation. As regards access to justice, the Council of the EU was asked to establish minimum standards for an adequate level of legal aid in cross-border litigation and for the protection of the rights of victims of crime. Further measures include the mandate to introduce common rules for simplified and accelerated cross-border litigation on small consumer and commercial claims and common minimum standards for multilingual legal forms and documents used in cross-border court cases. The principle of the mutual recognition of judicial decisions was endorsed by the HOSG as the future cornerstone of judicial co-operation in both civil and criminal matters, a major success for the British position. It was explicitly extended to a number of other areas such as pre-trial orders and lawfully gathered evidence. A comprehensive programme of measures to implement the principle of mutual recognition will have to be adopted by Council and Commission by December 2000. Yet the cause of those Member States arguing for more EU legislation and approximation and harmonization of national laws was not entirely lost: the Commission was invited to make proposals on fast-track extradition procedures and on new procedural legislation in cross-border cases, including such important elements as the taking of evidence and the setting of time limits. The issue of the approximation of national legislation on civil matters will be the object of an overall study on which the Council has to report back in 2001.

3. *The Fight Against Organized and Transnational Crime*: As regards crime prevention, the Tampere summit was not able to agree on more than the exchange of best practices and the strengthening of co-operation between national crime prevention authorities. National priorities and strategies on prevention continue to be very different and this prevented a more comprehensive common approach. Yet the possibility was opened of supporting co-operation between national crime prevention authorities through a specific Community project. The results on co-operation in the fight against crime were more substantial. The HOSG agreed on the creation of two new institutions: a unit called EUROJUST, composed of national prosecutors, magistrates or police officers, will have the task of facilitating the co-ordination of national prosecuting authorities and supporting criminal investigations in organized crime cases. The idea is that it will have, at least initially, a supporting, not an operational role, similar to that of Europol in the area of police co-operation. The summit also decided to establish a European Police College for the training of senior law enforcement officials, which will also be open to applicant countries. In addition, the European Council put pressure on national authorities to set up without delay the joint investigative teams foreseen by the Amsterdam Treaty and to create a special task force of European police chiefs for the exchange of experiences and for planning purposes. Money laundering was reconfirmed as a crucial issue in the Union's fight against organized crime. The European Council decided that legislation should be adopted to enable financial intelligence units to receive information on suspicious transactions regardless of secrecy provisions applicable to banking or other commercial activity. It also came out in favour of the approximation of criminal law and procedures on money laundering and for including money laundering in the remit of Europol.

In addition to the objectives set for each of the three areas above, the European Council also called for stronger external action, especially through the use of the new treaty-making possibilities of the EU after Amsterdam. The Council and Commission were asked to present proposals on policy objectives and measures for external JHA action before the European Council of June 2000. On this point, as well, the summit went much further than the Vienna Action Plan, which seems necessary considering the extent to which many internal JHA measures are dependent on effective co-operation with third countries and international organizations.

In all but name, Tampere was a summit on the implementation of the Amsterdam provisions on Justice and Home Affairs and the build-up of the AFSJ. The risk of the Council contenting itself with a mere reaffirmation of general principles and the resolution of some unfinished JHA Council business was averted. The Tampere decisions were more substantial than many observers had expected. They provide the Union with a fresh impetus in major areas of the AFSJ, and substantial new legislation is to be expected over the next few years on asylum matters, measures facilitating the integration of third-country nationals, access to justice, cross-border litigation and money laundering. EUROJUST could become the germ-cell of a European prosecution system. It remains to be seen, however, how much time it will take to implement some of the more ambitious objectives of Tampere.

References

Commission of the European Communities (1999) 'Communication ... Crime victims in the European Union. Reflexions on standards and action'. *COM*(1999) 349.

Commission of the European Communities (1999) 'Communication ... on a European Union Action Plan to Combat Drugs (2000–2004)'. *COM*(1999) 239.

Commission of the European Communities (1999) 'Proposal for a Council Decision creating a European Refugee Fund'. *COM*(1999) 686.

Commission of the European Communities (1999) 'Proposal for a Council Directive on the right to family reunification'. *COM*(1999) 638.

Council of the European Union (1999) 'Agreement concluded by the Council of the European Union and the Republic of Iceland and the Kingdom of Norway concerning their association with the implementation, application and development of the Schengen acquis'. *OJ* L 176/36, 10 July.

Council of the European Union (1999) 'Council Decision of 29 April 1999 extending Europol's mandate to deal with forgery of money and means of payment'. *OJ* C 149/16, 28 May.

Council of the European Union (1999) 'Council Decision of 20 May 1999 concerning the definition of the Schengen acquis ...'. *OJ* L 176/1, 10 July.

Council of the European Union (1999) 'Council Decision of 20 May 1999 determining ... the legal basis for each of the provisions or decisions which constitute the Schengen acquis'. *OJ* L 176/17, 10 July.

Council of the European Union (1999) 'Council Resolution of 27 May 1999 on combating international crime with fuller cover of the routes'. *OJ* C 162/1, 9 June.

House of Lords (2000) Select Committee on the European Union: UK Participation in the Schengen Acquis, Session 1999–2000, 5th Report, 15 February.

Journal of Common Market Studies

Volume 38, Annual Review
September 2000

Developments in the Member States

LEE MILES
University of Hull

I. Introduction

This section of the *Annual Review* examines the main political developments in the Member States that have implications for the European Union and some of the EU issues that reverberated in domestic debates on Europe. 1999 was, in many ways, the year in which the popularity of the Union in the Member States was, once again, tested. It represented a year of important 'highs' in which the Union moved forward on a number of critical fronts – the first year of the euro, CAP reform, and progress on enlargement and the CFSP; and also of distinct 'lows', such as the Commission crisis of March 1999. However, this section will examine only those areas where the 'Member State' dimension was particularly noticeable.

II. Elections and their Consequences

In one sense, each Member State held a relevant national election – to decide their national representation to the European Parliament (EP) by direct election between 10–13 June 1999. However, there were also a relatively large number of important national elections throughout the year, and some of them had important consequences for the Union.

Finland

Continuity seems to have been the watchword during and after a rather inconclusive Finnish general election held on 21 March 1999. Between 1995 and 1999, Finland had been governed by a relatively successful 'rainbow coalition' of five parties – the Social Democrats, Conservatives (National Coalition Party), Greens, the ex-communist Left Alliance and the Swedish People's Party – headed by the Social Democratic Party's leader, Paavo Lipponen. This coalition, which would seem over-large by normal western European standards since the only major political group not included was the Finnish Centre Party, had overseen among other things a return to prosperity, and, of course, Finland's participation in the euro.

The March 1999 general election saw the Social Democratic Party remain the largest party in the Finnish Parliament, even if its overall share of the vote fell to 22.9 per cent (from 28.3 per cent in the previous 1995 election) and its parliamentary seats were cut from 63 seats (1995) to 51 seats in 1999 (see Table 1). At the same time, Finland's other two largest parties – the opposing Centre Party led by ex-Prime Minister, Esko Aho, and the Conservatives (National Coalition Party) led by Finance Minister, Sauli Niinistö, registered slight increases in their vote. The Centre Party's voting share of 22.4 per cent in 1999 ensured that they remained the Finnish Parliament's second largest party with 48 seats. However, it was the Conservatives who were regarded, albeit to a limited degree, as the election's 'winners', turning in one of their best-ever performances and improving their share of the vote by more than three

Table 1: Finnish General Election, 21 March 1999

Party	% of Votes	Seats	Seats after 1995 Election
*Finnish Social Democratic Party (SSDP)	22.9	51	63
Centre Party (KESK)	22.4	48	44
*National Coalition Party (KOK)	21.0	46	39
*Left-Wing Alliance (VAS)	10.9	20	22
*Greens (VIHR)	7.3	11	9
*Swedish People's Party (SFP)	5.1	11	11
Finnish Christian League (SKL)	4.2	10	7
Remonttiryhma (REM)	1.1	1	–
Perussomalaiset (PS)	1.0	1	–
Representative from Åland	–	1	1
Others	4.1	0	4
Total	100.0	200	200

Source: Finnish Ministry of Justice.
Notes: * Member of Government Coalition 1995–99. A total of 13 parties contested the election. Turnout: 68%.

percentage points on the 1995 result. Turnout at 68 per cent was surprisingly low by Finnish standards.

Thus, the overall composition of Finland's new ruling coalition in 1999 was largely dependent on the preference of the Conservatives, especially since their parliamentary representation duly increased from 39 in 1995 to 46 in 1999. In the end, they opted to continue with the existing parliamentary alliance, ensuring that Paavo Lipponen's five-party 'rainbow coalition' remained in office for a second term, controlling 145 of the 200 seats in the *Eduskunta*. The five parties agreed to form the new government on 13 April 1999.

From the perspective of the other EU Member States, it seemed that it would be 'business as usual' as regards Finland. The country's reputation as the Nordic EU enthusiast would remain intact and there would be no major changes in the tone and/or direction of Finnish EU policy. This was widely regarded as 'good news' since Finland was due to take over the EU Council Presidency on 1 July 1999.

Italy

Carlo Azeglio Ciampi, Treasury Minister in the government of Massimo D'Alema, was duly elected the tenth President of Italy on 14 May 1999. His election by 707 votes in the first round of balloting – attaining the required two-thirds majority of an electoral college of 1,010 parliamentarians and regional leaders – was achieved comparatively smoothly. This was highly unusual since Italian presidential elections are usually marked by innumerable ballots and compromise choices. But it was possible largely because Ciampi enjoyed the support not only of the government, but also prominent opposition groups such as Silvio Berlusconi's *Forza Italia*, as well as the Italian public.

The other EU Member States also viewed Ciampi's assumption of the Italian Presidency positively. Ciampi had, after all, established a reputation as an effective politician, a successful former governor of the Bank of Italy (1979–93) and later as the architect of Italy's entry into the euro at the Treasury. Ciampi had, for example, also emphasized his EU credentials as the first president of the Commission's Advisory Group for Competitiveness in the Union. Moreover, his election provided an additional boost to Italy's profile inside the Union, especially since Romano Prodi had just been appointed by the European Council in March 1999 to be the next President of the European Commission from the following July.

United Kingdom

Elections in Scotland and Wales on 6 May 1999 marked the start of a new era of 'devolved politics' in the UK. They took place in accordance with the

Government of Wales Act and Scotland Act (enacted in July and November 1998 respectively). The Labour Party emerged as substantially the largest party in both the new Scottish Parliament and the Welsh Assembly, although without a clear majority in either case. The elections were also notable for another reason – they were the first in which candidates were elected in Great Britain by a system of proportional representation.

In Scotland, the election focused mainly on competition between the pro-UK Labour Party and the pro-independence Scottish National Party (SNP). In the end, Labour's party machine made its superiority felt, assisted by public concern about the economic and taxation consequences of an SNP-led government. After the result, in which Labour secured 56 seats (53 constituency seats by 'first past the post' and 3 'top-up' allocated according to percentage shares of the vote) with the SNP amassing 35 seats (7 plus 28 – see Table 2), Labour entered into a formal coalition with the Liberal Democrats, with Donald Dewar, the outgoing UK Secretary for Scotland, becoming the First Minister.

In Wales, Labour did less well. The party's campaign was damaged by the previous Welsh Labour Party leadership contest (February) which had angered many Labour supporters by Blair's treatment of the opposing candidate, Rhodri Morgan. This legacy, combined with a general lack of enthusiasm for the 'devolution project' among Labour voters contributed to the party's failure to win an overall majority and the emergence of Plaid Cymru as the main opposition party (see Table 3). Labour opted to form a minority administration under Alun Michael, the former UK Secretary for Wales. Voting turnout was 59 per cent in Scotland, but only 46 per cent in Wales – the latter perhaps reflecting that the Welsh Assembly's weaker constitutional powers and importance in the eyes of voters.

There was much speculation that the creation of these two new devolved assemblies (officially opened on 1 July 1999) and the emergence of the nationalist parties as the major opposition groups to Labour-led administra-

Table 2: Election in Scotland, 6 May 1999

Party	First (% Vote)	Second (% Vote)	Seats (Constituency	Top-up	Total)
Labour Party	38.8	33.8	53	3	56
Scottish National Party (SNP)	28.7	27.0	7	28	35
Conservatives	15.6	15.4	0	18	18
Liberal Democrats	14.2	12.5	12	5	17
Others	2.7	11.4	1	2	3

Note: Turnout: 59%.

Table 3: Elections in Wales, 6 May 1999

Party	First (% Vote)	Second (% Vote)	Seats (Constituency	Top-up	Total)
Labour Party	37.6	35.4	27	1	28
Plaid Cymru	28.4	30.5	9	8	17
Conservatives	15.9	16.5	1	8	9
Liberal Democrats	13.4	12.6	3	3	6
Others	4.7	5.1	0	0	0

Note: Turnout: 46%.

tions may lead to a stronger 'Scottish' and 'Welsh' voice appearing at the EU level, especially since these UK developments seem to be in line with the EU's commitment to a stronger 'Europe of the Regions'.

Belgium

1999 was a worrying year for most Belgians. The country held its election to the federal parliament, alongside elections to the European Parliament and the regional assemblies on 13 June 1999. However, rather than the political campaigns focusing on economic issues – as most people expected – they were instead dominated by 'Chickengate'. The discovery of high levels of cancer-causing dioxins in Belgian poultry and eggs prompted a nation-wide health scare and led to the resignation of the agriculture and health ministers prior to the election. In addition, the European Commission threatened (and on 21 June 1999 eventually took) legal action against the Belgian government over its failure to conform with EU rules on consumer protection and information. 'Chickengate' compounded difficulties for the four-party coalition government of Flemish and Walloon Christian Democrat and Socialist Parties, led by Jean-Luc Dehaene (leader of the Christian People's Party – CVP), which had already been battered by other recent scandals. Dehaene even took the unprecedented step of announcing the suspension of the CVP's campaign on 7 June in order to focus on resolving the crisis.

The electoral outcome ousted the four-party Christian Social–Socialist coalition from power. The Flemish Liberals and Democrats (VLD) made slight gains – emerging victorious as the single largest party (see Table 4). Most notably, the far-right Flemish separatist and anti-immigration party, Vlaams Blok, also did well in Flanders, raising the question of further constitutional reforms to the Belgian federal state. Given that voting was compulsory, turnout was, in comparative terms, high – averaging 90 per cent – and similar voting

Table 4: Belgian General Election Results, 13 June 1999

Party	% of Vote	Chamber (Seats)	% of Vote	Senate (Seats)
Flemish Liberals and Democrats (VLD)	14.3	23	15.4	6
*Christian People's Party (CVP)	14.1	22	14.8	6
*Socialist Party (PS -Walloon)	10.1	19	9.7	4
Liberal Reform Party (PRL-FDP)	10.1	18	10.6	5
Vlaams Blok	9.9	15	9.4	4
*Socialist Party (SP -Flemish)	9.6	14	8.9	4
Ecolo	7.3	11	7.4	3
Agalev	7.0	9	7.1	3
*Social Christian Party (PSC)	5.9	10	6.1	3
Volksunie	5.6	8	5.1	2
National Front (FN)	1.5	1	1.5	-
Others	4.6	0	4.0	0
Total	100.0	150	100.0	40

Note: * Member of outgoing coalition.

trends were noticed in the outcome for division of Belgium's seats to the European Parliament. The new six-party coalition government, consisting of the Flemish Liberals and Democrats (VLD), the Liberal Reform Party, the two Socialist parties and the two Green parties (Agalev) and (Ecolo), and led by Guy Verhofstadt, leader of the VLD, was sworn in on 12 July. It was the first Belgian government in 40 years that did not include the Christian Democrats.

Luxembourg

The Christian Social People's Party (CSV/PCS), the senior partner in the governing coalition, lost two seats in the general election on 13 June – held simultaneously with the EP elections. However, it retained its position as the country's largest party. Thus, its leader, the incumbent Prime Minister, Jean-Claude Juncker, again formed a government – this time with a different coalition partner in the Liberal Democratic Party (DP/PD) which came second in the general election. Interestingly, the former European Commission President, Jacques Santer, was elected as one of the country's two MEPs in the country's EP direct election.

Austria

The national election that caused the most shock waves amongst the other Member States was the result of the general election to the *Nationalrat*

(Austria's lower house) on 3 October 1999 (see Table 5). Although the Social Democratic Party (SPÖ) – the dominant partner in the previous ruling coalition – won the largest number of seats, most attention focused on the performance of the far-right Freedom Party (FPÖ) of Jörg Haider, which ran on an anti-immigration platform and managed narrowly to outpoll the centre-right People's Party (ÖVP), the Social Democrats' junior coalition partner. However, the formation of a new coalition government was problematic not just because of domestic difficulties as the Social Democrats did not have enough support to form a government outright, and had, in any case, ruled out bringing the FPÖ into the government. There was, too, international astonishment at the rise in popular support for the far right in Austria. On 13 November, for example, more than 50,000 people marched through the streets of Vienna to voice their opposition to the Freedom Party, fearing a 'coalition with racism' might come to power.

Tensions between Austria and the EU seemed to be even greater when it became clear that, as the negotiations on the future government progressed over the next few months, the new Conservative government would include members of the Freedom Party. Several Member States voiced their fears that an Austrian government influenced by the far right might exercise an Austrian veto on the development of the EU's more ambitious policies, especially since Haider, on 7 October, reaffirmed his reservations about further EU enlargement and the extension of majority voting. This could damage the EU's democratic credentials at the very time when it was accelerating negotiations on the accession of states from central and eastern Europe, discussing a deeper relationship with Israel, and at the Tampere summit (15–16 October), seeking agreement on the harmonization of policies in the field of Justice and Home Affairs, including working towards a common European asylum policy by 2004. Although Haider would eventually resign as Leader of the Freedom

Table 5: Results of Austrian General Election, 3 October 1999

Party	% of Votes (1999)	% of Votes (1999)	Seats (1999)	Seats (1999)
Social Democratic Party (SPÖ)	33.1	38.1	65	71
Freedom Party (FPÖ)	26.9	21.9	52	40
People's Party (ÖVP)	26.9	28.3	52	53
Greens	7.4	4.8	14	9
Liberal Forum	3.6	5.5	0	10
Others	2.1	1.4	0	0
Total	100.0	100.0	183	183

Note: Turnout: 80.42%.

Party, his continuing role as the *Landeshamptmann* of Carinthia, and his party's influence in the Conservative-led national coalition continued to worry the governments of several Member States into 2000. In fact, selective sanctions were imposed by other Member States when the new Austrian government took office in February 2000.

Portugal

In the elections to the 230-seat unicameral Assembly on 10 October, the Socialist Party was returned to power, unexpectedly winning 115 seats and falling just one seat short of an absolute majority (Table 6). In contrast to the edgy campaign in Austria, the campaigning in Portugal was muted as political parties and the electorate were, to some degree, distracted by events in East Timor (a former Portuguese colony) and the death of fado singer, Amália Rodrigues (6 October) which prompted three days of national mourning.

Prime Minster António Guterres unveiled a reshuffled government on 21 October. The most significant change was the replacement of Finance Minister António Sousa Franco, a political independent who had played a key role in leading Portugal to qualify for membership of the 'euro-zone'. Moreover, the new government assumed office during an ongoing dispute between Portugal and the EU over the government's veto of a takeover bid for the Champalimaud financial group by Spain's Banco Santander Central Hispanoamericano (BSCH). Nevertheless, the election results were viewed positively at the EU level since the outcome suggested that there would be no major change in the direction and/or substance of EU policy, especially since Portugal was in the process of preparing to take over the EU Council Presidency from Finland in January 2000.

Table 6: Results of the Portuguese General Election, 10 October 1999

Party	% of Votes (1999)	Seats (1999)	% of Votes (1995)	Seats (1995)
Socialist Party (PS)	44.0	115	43.9	112
Social Democratic Party (PSD)	32.3	81	34.0	88
Unified Democratic Coalition (CDU)	9.0	17	8.6	15
Democratic Social Centre/ People's Party (CDS/PP)	8.4	15	9.1	15
Left Bloc (BE)	2.5	2	–	0
Others	3.8	0	–	0
Total	100.0	230	100.0	230

Notes: The CDU comprised the Portuguese Communist Party and the Greens. Turnout: 61.87%.

Direct Elections to the European Parliament

Direct elections to the European Parliament were held in all 15 Member States between 10–13 June. The intention here is not to provide a broad resumé of the results or discuss their implications for the composition of the European Parliament, but rather to highlight the important electoral trends that featured across the Member States. Overall, the election was marked by low turnout (EU average of 49 per cent), with some countries registering particularly poor electoral participation (the UK at 23.1 per cent, Finland at 30.1 per cent and Sweden at 38.3 per cent), stressing the indifference of many domestic electorates. However, this was not uniform since in Portugal, Ireland and Spain there was a higher turnout than in 1994.

A brief analysis of the results showed an increase in support for centre-right parties in general, especially in Germany and the UK, with Italy's *Forza Italia* also maintaining the representation (25.9 per cent) that had first been secured in 1994. However, this trend was once again not universal across all the Member States, with the Socialists, for instance, increasing their share of the vote in France (21.95 per cent compared to 14. 5 per cent in 1994). There were also small increases in support for the Social Democrats in Austria. Another interesting development was the rise in support for the Greens and other small left-wing and regional and/or nationalist parties across the board, suggesting, in most cases, disillusionment with the mainstream, established parties. Yet, to some degree, these features are to be expected, since most of the election campaigns continued to be fought on mainly national issues. According to the polls, 46 per cent of EU voters cast their votes primarily with domestic issues in mind (66 per cent in Finland and Ireland). All indications suggest that the 1999 EP elections continued to be viewed by most EU citizens as 'mid-term referendums' on the performance of national governments and their component party compositions. Where EU issues were considered, then the Commission's resignation in March 1999 cast a negative picture in the minds of most voters. Ironically, the EP's reputation was not enhanced among voters despite its central role in bringing the Santer Commission to task.

III. Other Political Developments

Germany

1999 proved to be turbulent year for the SPD–Green coalition government of Gerhard Schröder. After Schröder's victory in September 1998 and the formation of the first 'Red–Green' coalition at the national level in Germany's post-war history, there seemed to be great optimism, especially since the new SPD–Green government was also due to hold the EU Council Presidency between January and June 1999.

Yet, early 1999 was a rather uncomfortable time for the new administration. The German government not only had to deal with some rather thorny issues during its EU Council Presidency, such as the Commission's resignation in March 1999, but also because the new government's relationship with Europe was less conciliatory than before. Schröder had, for instance, openly sought a reduction in Germany's budgetary contribution, and there had been visible tension between Oskar Lafontaine at the German Finance Ministry and the European Central Bank over the running of the euro. Several issues relating to the Presidency had substantial domestic implications. The Chancellor's desire for Germany to play a bigger world role, including *Agenda 2000* and German troop commitments to support NATO campaigns in Kosovo and Serbia, split opinion among his own Social Democrats and within the Greens. At the state elections in Hesse on 7 February 1999, the 'Red–Green' coalition suffered its first major electoral setback, when the improved performance of the Christian Democratic Union (CDU) left the federal coalition without a majority in Germany's upper house, the *Bundesrat.*

In addition, tensions between the Chancellor and Oskar Lafontaine, the popular left-wing SPD party chairman and Minister of Finance, reached the point where the latter resigned both posts on 11 March. Schröder duly went on to be elected SPD party chairman at a special party congress on 12 April, although the fact that only 76 per cent of the delegates supported Schröder – one of the lowest in the SPD's history – indicated the level of resistance amongst left-wingers within the party to the new Chancellor. The downturn in fortunes of the two governing parties seemed to continue throughout most of 1999 as the SPD, and especially the Greens, sustained a succession of electoral batterings in a series of German Länder elections. An SPD candidate, Johannes Rau was, nonetheless, elected the new Federal President by an electoral college in May 1999. Yet, although he enjoyed a good relationship with Foreign Minister Joschka Fischer, there was also obvious friction between the Chancellor and some of the Greens on a number of issues, such as the phasing out of nuclear power in Germany.

Nevertheless, there was a turn-around in the electoral performance of the SPD in late 1999. In part, this was due to the party financing scandal that affected Germany's main opposition group, the CDU, which unfolded throughout December 1999 and into 2000. Not only was the political credibility of the CDU harmed, but also the reputation of the former Chancellor, Helmut Kohl, was severely dented when he was eventually forced to admit his role in the operation of a system of secret 'slush fund' bank accounts (in parallel to his party's official finances) that had been used specifically for untaxed donations to the CDU. The CDU's poll ratings plummeted as the Bundestag opened a parliamentary enquiry on 16 December, and later the public prosecutor's office announced the start of a criminal investigation against Kohl on 29 December. However, the reputation of the Schröder government also improved in late 1999 after the German EU Presidency had proved reasonably successful and German–EU relations continued to improve. Hans Eichel, the new Finance Minister, for example, enjoyed a better rapport with the European Central Bank than his predecessor, Lafontaine.

Yet 1999 also illustrated how uncomfortable the process of the internationalization of business can be for German political leaders. Although the takeovers of Chrysler by Daimler-Benz and Bankers Trust by Deutsche Bank were generally welcomed by the German government, Schröder, initially, opposed the takeover of the German telecommunications giant, Mannesmann by Vodafone Airtouch in November. Vodafone was the first major hostile takeover bid of a German firm ever to succeed and was a telling comment on the inability of governments to constrain the internationalization of European business.

Italy

For Massimo D'Alema, Italy's Prime Minister, the year proved to be a rather bitter-sweet experience. It was sweet insofar as the government presided over a string of remarkable achievements in terms of Italian domestic politics and foreign policy. The D'Alema government in itself was historic since its formation in October 1998 ended half a century in which the once mighty Italian former communists and their heirs had been kept at arm's length from power, and it brought together ten political parties and some barely reconcilable foes. Yet, it was also largely responsible for several solid achievements in the first part of 1999. These included the continuing reduction in the public deficit to GDP ratio to well below the required 3 per cent that enabled Italy to qualify for entry into the euro in 1999; the appointment of Romano Prodi as the new President of the European Commission in March – the first time an Italian had held the Presidency in 30 years; the smooth appointment of a new Italian President in May; and most of all, the Prime Minister's performance during the conflict in Kosovo in maintaining government support for NATO's bombardment of Serbia for all of its 78 days.

Nevertheless, the experience of 1999 was also bitter since these achievements were not fully appreciated by the Italian public. In the European Parliamentary elections, the Premier's party – the Democrats of the left – sank to an all-time low – taking only 17.5 per cent of the vote. Even worse, D'Alema saw the Italian left's strong hold on Bologna removed for the first time since 1945 when it lost the mayoral election on 29 June. Moreover, the governing 'Olive Tree' coalition looked rather shaky in the latter part of 1999 and there were notable bouts of infighting between the coalition partners. D'Alema's attempts at constitutional reform also virtually collapsed in 1999, while the country's economy remained rather sluggish during the year, with the liberalization of the electricity and retail sectors proving difficult.

Shortly after the approval of the 2000 budget (18 December), D'Alema resigned in response to assertions from three governing parties – the Clover Group – that he would not be able to win the next general election in 2000, although a new, weaker, seven-party governing coalition under D'Alema assumed office later that month.

IV. Policy Developments

While in no way intended to be comprehensive, this section of the *Annual Review* examines those policy areas where the perspectives of, and developments in, the Member States have been particularly notable and influential.

Economic and Monetary Union

1999 was, of course, marked by an important development in the EU's history – namely the implementation of the third stage of the Maastricht timetable establishing the euro. Yet, the Member States' experiences of the euro were generally good, if rather mixed, given that from 1 January 1999, the European Central Bank was operating one monetary and exchange rate policy for the 'Euro-11'. The stability programmes of Austria, Belgium, Spain, Italy, Portugal, the UK, Sweden, France and Germany were all approved by the Union's Ecofin Council by March, although some criticism was made of the last two's lack of ambition when it came to budget deficits. However, tensions within the euro-zone existed, with the Irish and Finnish economies doing particularly well and requiring higher interest rates and the Italian economy remaining rather fragile. The EU was particularly pleased to see that Italy now had 'a genuine culture of stability' and the government's budgetary policies were leading to lower inflation and interest rates and a reduction in the deficit.

The relative success of the euro was perhaps marked more by the response of the four states outside the euro-zone – Britain, Denmark, Sweden and Greece. In a clear signal of the Labour government's warming attitude to British participation in the single currency, Prime Minister Blair unveiled on 23 February 1999 a 'national changeover plan' for the possible replacement of the pound sterling by the euro. He stressed that the plan represented 'a change of gear' rather than a change of policy. Yet, in spite of Blair's insistence that eventual participation would be subject to five 'economic tests' and would in any case require approval in a referendum, most commentators viewed the initiative as the clearest indication to date that the Labour government believed that the UK would eventually join the currency. However, Blair remained worried about the hardening of public opinion against UK participation evident in public opinion polls and also by the success of the Conservative Party's 'Keep the Pound' campaign during the June 1999 direct EP election.

There was also notable movement in the Danish and Swedish governmental positions during 1999. On 15 November 1999, for example, Sweden's Prime Minister in an interview with the *Financial Times* suggested that Sweden should no longer 'wait and see' but now had two options: 'Yes, we join now' or 'Yes, we join later'. In the same month, Greece announced it would apply to join the euro on 8 March 2000.

CAP Reform and Agenda 2000

The EU eventually secured provisional agreement on a limited reform of the CAP in March 1999, thereby, to a very limited degree, preparing the Union's agricultural policy for the impact of further enlargement (see also pp. 123–4). Agreement had proved elusive during the previous months since there were substantial divisions between key Member States. A four-day session of EU agriculture ministers (22–25 February) and an informal summit at Petersberg, near Bonn, failed to make significant progress on agricultural reform due to a dispute between France and Germany. France, in particular, rejected a proposal put forward by Germany and the European Commission for national co-financing, which would shift agricultural funding back to the national governments and keep agricultural spending within previously agreed limits. The French government was under strong pressure from its powerful domestic agricultural lobby. For example, French farmers ransacked the Paris office of French Environment Minister, Dominique Voynet, on 8 February 1999. Spain, as a notable beneficiary from present CAP allocations, was also opposed to most elements of the CAP reform that implied reductions in the present levels of agricultural spending. The UK Blair government was also keen to ensure the preservation of the UK budgetary rebate, which other Member States, once again, brought into question.

Two agricultural sectors – beef and milk – were regarded as especially difficult from the Member State perspective since the outcome of these reforms had dramatic and uneven consequences across EU countries. Four states – the UK, Italy, Sweden and Denmark – were in general in favour of quite radical reform, insisting on, amongst other things, the dismantling of milk quotas by 2006. The outcome at the Berlin European Council summit reflected the diversity of opinion between the Member States, with the Commission's proposals being watered down in most areas. Blair, for example, saw the deal as a 'very good result' since the UK retained its rebate in a revised form. Milk sector reforms were also deferred until 2006 and the other contentious areas of the reform package were largely tailored to placate French and Spanish objections. President Chirac downplayed Franco–German divisions and noted that the EU has reached 'a reasonable agreement', if one that perhaps did not address all the problems stemming from future EU enlargement.

Response to the Commission Crisis

The resignation of the Santer Commission (15 March 1999) was largely anticipated by the Member State governments, although some, such as the British, Danish and Swedish, were openly concerned about the negative impact on public support for the Union as a result. The only notably variation in reaction from Member States came in terms of their approaches to individual commissioners. The UK Blair government, for instance, immediately announced its confidence in its two Commissioners, whilst other governments, such as Denmark, were less forthright – perhaps enjoying the chance to replace unsatisfactory earlier appointments.

The appointment of Romano Prodi as the new Commission President was also comparatively smooth. However, several Member States were drawn into domestic debate on the suitability of their new Commission appointments. Some dissatisfaction was expressed in Italy over the preference of Mario Monti over Emma Bonino as Italy's other post-1999 Commissioner (alongside Prodi). The German government also sprang to the defence of Günter Verheugen's appointment, after Prodi was supposedly to have made derogatory remarks about his suitability and experience on 25 June 1999.

Dispute over the German Language

Small technical issues highlighted how easy it is to ruffle the national pride of EU Member States. The German and Austrian delegations boycotted the informal EU meetings in July after Finland, which had just assumed the EU Council Presidency, refused to include German as a working language at the meetings. The Finns insisted they were following the established practice of restricting working languages to English, French and the language of the host country. Germany and Austria objected on the grounds that German was the largest language group in the EU with around 92 million speakers. The Finnish Presidency eventually relented on the issue so that things were back to normal for the informal meetings later in the year.

The Beef War

On 14 July, the European Commission formally lifted the ban on UK beef exports, which had been imposed since March 1996 in the light of indications of 'mad cow disease' (BSE) affecting British herds and its possible transmission to humans. However, both France and Germany showed no inclination to remove their bans. After a long period of negotiation, Prime Minister Blair warned on 15 October that the UK government would take legal action against France if the latter did not lift its ban. The French government based its refusal on the recommendations of its Food Safety Agency (Afssa) and, with the German government, called for new scientific evidence to be considered by the EU, arguing that the lifting of the ban was 'premature'. The situation reached a new level of tension when the UK Agriculture Minister called on British shoppers to boycott French food that month, an EU scientific report was published on 22 October claiming that French animal feed regularly contained sewage, French farmers blockaded UK lorries at the Channel Tunnel terminal and, finally, the EU scientific committee (29 October) concluded that there were no grounds for maintaining the national bans. The next day, seven of the 16 German state governments announced their opposition to any speedy lifting of Germany's ban on UK beef – making life difficult for the Federal government since the legislation removing the ban required approval not only by the Länder parliaments but also from the *Bundesrat*, containing representatives of the Länder.

The UK government was further outraged when its French counterpart decided on 8 December, again on the advice of its statutory Food Safety Agency, to maintain its 'beef ban'. Blair described the French ban as 'totally wrong', claiming 'we have Europe on our side'. In response the French Prime Minister Lionel Jospin, stated that he was accountable 'first and foremost' to the French people, especially since there was widespread public support for the continuation of the French ban. In addition, the European Commission also sought 'urgent clarification' from the German government about the legislative delays in lifting Germany's ban. After the expiry of its final deadline, the European Commission duly announced on 30 December that it would initiate legal proceedings against France. In return, the French government declared its intention to sue the Commission over the decision to lift the EU ban on British beef in the first place.

Of course, although Anglo–French relations were strained, this did not prevent co-operation between the two Member States in other spheres. Both governments continued to push forward their joint proposal for the establishment of a EU military deployment force of peace-keepers, which was to form the basis of EU agreement at Helsinki in December 1999.

Tax Harmonization

The Member State perspective was also illustrated by the ongoing problems in agreeing an EU withholding tax on non-resident savings income in 1999. Discussions throughout the year and spanning two countries' EU Council Presidencies failed to deliver agreement on such a saving tax at the December

1999 Helsinki summit. The package of tax co-ordination measures proposed by the Commission to reduce tax evasion and harmful tax competition (affecting Germany especially) was resisted by the British government in particular. The inclusion of euro-bonds in the tax measures evoked the hostility of the City of London who wanted to protect London's $3,000 billion international bond market from a new EU tax regime. The Blair government insisted on a 'euro-bond' exemption from the proposed 20 per cent withhold-ing tax on interest income. This prompted severe criticism from Germany and Italy, with the Italian Finance Minister calling the UK position 'egoistic, nationalistic and myopic'. It was agreed at Helsinki to delay a final decision for another six months pending further study from 'a high-level working group'.

V. Public Opinion

According to *Eurobarometer*, it would seem that public opinion in the Member States is, on the whole, less positive in 1999 than it was in autumn 1998. Much of the drop in confidence can be attributed to the 'fall-out' from developments associated with the Commission's resignation in March 1999 after allegations of fraud, mismanagement and nepotism.

In spring 1999, public support for the European Union and the respective countries' full membership fell to an average of 49 per cent, a five percentage point drop on the 54 per cent recorded in autumn 1998. When asked if membership of the Union was a 'good thing' or a 'bad thing' for their country, 49 per cent concluded that it was a 'good thing', 27 per cent 'neither good nor bad' and 12 per cent of respondents thought it was a 'bad thing' for their country (*Eurobarometer*, No. 51, pp. 24–5). Interestingly, although there was a notable decline in the 'good thing' category, this did not translate into a rise in those viewing the EU as a 'bad thing'. Rather most people simply became more 'neutral' towards the Union and thus responded with 'neither good nor bad' and even more with 'didn't know'. Indeed, those registering 'neither good nor bad' increased the EU average by only one percentage point on the autumn 1998 figures and the 'bad thing' respondents actually stayed the same.

However, these averages hide substantial national variations. Support for EU membership continued to be higher in Ireland (78 per cent), Luxembourg (77 per cent) and the Netherlands (73 per cent). More than half of the people in Italy, Portugal, Spain, Greece and Denmark also supported their country's EU membership, although opposition levels in Denmark (23 per cent) are significantly above average. As usual, support for membership is lowest in the UK (31 per cent), Sweden (34 per cent) and Austria (36 per cent), with highest opposition levels recorded in Sweden (33 per cent).

Nevertheless, there was a more notable deterioration in the results for some countries in 1999 as, no doubt, the media coverage effects of the March 1999 Commission crisis had varying influences upon public opinion in the EU Member States. However, the results are very mixed at the individual Member State level. There were, in fact, three countries – Portugal (–5), Luxembourg and Sweden (–3) – where the proportion of people regarding EU membership as a 'bad thing' actually fell between 1998–99 at the very time when the Commission crisis was taking place. Support levels in Ireland, Luxembourg, and the Netherlands were also hardly affected. In contrast, *Eurobarometer* registered a 13 percentage point drop in 'good thing' support ratings in Greece and a larger than average 8 percentage points was also recorded for Spain. In these particular cases, the image of EU institutions as more efficient organizations than those operating nationally has been severely dented. Denmark is the only country where there was a significant increase in the proportion of people who regarded their country's membership as a 'bad thing' (+3 percentage points), reflecting the fact that there is already deep scepticism amongst the Danes about the level of democratic accountability operating at the EU level.

In a related question on the perceived benefits stemming from EU membership, 44 per cent of those interviewed felt that their respective country had benefited – a similar decline of 5 percentage points on the EU average recorded for autumn 1998. However, it would also seem that the proportion of negative responses also dropped (though not significantly) from 31 per cent to 29 per cent, which suggests that, in spring 1999, more people were likely to reserve their opinion on the Union's performance. Nonetheless, there were striking differences across the Member States. In early 1999, most people in Ireland (86 per cent) and Portugal (71 per cent) believed they benefited from their country's membership with also higher than average figures for Luxembourg (65 per cent), the Netherlands (67 per cent), Greece (67 per cent) and Denmark (62 per cent). In contrast, only a small section of the populations of Sweden (21 per cent), the UK (31 per cent), Germany (35 per cent) and Austria (37 per cent) believed that their country benefited from EU membership in 1999.

Nevertheless, Portugal and Finland saw increases between autumn 1998 and early 1999 in those who thought that their respective country had benefited (both +4 percentage points) from EU membership (see Table 8). In Italy and the Netherlands, positive responses remained the same, but negative responses were also less frequent. In contrast, in Spain, the UK, France, Greece and Sweden, people were less positive about the Union, but this does not translate into significant increases in those who perceived the country as 'not benefiting', but merely that they were more likely to be unsure in early 1999. Interestingly, only in Austria, Denmark and Germany were respondents to *Eurobarometer* significantly more negative.

Table 7: National Attitudes Towards EU Membership (% by Member State)

	B	DK	D	GR	E	F	IRL	I	L	NL	A	P	FIN	S	UK	EU15
A good thing	47 0	51 –5	44 –4	54 –13	55 –8	47 –5	78 –1	62 –6	77 0	73 –2	36 –2	59 +1	45 0	34 –1	31 –6	49 –5
A bad thing	8 –1	23 +3	11 0	11 +2	4 –3	14 +2	3 –1	5 0	3 –3	5 –1	23 +4	4 –5	19 –2	33 –3	23 +1	12 0
Neither good nor bad	35 –1	22 0	32 +2	29 +6	26 +1	31 +|1	12 +2	22 +5	17 +2	18 +2	31 –5	24 0	31 +1	28 +3	26 –3	27 +1
Don't know	10 +3	4 +1	14 +4	6 +4	15 +10	9 +3	8 +1	12 +3	3 0	4 +1	10 +3	13 +4	6 +1	6 +2	20 +8	12 +4
Total	100	100	101	100	100	101	101	101	100	100	100	100	101	101	100	10

Source: Eurobarometer 51, 1999: B26.

Table 8: Perceived Benefits of EU Membership (% by Member State)

	B	DK	D	GR	E	F	IRL	I	L	NL	A	P	FIN	S	UK	EU15
Benefited	44 0	62 – 8	35 –4	67 –9	48 –10	44 –9	86 +1	51 0	65 –4	67 0	37 –4	71 +4	43 +4	21 –6	31 –6	44 –5
Not Benefited	32 0	23 +3	39 +3	18 +1	21 –4	27 0	3 –2	19 –8	15 +1	19 –3	40 +6	11 –7	40 –4	55 +2	37 –5	29 –2
Don't know	24 0	15 +5	26 +1	15 +8	32 +14	28 +7	11 +1	30 +8	20 +2	14 +2	23 –2	18 +3	18 +1	24 +4	32 +11	27 +7
Total	100	100	100	100	101	99	100	100	100	100	100	100	101	100	100	100

Source: Eurobarometer 51, 1999: B28.

Note: Figures for late 1999 were unavailable at the time of writing.

VI. Implementation

The enhanced focus by the Commission on the implementation of Community law in the Member States continues. In June 1998, the Commission evaluated the operation of its working methods in relation to infringement proceedings (Art. 169). It decided on a range of new internal measures aimed at ensuring the faster handling of cases, greater transparency and also better relations with complainants. The Commission is now better placed to monitor accurately the implementation performances of the Member States, and the Commission's responses in terms of decision-making action have been speeded up significantly so that proceedings are now more commonly opened the same year.

The overall impact has been a more balanced picture. According to the *Sixteenth Annual Report on Monitoring the Application of Community Law*, the Commission issued an all-time high number (675) of reasoned opinions in 1998 (compared with 334 in 1997 – an increase of 102 per cent), a lower number of letters of notice under Art. 169 (1101 in 1998 compared to 1461 in 1997) and 123 referrals to the European Court of Justice (Commission, 1999). Provisional figures for 1999 outlined in the Commission's *General Report on Activities* (Commission, 2000, p. 383) suggest that the number of infringement proceedings is down (1075) as are issued reasoned opinions (469 cases), but the number of cases referred to the European Court rose to 165. This suggests that, although Member States do implement EC legislation more effectively, especially since most of the internal market legislation is firmly in place, some of the remaining areas are the more controversial and require Court action to coerce Member States into action.

The figures also tend to hide the fact that implementation remains uneven between the Member States. The provisional figures on the referral of cases to the European Court of Justice (165 cases in 1999) on the basis of Member State distribution, suggest that Finland (0 actions), Denmark, Sweden and the Netherlands (1 action each) are the most 'law-abiding', while the worst culprits for slow action are France (32), Italy (32) and Luxembourg (18 actions) (Commission, 2000, p. 383).

Yet, the *Sixteenth Annual Report* covering 1998 concludes that the level of implementation duly improved, insofar as 95.7 per cent of national measures needed to implement the directives were taken by 31 December 1998 (Commission, 1999). The general rise in the transposition rate from the 1997 figure of 94 per cent was, in part, due to the tougher means applied by the Commission to enforce Community law, either by infringement proceedings, increased administrative efficiencies and/or greater peer pressure generated by the plan of action for the internal market. Denmark continued to occupy the first position on the league table (98 per cent of applicable directives transposed).

Table 9: Notification of Transposition of European Community Law

Member State	Directives Applicable 31.12.1998	Measures Notified	(%)
Denmark	1453	1427	98.21
Spain	1458	1420	97.39
Finland	1453	1411	97.11
Sweden	1454	1411	97.04
Germany	1459	1411	96.71
Netherlands	1459	1410	96.64
United Kingdom	1455	1402	96.36
Ireland	1452	1387	95.52
Austria	1461	1388	95.00
Portugal	1462	1386	94.80
Belgium	1459	1382	94.72
France	1458	1377	94.44
Luxembourg	1457	1372	94.17
Greece	1456	1366	93.82
Italy	1457	1364	93.62
EC Average	1457	1394	95.70

Source: Commission (1999, p. 7).

There were also noticeable improvements in the performances of Spain (97.39 per cent in 1998 compared with 95.1 per cent in 1997), Belgium (94.72 per cent in 1998 against 91.8 per cent in 1997) and Germany (96.71 per cent in 1998 from 93.6 per cent in 1997). However, the Commission did express concern over the comparatively weaker implementation rates of France, Luxembourg, Greece and Italy – the latter of which continues to find itself at the bottom of the league table (see Table 9).

References

Commission of the European Communities (1999) *Sixteenth Annual Report on Monitoring the Application of Community Law – 1998. COM* (1999) 301 final, 9 July.

Commission of the European Communities (2000) *General Report on the Activities of the European Union –1999. SEC* (1999) 1000 final, 28 January.

Keesing's Record of World Events (various issues).

European Voice (various issues).

Agence Europe (various issues).

Journal of Common Market Studies

Volume 38, Annual Review
September 2000

Developments in the Economies of the European Union

NIGEL GRIMWADE
South Bank University

1. Overview

Twelve months ago, there was concern in some quarters that unfavourable developments in the global economy would lead to significantly weakened growth in the EU economy during 1999. A marked slowing down in the level of economic activity did, indeed, take place in the first half of the year, with real GDP growth falling to about 1.5 per cent. However, in the second half of the year, growth picked up to an annualized rate of 3 per cent. The overall growth rate for the entire year stood at 2.3 per cent, a little higher than was forecast by the European Commission in the spring of 1999 (Commission, 1999a). The Commission now expects a further acceleration to 3.4 per cent in 2000 and 3.1 per cent in 2001 (Commission, 2000).

One of the reasons for this benign outcome was that the monetary authorities in the EU made sufficiently appropriate and timely adjustments in short-term interest rates to ensure that private domestic demand remained buoyant. Thus, the European Central Bank (ECB) made two reductions in interest rates in December 1998 and April 1999, which brought base rates in the euro-zone down to 2.5 per cent. Official interest rates were also lowered in several of the other 'pre-in' countries. Another factor was the robustness of economic activity in the more 'sheltered' sectors of the EU economy, including construction, public investment and services.

Finally, in the second half of the year, the EU economy enjoyed a major impetus from exports. One reason for this was a faster than expected pick-up in world economic growth. Economic growth has remained strong in the United States, while a more rapid recovery took place in the east Asian region than many had once thought possible. The second factor was the sharp fall in the external value of the euro in the first half of the year, which raised the competitiveness of EU exports. However, growth within the EU remained very uneven. Among the EU's largest Member States, Germany and Italy continued to experience relatively sluggish growth, while France and Spain enjoyed very favourable growth. Outside the euro-zone, Sweden also had above average growth. Among the smaller Member States, Ireland, Luxembourg, the Netherlands, Finland and Greece all showed exceptionally strong growth.

Partly as a result of rapid output growth, the employment rate in the EU also rose, leading to a further reduction in the EU's unemployment rate. Over the course of the year, employment in the EU rose by 1.3 per cent and the average unemployment rate fell to 9.2 per cent, down from 9.9 per cent in 1998. (In the euro-zone, unemployment remains slightly higher at 10 per cent, down from 10.8 per cent in 1998.) This was a somewhat lower rate than the Commission had forecast in the spring of 1999 (Commission, 1999a), reflecting the improved growth performance. Nevertheless, Europe's average unemployment rate remains significantly higher than in other developed market economies (more than twice the rate in the United States and Japan). Moreover, the average continues to conceal exceptionally high rates of unemployment in particular Member States (notably, Spain, Italy and France).

Towards the end of 1998, inflation in the EU reached an all-time low, helped by a low rate of economic activity, falling commodity prices and global excess capacity in many branches of manufacturing due largely to the East Asian crisis. In January 1999, the inflation rate for the EU area as a whole fell to 0.9 per cent. In the remainder of the year, however, the inflation rate crept up, reaching 1.2 per cent in September. This reflected the faster rate of increase in global economic activity, rising oil prices and the depreciation of the euro. The sharp rise in world oil prices, following the decision of the world's major oil producers in March to cut production, was an important factor. During the course of the year, a barrel of Brent crude oil rose from about $10 to just over $25. In the faster-growing Member States (Ireland, Spain and Denmark), there was evidence of a considerable amount of over-heating taking place. These considerations were, no doubt, a major reason for the decision by the ECB to raise short-term interest rates in November to 3 per cent (a decision taken at the same time as the Bank of England raised the UK rate to 5.5 per cent). In December, due to a further surge in energy prices, the headline inflation rate reached 1.8 per cent (1.7 per cent for the members of the euro-zone), raising the prospect of the ECB's target ceiling of 2 per cent being exceeded.

Throughout the year, much attention was focused on the performance of the euro following its successful introduction on 1 January (see also Alison Cottrell's article pp. 77–80). At the time of the changeover, the euro was valued at $1.167. By July, it had fallen to $1.01, a depreciation of more than 13.5 per cent. Despite a brief recovery in the third quarter, the euro fell further, reaching more or less parity by the end of the year. Against the Japanese yen, the depreciation was greater, while a slightly smaller depreciation occurred against the pound sterling. This was despite the fact that the euro-zone continued to enjoy a current account surplus equivalent to approximately 1 per cent of GNP. By way of contrast, the US has run a current account deficit equivalent to about 4 per cent of GNP. In part, the depreciation of the euro could be seen as a correction for the appreciation of ERM currencies in the six months immediately preceding the launch of the euro. In part, too, the fall reflected the economic state of the two regions, with growth remaining strong in the US but sluggish in at least two of the EU's largest economies. This appears to have attracted large flows of capital into the US, encouraged by the continuing buoyancy of the US stock market. Likewise, despite zero short-term nominal interest rates in Japan, real rates of interest have remained high, attracting funds back into the Japanese yen. Uncertainty about the intentions of the ECB appears also to have depressed confidence in the euro.

II. Main Economic Indicators

Economic Growth

Table 1 sets out the estimated annual rate of change in gross domestic product (GDP) measured at constant prices for individual Member States and for the EU as a whole. In 1999, GDP growth in the EU as a whole and the euro-zone averaged 2.3 per cent, compared with 4.1 per cent in the United States and only 0.3 per cent in Japan. Although EU growth was modest in comparison with that of the United States, it was a better out-turn than had been forecast 12 months earlier. Moreover, the rate of output expansion is expected to accelerate during 2000, while growth in the US will fall. By 2001, growth in the EU economy may exceed that of the United States.

But these figures mask big differences in growth performance among the Member States with Ireland, Luxembourg, Sweden, Spain, the Netherlands, Finland and Greece all enjoying relatively rapid rates of growth, and Italy, Germany and Denmark experiencing much more disappointing results. One of the reasons for these differences was that certain Member States were more adversely affected by the slowdown in the global economy. Both Germany and

Table 1: Gross Domestic Product (Annual Average % Change) 1961–2000

	1961 –73	1974 –85	1986 –90	1991 –95	1996	1997	1998	1999 Estimate	2000 Forecast
Austria	4.9	2.3	3.2	1.9	2.0	1.2	2.9	2.3	3.2
Belgium	4.9	1.8	3.0	1.5	1.3	3.5	2.7	2.3	3.5
Denmark	4.3	2.0	1.3	2.6	3.2	3.1	2.7	1.4	2.0
Finland	5.0	2.7	3.3	0.7	4.1	6.3	5.0	3.5	4.9
France	5.4	2.2	3.1	1.1	1.6	2.0	3.2	2.8	3.7
Germany	4.3	1.7	3.4	2.0	1.3	1.5	2.2	1.5	2.9
Greece	8.5	1.7	1.2	1.2	2.4	3.4	3.7	3.5	3.9
Ireland	4.4	3.8	4.6	4.6	8.3	10.7	8.	8.3	7.5
Italy	5.3	2.7	2.9	1.3	0.7	1.8	1.5	1.4	2.7
Luxembourg	4.0	1.8	6.4	5.4	3.0	7.3	5.0	5.0	5.6
Netherlands	4.9	1.9	3.1	2.1	3.1	3.8	3.7	3.5	4.1
Portugal	6.9	2.2	5.5	1.8	3.2	3.5	3.5	2.9	3.6
Spain	7.2	1.9	4.5	1.3	2.4	3.8	4.0	3.7	3.8
Sweden	4.1	1.8	2.3	0.6	1.3	2.0	3.0	3.8	3.9
UK	3.2	1.4	3.3	1.6	2.6	3.5	2.2	2.0	3.3
EUR 11	5.2	2.1	3.3	1.5	1.6	2.3	2.7	2.3	3.4
EUR 15	4.8	2.0	3.2	1.5	1.8	2.5	2.7	2.3	3.4

Source: Commission (2000).

Italy, for example, were more dependent on exports to emerging economies adversely affected by the crisis in east Asia and central and eastern Europe. Both countries also have a stronger specialization in exports of capital and intermediate goods that are generally more sensitive to shifts in external demand. Another factor concerned the adjustments in macroeconomic policies made by different Member States in the run-up to EMU. Whereas private investment benefited from the fall in interest rates in Finland, Spain and Portugal, the effects of declining interest rates in Italy were offset by a highly restrictive budgetary policy.

Finally, the differences in growth rates may also reflect disparities in potential growth rates between Member States. Countries with lower per capita GDP have greater potential to grow more quickly than countries with high per capita GDP. Some evidence exists for a negative correlation between rates of growth of output per worker in the EU between 1996–98 and initial levels of output per worker (IMF, 1999). In other words, differences in growth rates may reflect growing convergence not divergence within the EU.

Unemployment

The EU measures the average rate of unemployment as the numbers of unemployed measured on the basis of a survey of the labour force in the Member States expressed as a percentage of the civilian labour force. Table 2 shows the average unemployment rates for the EU for the period since 1964.

For the EU as whole, the average unemployment rate fell from 9.9 per cent in 1998 to 9.2 per cent in 1999. This continues to compare very unfavourably with 4.2 per cent in the USA and 4.9 per cent in Japan. However, there was some evidence for an improvement in labour market performance in the EU in 1999, as shown by a rise in the EU's employment rate. This measures the proportion of the population of working age in employment. Although this remains below the rate current in the USA and Japan, the rate rose by 0.8 per cent in 1999. There is some evidence that economic growth in the EU is, at last, resulting in the creation of a significant number of new jobs. In part, this may be due to a structural shift towards the more labour-intensive service sector. However, there is also evidence that, after a period of job restructuring, the

Table 2: Annual Average Rates of Unemployment, % of the Civilian Labour Force, 1964–2000

	1964 –73	1974 –85	1986 –90	1991 –95	1996	1997	1998	1999 Estimate	2000 Forecast
Austria	1.7	2.5	3.4	3.7	4.3	4.4	4.7	4.4	4.0
Belgium	2.0	7.7	8.7	8.5	9.7	9.4	9.5	9.0	8.6
Denmark	0.9	6.4	6.4	8.6	6.8	5.6	5.1	4.5	4.2
Finland	2.8	4.8	4.1	13.3	14.8	12.7	11.4	10.2	8.9
France	2.2	6.4	9.7	11.1	12.4	12.3	11.7	11.0	10.0
Germany	0.7	4.2	5.9	7.3	8.9	9.9	9.4	9.1	8.6
Greece	4.2	3.8	6.6	8.3	9.6	9.8	10.7	10.4	10.0
Ireland	5.7	10.6	15.5	14.5	11.6	9.8	7.7	6.5	5.7
Italy	5.2	7.0	9.5	10.1	12.0	11.7	11.9	11.3	10.9
Luxembourg	0.0	1.7	2.1	2.5	3.0	2.8	2.8	2.7	2.6
Netherlands	1.3	7.1	7.4	6.4	6.3	5.2	4.0	3.1	2.4
Portugal	2.5	6.9	6.1	5.6	7.3	6.8	5.1	4.5	4.5
Spain	2.8	11.3	18.9	20.9	22.2	20.8	18.7	15.8	13.8
Sweden	2.0	2.4	2.0	7.2	9.6	9.9	8.3	7.0	6.3
UK	2.0	6.9	9.0	9.5	8.2	7.0	6.3	6.1	5.8
EUR 11	2.5	6.6	9.3	10.2	11.8	11.5	10.8	10.0	9.2
EUR 15	2.4	6.4	8.9	10.0	10.9	10.6	9.9	9.2	8.5

Source: Commission (2000).

manufacturing sector is beginning to make a positive contribution to growth. Labour market reforms in certain Member States (resulting in greater labour flexibility, more part-time and temporary employment, and reduced employment taxes), and sustained wage moderation also contributed to the expansion of employment. It is clear, however, that much remains to be done in bringing EU unemployment rates closer to the average rates prevailing in other developed market economies. Moreover, unemployment rates well above the EU average continue to prevail in certain Member States.

Inflation

Table 3 shows the average inflation rate in the individual Member States. This is measured by the deflator of private consumption for the period up to and including 1995, but by the harmonized index of consumer prices (HICP) thereafter. In 1999, so-called core inflation in the EU fell to its lowest rate for

Table 3: Inflation Rates, Annual % Change in the Deflator of Private Consumption until 1995 and the Harmonized Index of Consumer Prices from 1996 Onward, 1961–2000

	1961 –73	1974 –85	1986 –90	1991 –5	1996	1997	1998	1999 Estimate	2000 Forecast
Austria	4.1	5.8	2.0	3.0	2.8	1.2	0.8	0.5	1.3
Belgium	3.7	7.4	2.2	2.3	2.3	1.5	0.9	1.1	1.3
Denmark	6.6	9.6	3.8	1.6	1.7	1.9	1.3	2.1	2.4
Finland	5.7	10.7	4.3	3.0	1.6	1.2	1.4	1.3	2.3
France	4.7	10.6	3.1	2.5	1.8	1.3	0.7	0.6	1.1
Germany	3.4	4.3	1.4	3.3	1.7	1.5	0.6	0.6	1.6
Greece	3.6	18.2	17.6	13.8	8.3	5.4	4.5	2.1	2.3
Ireland	6.3	13.8	3.2	2.6	1.4	1.2	2.1	2.5	3.7
Italy	4.9	15.9	6.1	5.8	4.3	1.9	2.0	1.7	2.1
Luxembourg	3.0	7.4	2.4	3.0	1.6	1.4	1.0	1.0	2.0
Netherlands	5.1	5.7	0.9	2.5	1.6	1.9	1.8	2.0	2.4
Portugal	3.9	22.2	12.2	7.7	3.6	1.9	2.2	2.2	2.2
Spain	6.5	15.4	6.6	5.6	3.4	1.9	1.8	2.2	2.5
Sweden	4.8	10.3	6.7	4.7	1.2	1.8	1.0	0.6	1.6
UK	4.8	11.9	5.4	4.2	3.1	1.8	1.6	1.3	1.4
EUR 11	4.6	10.4	3.8	3.9	2.5	1.6	1.1	1.1	1.8
EUR 15	4.6	10.9	4.4	4.2	2.7	1.7	1.3	1.2	1.8

Source: Commission (2000).

over 40 years. In the Fifteen, core inflation fell a further 0.1 per cent to 1.2 per cent, taking the year as whole. However, during the year, inflation was clearly on a rising trend. The main reasons for the relatively modest rate of inflation recorded for the year as a whole were several. First, the existence of a significant margin of spare capacity in manufacturing meant that the economy could grow relatively quickly without running into shortages and inflationary bottlenecks. Second, levels of wage settlement remained reasonably modest throughout the year. Third, pro-competition measures implemented as part of the EU's ongoing single market programme helped hold down prices. However, in the second half of the year, other factors began to exert an upward pressure on prices, including the dramatic increase in world oil prices referred to above. Significant differences in rates of inflation existed between the Member States in 1999. At one extreme, there were the fast-growing economies (Ireland, Spain and Portugal) which experience high and rising inflation. At the other extreme, inflation remained relatively low in the Member States experiencing more subdued growth (Germany and France).

Public Finances

As part of the attempt to bring government borrowing into line with the requirements of the EU's Stability and Growth Pact (SGP), the Member States continued their efforts at budgetary consolidation. The SGP requires the members of the euro-zone to achieve budget positions close to balance or in surplus over the medium term in order to avoid a deficit in excess of 3 per cent of GDP in periods of normal cyclical slowdown. The Commission has estimated that, in order to meet these requirements, most Member States should aim to achieve an underlying deficit of 0–1 per cent of GDP. However, in the case of certain countries (Spain and Finland) with large public sectors and larger cyclical fluctuations, the minimal benchmark is a budget surplus. The Member States have agreed to achieve these positions by the year 2002. Table 4 indicates the progress made during 1999.

In 1999, general government borrowing fell from 1.5 to 0.6 per cent of GDP in the EU as a whole and from 2 to 1.2 per cent in the euro-zone. This represented a much bigger improvement in the EU's public finances than had been expected as late as the autumn of 1999. Three factors can explain this. First, GDP growth proved slightly faster over the year as a whole than most people expected. Second, tax receipts proved more buoyant than had been anticipated. Third, most of the budget deficits from the previous year were revised downwards during the course of the year, making the improvement in 1999 appear better than it was.

A major factor in the reduction of budget deficits was the fall in interest payments that governments were obliged to make on outstanding debt. This

Table 4: General Government Net Borrowing(–) or Lending (+) as % of GDP, 1970–2000

	1970 –3	1974 –85	1986 –90	1991 –5	1996	1997	1998	1999 Estimate	2000 Forecast
Austria	1.4	–2.3	–3.2	–3.8	–3.7	–1.9	–2.5	–2.0	–1.7
Belgium	–3.4	–7.9	–7.0	–5.9	–3.1	–2.0	–1.0	–0.9	–0.5
Denmark	4.2	–2.7	1.3	–2.4	–0.9	0.5	1.2	3.0	2.4
Finland	4.5	3.7	4.0	–5.0	–3.1	–1.5	1.3	2.3	4.1
France	0.6	–1.6	–1.8	–4.5	–4.1	–3.0	–2.7	–1.8	–1.5
Germany	0.2	–2.8	–1.5	–3.1	–2.6	–2.6	–1.7	–1.1	–1.0
Greece	0.2	–4.9	–12.0	–11.5	–7.5	–4.6	–3.1	–1.6	–1.3
Ireland	–3.9	–10.0	–5.3	–2.2	–0.3	0.8	2.1	2.0	1.7
Italy	–5.4	–9.6	–10.8	–9.1	–6.6	–2.7	–2.8	–1.9	–1.5
Luxembourg	2.5	1.8	–	–1.8	2.8	3.6	3.2	2.4	2.6
Netherlands	–0.5	–3.4	–4.9	–3.5	–2.0	–1.2	–0.8	0.5	1.0
Portugal	2.0	–7.0	–4.4	–5.0	–3.3	–2.6	–2.1	–2.0	–1.5
Spain	0.4	2.6	–4.0	–5.6	–3.5	–3.2	–2.6	–1.1	–0.7
Sweden	4.3	–1.7	3.1	–7.6	–3.5	–2.0	1.9	1.9	2.4
UK	0.1	–3.6	–0.7	–5.7	–4.4	–2.0	0.3	1.2	0.9
EUR 11	–0.7	–3.9	–4.1	–4.9	–4.1	–2.6	–2.0	–1.2	–0.9
EUR 15	–0.3	–3.7	–3.3	–5.1	–4.1	–2.4	–1.5	–0.6	–0.4

Source: Commission (2000).

reflected both the fall in debt levels achieved in previous years and lower interest rates. If interest payments are omitted, however, it is apparent that Member States still did better in 1999 than in 1998. The primary budget surplus (which omits interest payments) rose from 3.3 to 3.5 per cent in 1999. Allowing, too, for the influence of cyclical factors on public finances, it is clear that some element of discretionary adjustment took place. The cyclically-adjusted deficit fell from 1.2 per cent of GDP in 1998 to 0.2 per cent in 1999. This was a reflection mainly of the continuing efforts made by Member States to restrain public expenditure growth. From a peak of just over 51 per cent of GDP in 1993, general government expenditure in the Fifteen has fallen to just over 46.5 per cent today. By way of contrast, the tax burden has risen from about 41.5 per cent in 1993 to 43.5 per cent today.

The reduction in the level of government borrowing as a percentage of GDP has made possible further reductions in the ratio of government gross debt to GDP as shown in Table 5. Public debt ratios remain high in a number of

Table 5: General Government Gross Debt as a % of GDP, 1980–2000

	1980	1985	1990	1994	1995	1996	1997	1998	1999 Estimate	2000 Forecast
Austria	35.8	48.8	56.8	68.0	68.3	69.8	63.9	63.5	64.5	64.0
Belgium	76.6	119.3	124.7	129.8	128.3	128.0	123.0	117.4	114.4	110.0
Denmark	37.6	70.4	57.7	69.3	65.0	67.4	61.3	55.6	52.6	49.3
Finland	11.5	16.2	14.3	56.6	57.1	57.8	54.1	49.0	47.1	42.6
France	19.3	30.3	34.8	51.9	57.1	55.7	59.0	59.3	58.6	58.2
Germany	31.7	41.7	43.8	57.0	59.8	60.8	60.9	60.7	61.0	60.7
Greece	23.6	50.9	89.0	108.7	111.3	112.2	108.5	105.4	104.4	103.7
Ireland	67.6	98.9	2.6	80.8	74.1	69.4	65.3	55.6	52.4	45.2
Italy	57.7	81.7	97.3	123.2	122.1	124.6	119.8	116.3	114.9	110.8
Luxembourg	11.8	12.3	4.5	5.6	6.2	6.3	6.0	6.4	6.2	5.8
Netherlands	45.1	68.7	75.6	75.5	75.3	77.0	70.3	67.0	63.6	58.7
Portugal	31.9	60.8	64.2	64.7	63.6	64.9	60.3	56.5	56.7	57.0
Spain	16.8	41.9	43.2	63.2	68.0	68.6	66.7	64.9	63.5	62.3
Sweden	39.6	61.6	42.1	76.6	76.0	77.2	75.0	72.4	65.5	61.3
UK	54.7	54.1	35.0	52.0	52.6	53.6	50.8	48.4	46.0	42.4
EUR 11	34.6	51.8	58.0	71.4	74.7	75. 7	4.5	73.1	72.3	70.5
EUR 15	37.8	52.9	54.4	69.5	72.1	72.8	71.0	69.0	67.6	65.1

Source: Commission (2000).

Member States (Belgium, Greece and Italy). In 11 of the 15 Member States, these exceeded the 60 per cent of GDP threshold set as pre-condition for entering the euro. However, with the exception of three countries (Germany, Austria and Portugal), these ratios fell during the course of 1999, continuing the downward trend of previous years.

III. Economic Developments in the Member States

Germany

In 1999, Germany's GDP grew at a rate of only 1.5 per cent, the second poorest performance of any Member State. This followed several years of below average growth. The low point was reached in the first quarter of the year when growth plunged to an annualized rate of only 0.8 per cent. The relatively steep downturn of the German economy appears to have been due, in part, to the much greater exposure of German exports to the crisis in the emerging nations. Whereas, on average, only 12 per cent of the exports of euro-zone countries went to emerging countries in east Asia and central and eastern Europe in 1998, over 17 per cent of Germany's exports went to these countries (Commission, 1999). In addition, a relatively high proportion of Germany's exports consisted of capital goods, which are more sensitive to shifts in external demand.

However, by the middle of the year, it was apparent that the worst had past and that growth was picking up. By the end of the year, growth at an annualized rate in excess of 2.5 per cent took place. The Commission's spring forecast was for 2.9 per cent growth in 2000, an upward revision of 0.4 percentage points from the autumn 1999 forecast. A key factor in this improvement was strong export growth assisted by a weak euro and increasing demand in neighbouring countries. Tax changes announced during the year, which lower the tax burden on both companies and individuals, also helped boost consumption and restore the confidence of the industrial sector. Despite the growth acceleration during the year, however, unemployment has fallen only slightly from 9.4 to 9.1 per cent. Total employment barely increased at all, growing by only 0.3 per cent, lower than in any other Member State except Denmark. This may have been the result of a conscious decision by firms to use the opportunity of faster growth to raise productivity rather than recruit extra staff.

At 0.6 per cent, Germany enjoyed one of the lowest rates of inflation in the EU. This might suggest that there exists substantial scope for faster growth in the Germany economy without the risk of inflation taking off. For this reason, Germany is reluctant to see short-term interest rates in the euro-zone rise too fast. However, during 1999, the rate of inflation did, indeed, rise quite quickly in Germany. In the autumn, EU Commission forecasts predicted that the rate would rise to 1.2 per cent in 2000. Subsequently, however, these forecasts have been revised upwards to 1.6 per cent.

France

In France, the rate of GDP growth fell from 3.2 per cent in 1998 to 2.8 per cent in 1999. However, the decline was concentrated mainly in the first quarter of the year, with a marked acceleration taking place in the second half of the year when the annualized growth rate reached as high as 4 per cent. A sharp increase in export demand, combined with steady growth of both private consumption and fixed investment, were the contributory factors. As a result, employment growth accelerated and the unemployment rate fell to 11 per cent.

Although France continues to suffer from the third highest unemployment rate in the EU, the decline in the unemployment rate during the year was better than many had expected. Moreover, the fastest decrease appears to have occurred among the under-25s, largely as a result of government policies targeted at young unemployed workers (*Financial Times,* 25.2.2000). The extent to which the introduction of the 35-hour week has contributed also to the fall in unemployment remains the subject of heated debate within France. Structural shifts towards the more labour-intensive services sector and a growth of temporary and part-time employment appear also to have assisted the process of job creation.

Despite accelerating output growth, inflation remained modest, with prices rising by only 0.6 per cent over the year as a whole, the second lowest rate in the EU. A significant factor appears to have been relative wage moderation, as companies have sought to offset the costs of reduced working time with a slower rate of wage increase. Some concern, however, has been expressed about the level of government borrowing. Although the budget deficit did fall from 2.7 per cent in 1998 to 1.8 per cent in 1999, France still has a higher level of government borrowing than any Member State except for Austria.

Italy

In 1999, Italy was, once again, the EU's slowest-growing economy. GDP grew by 1.4 per cent compared with 1.5 per cent in the previous year. However, in the second half of the year, a recovery was fully underway and the Commission is forecasting a growth rate of 2.7 per cent for 2000. The reason for the severity of the slowdown in the Italian economy is mainly to be found in weak export demand. Compared with other Member States, a relatively high proportion of Italian exports (nearly 14 per cent compared with 12 per cent for the Euro-11) went to emerging market economies in 1998. An additional factor may have been the concentration of Italian exports on relatively labour-intensive sectors such as textiles, clothing and footwear where international competition has been more intense (Commission, 1999b). However, in the second half of the year, Italian exports benefited greatly from the depreciation of the euro and improved external demand.

Despite disappointing growth, employment continued to increase in Italy in 1999 and the unemployment rate fell to 11.3 per cent. Nevertheless, Italy continues to suffer from the second highest rate of unemployment in the EU. Many observers have argued that structural factors account for much of the difference in unemployment levels between Italy and the other members of the EU. High taxes, an inefficient welfare system and labour market rigidities are often cited as major causes of Italy's below-average performance in the 1990s (IMF, 1999). If this is true, it must be a cause for concern that little progress was made in 1999 in tackling these structural weaknesses. On the positive side, however, some improvement was made in Italy's public finances in 1999, with the level of government borrowing falling from 2.8 per cent of GDP in 1998 to 1.9 per cent in 1999. A further reduction is expected in the next two years, although Italy's debt to GDP ratio will remain the highest in the EU.

Spain

In 1999, Spain continued to be one of the EU's fastest-growing economies, growing by 3.7 per cent a year compared to 4 per cent in the previous year. For the previous five years, the Spanish economy has grown at a rate well above the EU average. The Commission expects this to continue at a rate of 3.8 per cent in 2000. The main cause of this expansion has continued to be increasing domestic demand. Private consumption was stimulated by strong job creation and cuts in personal income tax. Private investment demand was boosted by low short-term interest rates and the increase in private consumption.

In 1999, employment increased at a rate of 3.4 per cent, the third fastest rate in the EU. In absolute terms, Spain has become the main source of job creation in the EU. Although Spain still has the highest rate of unemployment in the EU, this fell from 18.7 per cent in 1998 to 15.8 per cent in 1999. This should be compared with an unemployment rate of nearly 23 per cent three years ago. Labour market reforms have contributed much towards this improvement. However, large regional differences in the unemployment rate continue to exist. While there are labour shortages in the more prosperous regions of Spain, high levels of unemployment are still apparent in regions hit by the restructuring of heavy industries (*Financial Times*, 25.2.2000).

Despite rapid growth, inflation remained relatively controlled during 1999. Prices rose at an annual rate of 2.2 per cent, due mainly to higher oil prices. Wage increases remained modest. However, the rate of inflation is expected to accelerate to 2.5 per cent in 2000, which will be considerably higher than in the rest of the euro-zone. Already in 1999, Spain experienced a substantial worsening of its current account balance of payments, with the deficit rising to 1.8 per cent of GDP. There is some concern that, if prices continue rising at a rate well above that of other euro-zone countries, this deficit will widen still further. On the other hand, providing the rate of wage increase remains moderate, increases in productivity may still ensure that unit labour costs do not rise significantly faster than in other Member States.

United Kingdom

In 1999, the UK economy grew at a rate of 2 per cent, a little below the EU average. However, by the second half of the year, a strong recovery was underway, which is forecast to continue into 2000. The main source of more rapid growth was an increase in private consumption, the result of improved consumer confidence, rising real wages, rising asset prices and lower interest rates. Despite the rise in the external value of sterling, exports also remained buoyant. As a consequence of rapid output growth, employment continued growing and the unemployment rate fell to a 20-year low of 6.1 per cent.

However, by the end of the year, it was apparent that domestic demand was growing too strongly. Inflation as measured by the Retail Price Index (less mortgage interest payments) (RPIX) was close to the UK's target rate of inflation. As a consequence, interest rates were raised by the Bank of England's Monetary Policy Committee (MPC) in a series of small steps to a level of 5.5 per cent in an attempt to prevent the target from being exceeded. Measured by the EU's harmonized index of consumer prices, however, the UK's rate of inflation was only 1.3 per cent during the year, one of the lowest in the EU. An important factor in holding down the rate of inflation was the strength of sterling. A concern that higher interest rates might result in a further strengthening of sterling, with a consequent tightening of the profits squeeze on the manufacturing export sector, means that more reliance may have to be placed on fiscal policy to contain excess demand.

In 1999, the UK ran a budget surplus of 1.2 per cent of GDP, larger than had been forecast at the start of the year. In part, this reflected much stronger growth in the economy than had been at first foreseen, resulting in higher tax receipts and lower spending. However, the cyclically-adjusted surplus was of roughly the same magnitude.

Other Member States

In 1999, *Austria* experienced a rate of economic growth in line with the average for the EU as a whole, but is forecast to enjoy to strong acceleration in 2000. Employment grew slowly and the unemployment rate fell further to a level of 4.4 per cent, well below the EU average. Inflation at 0.5 per cent was the lowest rate recorded for any Member State and the lowest for any year since World War II. With wages increasing at a moderate rate and productivity rising fast, Austria enjoyed a big increase in competitiveness in the EU.

Belgium experienced a mild slowing down of the economy in 1999 with GDP growth declining to 2.3 per cent. However, a strong recovery, generated by sustained domestic demand and a positive contribution from net exports, took place in the second half of the year. The rate of unemployment fell 0.5 per cent to 9 per cent, just below the EU average. Inflation remained modest at 1.1 per cent due largely to a moderate rate of wage increase. The budget deficit was reduced to 0.9 per cent of GDP, making possible a further reduction in Belgium's very high gross indebtedness ratio to 114.4 per cent.

Denmark saw a further slowing down in her rate of output expansion, with GDP growing by only 1.4 per cent which, alongside Italy, was the slowest rate of growth in the EU. A decline in private consumption, brought about by a contractionary fiscal package in May intended to prevent overheating, was a major cause of the slowdown. On the other hand, exports grew at a faster rate than in 1998 as firms switched sales away from the depressed domestic market.

A favourable outcome was a marked improvement in Denmark's external balance from a deficit of 15.2 billion DKK in 1998 to a surplus of 10.6 billion DKK in 1999. With slow output growth, employment increased by only 0.8 per cent. Unemployment fell from 5.1 per cent in 1998 to 4.5 per cent in 1999. Inflation, however, remained relatively strong at 2.1 per cent, due partly to higher energy taxes. Public finances remained sound, with Denmark recording a budget surplus equivalent to 3 per cent of GDP, the healthiest of any EU Member State.

In 1999, *Finland*'s GDP grew at a rate of 3.5 per cent down from 5 per cent in 1998. This was due to both weak export demand in the first half of the year and a slowing down in the growth of domestic demand. Nevertheless, employment grew at a faster rate than in 1998 with most job creation occurring in the private services sector. As a result, the unemployment rate fell by 1.2 percentage points to 10.2 per cent. A further reduction in the unemployment rate is forecast for 2000, although structural factors will make it difficult for unemployment to fall as quickly as in the past (Commission, 2000). Inflation remained close to the EU average at 1.3 per cent, but is expected to increase in 2000 as the effects of higher oil prices feed through to the domestic economy. At 2.3 per cent of GDP, Finland continued to run one of the largest budget surpluses in the EU.

Greece's most important achievement in 1999 was, undoubtedly, her success in bringing the rate of inflation down to 2.1 per cent from a rate of nearly 14 per cent in the early 1990s. This brings her inflation to within 1.5 percentage points of the three best performing Member States, a requirement for Greece to qualify for entry to the euro at the next stage. Despite this, growth remained strong at 3.5 per cent, down only slightly from 3.7 per cent in 1998. Employment grew at a rate of 1.2 per cent, making possible a small decline in the unemployment rate to 10.4 per cent. A deceleration in the rate of wage increases was an important factor in making possible a slower increase in unit labour costs. This, combined with falling commodity prices, contributed to the decline in inflation. At the same time, Greece has managed to sustain the improvement in public finances that has been taking place since 1994. The budget deficit fell further to 1.6 per cent of GDP, making possible a further reduction in the debt-to-GDP ratio to 104.4 per cent.

Ireland continued to grow at the fastest rate of any economy in the EU, although the growth moderated somewhat to a rate of 8.3 per cent compared with 8.9 per cent in 1998. Domestic demand contributed the most, as household consumption continued rising in response to higher real incomes, rising asset prices and increasing employment. However, both private investment and net exports also contributed positively to economic growth. Employment rose at a rate of 5 per cent, making possible a further reduction in the unemployment rate to 6.5 per cent. However, there were signs of a tightening of the labour market with the rate of wage increases rising to 6 per cent.

Inflationary pressures are mounting. At 2.5 per cent, Ireland's inflation rate was the highest in the EU in 1999 and is forecast to increase to 3.7 per cent in 2000. Rising house prices continue to fuel increased private consumption, while wage inflation is also accelerating. On the other hand, there is very little that Ireland can do to curb excess demand. In 1999, Ireland recorded a budget surplus of 2 per cent of GDP. The budget announced in December 1999 was widely criticized for adding to inflationary pressures within the economy.

Luxembourg enjoyed the second highest growth rate in the EU in 1999, with GDP rising by 5 per cent, exactly the same rate as in the previous year. For the whole of the past decade, the Luxembourg economy has grown at an annual average rate of over 5 per cent, a performance not matched by any other Member State. Most of this growth has been based on a growth of the services sector, especially financial services. As a result, at 2.7 per cent, Luxembourg continued to enjoy the lowest rate of unemployment of any country in Europe. In 1999, employment grew at a rate of 4.8 per cent, the bulk of which occurred in the services sector. At the same time, inflation remained very modest at an annual rate of only 1 per cent. Towards the end of the year, however, inflation had accelerated to an annual rate of 2 per cent due partly to rising oil prices.

The Netherlands continued to enjoy strong growth in 1999 at a rate of 3.5 per cent a year, down only slightly from a rate of 3.7 per cent in 1998. Economic activity was much less affected by the slowdown in world output growth than had been anticipated. Although export demand did fall somewhat, this was offset by buoyant domestic demand. In particular, consumer demand was boosted by rising employment levels, increasing real wages, tax cuts and rising asset prices. Employment continued to grow and the average rate of unemployment fell further to 3.1 per cent, the second lowest rate in the EU. However, during the year, there were signs of growing inflationary pressures, acting through rising wages. After several years of a modest rate of wage increase, the rate rose to 3.7 per cent in 1999 and is forecast to rise further to 4 per cent in 2000. Although this was partially offset by strong productivity growth in the export-oriented manufacturing sector, there remains a danger that the competitiveness of the Dutch economy could be undermined if wage claims are not moderated.

In 1999, *Portugal's* GDP grew at a rate of 2.9 per cent a year compared with 3.5 per cent in 1998. The slowdown was due both to a fall in domestic demand and external demand. Employment continued to rise a rate of 1.8 per cent and unemployment fell further to 4.5 per cent, well below the EU average. However, for the second year running, the rate of inflation stood at 2.2 per cent which, with Spain, was the second highest in the EU. With nominal wages rising at a relatively fast rate of 5 per cent, unit labour costs rose sharply, undermining the competitiveness of Portuguese exports in the euro-zone. This was reflected in a widening trade gap equivalent to 12.6 per cent of GDP.

Finally, *Sweden* was the only Member State to enjoy faster growth in 1999 than in the previous year. In 1999, GDP grew by 3.8 per cent compared with 3 per cent in 1998. Growth in private consumption and investment, assisted by favourable monetary conditions, were the main factors contributing to this performance. As a result, employment grew by 2.2 per cent and the rate of unemployment fell further to 7 per cent. Inflation remained low at 0.6 per cent, but there were signs that inflationary pressures were building up towards the end of the year. In November, concern that the inflation target might be exceeded in 2000 prompted the Riskbank to raise interest rates. This was followed by a second increase in February, 2000. Some slowing down of the economy will be needed to prevent overheating from taking place.

III. Conclusion

Overall, 1999 proved a better year for the EU economy than seemed likely 12 months ago. In part, this was because the world economic slowdown proved less severe and shorter lived than at one time looked probable. In part, too, it reflected the fact that the Member States made the necessary adjustments to macroeconomic policies to ensure that a steep and prolonged downturn was avoided. Although unemployment levels remain high in certain Member States, especially in comparison with other developed market economies in the world, some progress has been made in all countries in bringing these rates down to more reasonable levels. More effort is still needed in some countries to ensure that continued output growth translates into employment creation. However, it remains important that economic growth is maintained at existing levels without jeopardizing the price stability objective.

The Commission is forecasting an increase in GDP growth to 3.4 per cent in 2000. However, this depends heavily on global conditions. Although growth is expected to slow down in the United States, much will depend on whether this takes the form of a soft landing (a gradual slowing down in the rate of economic expansion) or a hard landing (sharp and sudden contraction of output). A further external factor remains the uncertainty surrounding the future direction of world oil prices. On the other hand, the possibility exists that growth within the EU could prove stronger than expected. This would be the case if private investment demand were to prove more vigorous than otherwise, or if the effects of the growth of the 'knowledge-based economy' on EU productive potential proved stronger than has thus far been the case.

References

Commission of the European Communities (1999a) *Spring Economic Forecasts* (Brussels: CEC), March.

Commission of the European Communities (1999b) *The EU Economy 1999 Review* (Brussels: CEC) EC/FIN/646/99-EN.

Commission of the European Communities (2000) *European Economy, Supplement A, Economic Trends*, No 1/2, April.

Financial Times (2000) 'Financial Times Survey – the Eurozone Economy'. 25 February.

International Monetary Fund (1999) *World Economic Outlook* (Washington, D.C.: IMF), October.

Journal of Common Market Studies

Volume 38, Annual Review
September 2000

Chronology of Key Events in 1999*

GEORG WIESSALA
University of Central Lancashire

I. Main Events of the Year

- The Member States deposit the instruments of ratification for the Amsterdam Treaty
- The euro (€) is introduced
- The Santer Commission resigns
- Germany and Finland hold the Presidencies of the Council of Ministers
- The European Parliament elections take place in June
- The preparations for a reform-oriented Intergovernmental Conference (IGC) in 2000 are made
- The EU is given a new security and defence framework
- The first EU High Representative for the CFSP is appointed
- Human Rights Protection takes a further step forward in EU politics

II. Month-by-Month Overview

January

1   Germany takes over Presidency of the Council of Ministers. Germany also holds the chair of the G-7/8 (US, Canada, Japan, Germany, France, Italy, UK and Russia) and the WEU in the first half of 1999.
«http://www.eu-praesidentschaft.de»

---

* Additional material has been contributed by Ian Mayfield, EDC Librarian, University of Portsmouth and Patrick Overy, EDC Librarian, University of Exeter.

1   Official launch of the euro (€). Austria, Belgium, Finland, France, Germany, Ireland, Italy, Luxembourg, the Netherlands, Portugal and Spain (the 'Euro-11'), adopt the new currency.

12   Jacques Santer, ex-President of the Commission, seeks a vote of confidence from the European Parliament.

27–28   The President of the European Parliament, José María Gil-Robles, announces the five members of a Committee of Independent Experts, whose remit is to investigate allegations of fraud and mismanagement in the Commission, following the vote, in December 1998, to censure the EU Executive.

February

1   Entry into force of the EU–Slovenia Europe Agreement and Framework Co-operation Agreement with Chile.

8–9   EU–ACP ministerial meeting in Dakar, Senegal. Cuba attends, for the first time in an observer capacity. The meeting aims to negotiate a successor agreement to Lomé IV and is followed by ministerial conferences in Brussels in July and December.

17   Updated *avis* on Malta's renewed application. It recommends that the Council give the go-ahead for a screening process of the island's legislation. The screening exercise begins on 21 March.

18   EU–Russia summit in Moscow develops the EU–Russia Partnership and Co-operation Agreement (PCA) and hears ex-President Yeltsin re-affirm his opposition to NATO bombardment in Serbia. Referring to the Rambouillet talks, both sides stress the urgent need for an end to the Kosovo war.

21–22   A special meeting of EU foreign ministers in Luxembourg fails to make progress with regard to the *Agenda 2000* blueprint.

26   Summit meeting at Petersberg, near Bonn. The Heads of State or Government (HOSG) discuss, amongst other topics, *Agenda 2000*, budget reform and the UK rebate, the 2000–06 financial perspective, structural funds, CAP, asylum and immigration and duty-free shopping, due to end July 1999.

March

7   World Trade Organization (WTO) General Council appeals to both the EU and the US to come to an agreement over the banana dispute.

9   Commission adopts communication on EU–Latin America relations in the twenty-first century.
         «http://europa.eu.int/en/comm/dg1b/pol-orientations/en/en-projet.htm»

11   New Code of Conduct for Commissioners published by President Jacques Santer to replace an earlier one, dating back to 1995.

12   At a meeting of JHA ministers the UK indicates, for the first time, its willingness to join parts of the Schengen Convention, including the Schengen Information System (SIS) and the common asylum rules.

15   First report published on allegations regarding fraud, mismanagement and nepotism in the European Commission of the Committee of Independent Experts. The Santer Commission resigns *en masse*, though it remains in a caretaker role until September. «http://www.europarl.eu.int/experts/en/report1. htm»

22   Special plenary session of the European Parliament.

24–25   Berlin *Agenda 2000* summit decides reforms of the EU's finances, agricultural, regional and social policies. The meeting also addresses the British budget rebate, the Middle East Peace Process, the Kosovo war and the Trade and Cooperation Agreement with South Africa. Romano Prodi, former Prime Minister of Italy, nominated new Commission President.

30   ASEM Meeting in Berlin. Official opening of the Asia–Europe Environment Technology Centre in Bangkok.

30   France is the last Member State to deposit the instrument of ratification regarding the Treaty of Amsterdam (Spain: 5 January, Belgium: 19 February, Portugal: 19 March, Greece 23 March. The other ten Member States deposited their instruments of ratification in 1998).

April

7   Justice and Home Affairs emergency meeting in Luxembourg discusses the worsening refugee crisis in Kosovo.

8   Foreign ministers hold a special meeting on Kosovo, and express support for NATO bombing of Serbian targets. They hint at future EU membership for Balkan countries as a way to stabilize peace in the region.

13   The Commission recommends that the three-year transition period for the euro should not be shortened.

15–16   Third Euro-Mediterranean Conference in Stuttgart, with the aim of continuing to develop the Barcelona Process. Libya attends as a 'special guest of the Presidency'.

20   Foreign ministers from the EU and the Middle East meet in Stuttgart, to discuss the EURO-MED programme and prospects for a lasting peace in the Middle East.

26   The General Affairs Committee (GAC) calls for UN Peacekeeping Force in East Timor.

28   Decision to create an Independent Fraud Office is agreed. Commission adopts Preliminary Draft Budget for 2000.

28–29   The President of the Committee of the Regions, Manfred Dammeyer, is, for the first time, invited to speak at a plenary session of the Economic and Social Committee, following the conclusion of a 'Co-operation Agreement' between the two bodies.

29   The Council of Industry Ministers adopts a measure banning new aircraft equipped with 'hush-kits', but with a one-year delay.

May

1   The Amsterdam Treaty enters into force, having been ratified by all 15 Member States. It was signed on 2 October 1997.

3–7   EP overwhelmingly approves the nomination of Romano Prodi as head of the European Commission for the next five years. It also gives its support to 19 reports on *Agenda 2000* and the EU's budget for 2000–06.

4   Joint EU–New Zealand Declaration is signed in Strasbourg.

17–18   Council discusses a future EU Charter for Fundamental Rights, a new Russia policy and the merger of the EU and the WEU.

28   The President of the European Court of Justice (ECB), Gil Carlos Rodríguez Iglesias, initiates the Court's reflections on the future of the EU's judicial system.

31   Council adopts conclusions on the implementation of a 'Northern dimension' in EU policy-making.

June

1   The European Anti-Fraud Office (OLAF) is established and continues the work of the Commission Fraud Prevention Task Force.

3–5   Cologne summit of Heads of State or Government (HOSG) ends the German Presidency. The summit agenda includes:
- Peace in Kosovo
- Common strategy for Russia
- Unemployment and the European Employment Pact
- Security and defence
- Development and institutional reform in the EU
- Enlargement and foreign affairs. Javier Solana Madariaga is designated EU High Representative for the CFSP
- The codification of an EU Charter of Fundamental Rights «http://europa.eu.int/council/off/conclu/june99/june99_en.htm»

10–13   Fifth direct elections for the EP. At 49.8 per cent, the turnout is the lowest since 1979. European People's Party (EPP) becomes strongest political force ahead of the Party of European Socialists (PSE). The UK, Denmark and the Netherlands vote on 10 June, Ireland on 11 June. Austria, Belgium, Spain,

Finland, France, Germany, Greece, Italy, Luxembourg, Portugal and Sweden on 13 June. «http://www2.europarl.eu.int/election/»

17   EU–Canada summit in Bonn.

17   Parliament and Council adopted the 'Eurovignette' directive on charging of heavy goods vehicles.

18–20   Annual G-8 summit in Cologne discusses issues as varied as globalization, Russia, the WTO and the reduction of debt for developing countries.

20   Eighth EU–Japan summit in Bonn. The emphasis is on the political side of the EU–Japan dialogue.

21   EU–US summit in Bonn. The meeting debates security and trade matters and the development of the New Transatlantic Agenda.

21   The GAC agrees mandate for the Commission to negotiate association agreements with the four countries of Mercosur (Mercado Común del Sur: Argentina, Brazil, Paraguay and Uruguay) and Chile, which has been an associate member since 1996. Ministers also agree on a new Association Agreement with Egypt.

22   Association Conference with Cyprus, Estonia, Hungary, Poland, the Czech Republic and Slovenia in Luxembourg. Luxembourg also hosts an EU summit meeting with Armenia, Azerbaijan and Georgia.

23   Commission propose the establishment of a European Agency for Reconstruction in Kosovo.

24–25   Environment ministers agree an amendment to the directive which stipulates the approval mechanism for new genetically modified (GM) organisms.

28–29   First EU–Latin America/Caribbean summit in Rio de Janeiro. The Rio Declaration stresses 55 priorities for action in the fields of political dialogue, economic and trade relations, fighting organized crime, sustainable development and disaster prevention, education, culture and the human dimension of the relationship.

July

1   Finland assumes the Presidency of the EU. «http://www.presidency.finland.fi/frame.asp»

The Europol Police Agency begins work (the relevant Convention entered into force in October 1998).

Duty-free sales within the EU are abolished.

Partnership and Co-operation Agreements (PCAs) with Armenia, Azerbaijan, Georgia, Kazakhstan, Kyrgyzstan and Uzbekistan enter into force.

Interregional framework co-operation agreement with Mercosur enters into force.

8   Senior troika officials travel to the Union of Myanmar (Burma) for the first high-level EU–Burma meeting for two years.

14   The Commission agrees that British farmers should be able to resume exports of beef products from 1 August. This move ends a ban imposed in March 1996.

19   The European Conference meets in Brussels. It brings together the foreign ministers of the 15 EU Member States, the 10 CEECs, Cyprus, Malta and Switzerland.

20–23   First session of the newly elected EP in its new HQ in Strasbourg. The French Christian Democrat MEP Nicole Fontaine is elected Parliament' s first female President in 20 years.

21   The new Commission is informally presented to the EP. The decision is announced that restrictive ticket sales by the French organizers of the 1999 football World Cup contravened EU competition law.

23   Third EU–Ukraine summit in Kiev intensifies relations. The Partnership and Co-operation Agreement (PCA) had entered into force on 1 March 1998.

29–30   The EU takes part in an international summit on the Balkans, discussing economics, democracy and proposals for a stability pact for south eastern Europe.

August
30   Until 7 September: European Parliament hearings with each new member-designate of the new Prodi Commission.

September
7   New Commission President Prodi outlines a strategy for good relations with the EP.

8   Outgoing Santer Commission meets for the last time, having acted in a caretaker capacity for the last six months.

9   A second, 290-page report, *Reform of the Commission. Mismanagement, Irregularities and Fraud* published (*see also* 15 March 1999). «http://www.europarl.eu.int/experts/en/default.htm»

13–14   EU foreign ministers decide to end civilian sanctions against Libya, impose an arms sales embargo on Indonesia to help end the violence in East Timor and agree to improve contact with the opposition in Yugoslavia, in order to counter the influence of Slobodan Milosevic.

13–17   The EP welcomes the Committee of Independent Experts' Second Report and votes (on 15 September) to approve the new Prodi Commission by 404 votes to 153.

18   First official meeting of the New Commission.

October
1   The GAC approves the EU's first Trade, Co-operation and Development Agreement with South Africa.

11–14   29th EU–ACP Joint Assembly in Nassau, the Bahamas.

12   Commission adopts a communication on relations between the EU and Macao: *Beyond 2000*, approving of China's one-country-two-systems approach towards Macao.

15–16   Special Justice and Home Affairs summit in Tampere, Finland. Priorities include: fighting crime, access to justice, asylum, drugs and immigration. Decisions are also taken on the drafting of the European Union Charter of Fundamental Rights and membership of the drafting body. «http://europa.eu.int/abc/doc/off/bull/en/9910/i1002.htm»

18   Task Force for Administrative Reform is set up, supported by the Commissioners' Reform Group under Commissioner Neil Kinnock.

18–19   WEU Assembly special session on security and defence following the Cologne summit.

19   The Council publishes its first Annual Report on the Human Rights Situation in the World, in the wake of the EU declaration of 10 December 1998, on the 50th Anniversary of the Universal Declaration of Human Rights.

22   EU–Russia summit in Helsinki. The war in Chechnya dominates discussions.

24   General election in Switzerland.

28   First ever judgment is delivered in the format of a single judge at the European Court of First Instance.

November
16   Commission launches the first stage of formal infringement proceedings against France, as a result of the continued French ban on British beef.

18–19   Commission President Romano Prodi and Commissioner Chris Patten attend the summit meeting of the Organization for Security and Co-operation in Europe (OSCE) in Istanbul.

23   WEU Ministerial Council approves the appointment of Javier Solana as new WEU Secretary-General.

23   The European Court of Justice in Luxembourg rules that the agreement establishing the WTO does not have direct effect in the Community legal system and therefore has to be implemented into national legal systems.

25   Philippe Maystadt appointed President of the European Investment Bank (EIB).

30   WTO Third Ministerial Conference starts 'Millennium' trade talks in Seattle with inconclusive results (until 3 December). The violent protests accompanying the meeting highlight the widespread mistrust of the WTO and its liberalization policies.

December

7   Association conference at ministerial level with Cyprus, the Czech Republic, Estonia, Hungary, Poland and Slovenia in Brussels.

10–11   The Helsinki summit concludes the Finnish term of office. The main points under discussion are:
- a more independent military capacity for the EU, including a 'Rapid Intervention Force'
- the 2000 IGC agenda and its restriction to the 'Amsterdam leftovers', i.e. the size of the Commission, the weighting of votes in the Council and the issues of qualified majority voting (QMV)
- sanctions against Russia and the war in Chechnya
- the first common strategy on Ukraine
- Turkey's full candidate status for accession
- a further six countries were invited to begin formal accession talks, according to the 'Regatta principle' (Latvia, Lithuania, Slovakia, Bulgaria, Romania and Malta)
- no agreement was reached on an EU-wide savings tax. «http://europa.eu.int/council/off/conclu/dec99/dec99_en.htm»

14   Commission takes second stage of formal infringement proceedings against France over British beef. France is given five working days to lift its ban.

16   EU–Canada summit in Ottawa adopts various statements, e.g. on e-commerce and the information society. Portuguese Foreign Secretary Jaime Gama launches the Portuguese Presidency's programme.

17   EU–US summit in Washington adopts a number of statements on, for instance, the WTO, the 'northern dimension' of Europe, and co-operation in areas such as biotechnology.

21   Second EU–China summit in Beijing. It continues the work programme initiated by the first summit in London, in April 1998. Discussions focus

again on China's application to join the WTO, and on the establishment of the EU–China Chamber of Business and Commerce in Beijing.

IV. Sources

Commission of th European Communities (2000) *General Report on the Activities of the European Union 1999*, Luxembourg.

The Week in Europe (1999), various.

The European Voice 1999 – For The Record – «http://europa.eu.int/abc/ history/1999/1999_en.htm»

Committee of Independent Experts (1999) *First Report on Allegations regarding Fraud, Mismanagement and Nepotism in the European Commission*, 15 March «http://www.europarl.eu.int/experts/en/report1.htm»

Committee of Independent Experts (1999) *Second Report on Reform of the Commission. Analysis of Current Practice and Proposals for Tackling Mismanagement, Irregularities and Fraud*, 10 September «http://www.europarl.eu.int/experts/en/default.htm»

Journal of Common Market Studies

Volume 38, Annual Review
September 2000

Documentation of the European Union in 1999

PATRICK OVERY
Exeter University
and
IAN MAYFIELD
University of Portsmouth

SECTION A:
Recent Trends in EU Documentation

The dominant trend in EU documentation over the past year or so has been the continued development of the world wide web as the platform of choice for delivery of information. Most major databases had already migrated to the web from their traditional, complex software systems to more user-friendly, web-based interfaces and this process reached its logical conclusion with the closure, around the end of 1998, of the official database host Eurobases (the other host, ECHO, had already closed). The few remaining, mostly obscure and specialized Eurobases services either moved to the web or disappeared entirely. These developments were part of a general trend towards the provision by the EU institutions and agencies of high-quality, often free resources on the web so that it is now easier than ever before – for those with access to the internet – to access information about EU legislation, policies and activities.

This trend has brought benefits in increased openness. For the first time, for example, a register of Council documents is available at «http://register.consilium.eu.int/ isoregister/ introEN.htm», as well as a growing range of primary documentation. However, there continues to be contradiction and confusion surrounding certain aspects of the EU's provision of information, so that enthusiasm for the general trend towards wider availability via the web must be qualified by concern about particular issues to do with access to and the durability of information.

One aspect of this currently rather muddled picture is duplication of effort. Among the databases lost with Eurobases was APC, a little used French-language database, the purpose of which was to enable users to track the progress of EU legislation through the various stages of the legislative process. This loss was more than offset by the continued development of the European Legislative Observatory (OEIL) at «http://www.europarl.eu.int/r/dors/oeil/en/ default.htm», housed on the Parliament's website. It was somewhat surprising, therefore, to learn, early in the year 2000, of the new Pre-Lex website «http://europa.eu.int/prelex/ rech_simple.cfm?CL=en», subtitled 'Decision-making process between institutions' which appears to perform a very similar task. This is presumably explicable as independent activity by separate institutions but is, nonetheless, of concern in resource terms at least.

A more complex issue is the conflict within the Commission between the political imperative of reducing the democratic deficit and increasing transparency by making information freely available, and the economic imperative of regarding information as an economic good from which income can be earned. This is perhaps seen most clearly in the continued development of the free legislative database Eur-Lex «http://europa.eu.int/eur-lex/en/index.html» to the point at which it contains almost as much information, albeit with a less powerful search engine, as the official legislative database Celex, which costs around £1,000 p.a. Those intrigued by the economics of this situation would have been interested in the announcement towards the end of the year that the two databases, together with the document delivery service EUDOR, were to be integrated within 'a single portal'. Quite what this means remains to be seen.

In the purely commercial arena, leading players such as Context, ILI and Ellis continue to vie for pre-eminence by adding ever more sophisticated value-added information and technical features to their versions of Celex: for example, now predominantly following the trend towards web delivery. For example, Context's J-link facility allows cross-referencing between different databases, email, word processing and web applications. This is a competitive field in which the major players Context, ILI and Ellis publications can be expected to continue to develop their existing range of products. However, the commercial sector has also seen a number of new products during 1999. According to Hudson, 'we are experiencing a wave of new generation web-based products which may change the face of EU information and cause us all to re-evaluate the tools we currently use' (Hudson, 1999a, p. 34). The approach is the assembly of a range of EU-related information, much of it full text rather than merely references, and the presentation of this information by means of a common, user-friendly interface. Butterworths' *EU Direct* and *EU Interactive* from Lawtel are aimed primarily at lawyers, but will also hope to attract interest from the higher education sector. Chadwyck-Healey's *Know Europe* is aimed at a more general audience and it remains to be seen how widely this will be adopted, with a price tag around £2,000, by public and education libraries. One of its constituent parts, *European Access Plus,* seems more assured of its market given its more modest costs, and the fact that it represents a long-awaited electronic version of the highly-respected bibliographic tool, *European Access*. Interestingly, the business of gathering and organizing EU information has also been attempted on a no-fee basis both by commercial sites such as *EU Business* «http://www.eubusiness.com/» and educational institutions, for example the University of Mannheim's EDC site «http://www.uni-mannheim.de/users/ddz/edz/eedz.html» and the *European Integration Current Contents* service offered by the Academy of European Law and Harvard Law School «http://www.law.harvard.edu/programs/JeanMonnet/TOC/index.html».

The immense and growing importance of the internet for delivery of European information does not appear so far to have been paralleled in the use of the web for teaching about Europe. A number of resource collections exist, such as *Eurotext* «http://eurotext.ulst.ac.uk:8017/», which became a subscription-based service in June 1999, the *European Legislative Virtual Library* (ELVIL, «http://www.sub.su.se/elvil.htm» and *European Integration Online Papers* «http://olymp.wu-wien.ac.at/eiop/». However, thus far, the pedagogic elements necessary to transfer such resources into online teaching materials do not seem to have been developed. Petzold, overviewing available materials in *European Access* concluded that 'beyond a limited number of project-based resources publishers seem not to have defined possibilities for alliances with the academic world' (Petzold, 1999, p. 21).

Of wider concern is the long-term availability of the information which is now available on the internet. Many documents up to a few years old are relatively easy to come by, but, what about older material? And for how long will the information remain on the servers, freely available in the public domain? These questions become particularly acute in an environment in which there is a trend towards making electronic access to information the only available means, rather than an easily-accessible complement to printed resources. For example, the *Official Journal C E* (i.e. electronic) was recently introduced, carrying information, including proposed legislation, which is no longer made available in the printed *Official Journal C*. More recently still, it was announced at very short notice that, from March 2000, members of the Commission's network of information 'Relays' would no longer be entitled to free receipt of the *OJ* in print form. This decision, though not entirely unexpected, was taken despite the presentation, by European Documentation Centres in particular, of a strong case based on their role as primary repositories of the documentation, difficulties of access to electronic information and the status of the printed *OJ* as the only legally binding text.

There is also concern about the effect on access to information of two items of legislation currently in the pipeline. In the information professions, there is anxiety that the proposed copyright directive (*COM* (1999) 250 final) may inhibit the provision of a quality service to users. Concern regarding the draft regulation on access to documents (*COM* (2000) 30 final) has been more widespread, the *Guardian* observing that 'plans being drawn up by European officials would introduce sweeping new restrictions on citizens' rights to information about EU decision-making' (*Guardian*, 8.12.1999). It would appear that the intentions behind the regulation are worthy. However, the exceptions listed in Art. 4 are so numerous and so general that there is plenty of scope for access to be denied by officials with a wish to do so. The democratic impact of the legislation is likely to be determined not by those who drafted it but by those who operate it in practice.

It is clear that, despite many welcome developments in information provision, there are areas of concern and battles still to be fought. The importance of ready access to information needs to be emphasized by academics and the general public as well as by information professionals. It is also important that the delivery of information is effected at the right level; as Hudson says, 'the laudable aim of easy access to EU law for the citizen must not preclude effective search options for the professional user' (Hudson, 1999b, p. 31). We should be ready to forge liaisons in order to ensure that our representatives, elected or otherwise, are fully aware of these concerns.

References

Hudson, G. (1999a) 'EU Electronic Information Column'. *European Access* 5/6 December, p. 34.
Hudson, G. (1999b) 'EU Electronic Information Column'. *European Access* 5/6 December, p. 31.
Petzold, W. (1999) 'The Challenge of Virtual Mobility: Using Information Technologies in European Studies'. *European Access* 3, June, p. 21.

SECTION B:
Key Documentation

N.B: Entries within sub-headings are in alphabetical order

I. Governance and Institutional Developments

Amsterdam Treaty

The Amsterdam Treaty entered into force on 1 May 1999, the 15 EU Member States having completed their ratification procedures on 30 March. IP/99/269.

The European Commission

The *General Report on the Activities of the European Union 1999* is available. ISBN 92-828-8155-5 cat.no. CM-25-99-891-EN-C «http://europa.eu.int/abc/doc/off/rg/en/1999/index.htm»

The Commission resigned in March following the publication of the first report of the Committee of Independent Experts on 15 March 1999 «http:/www.europarl.eu.int/experts/ en/report1.htm»

A second report was published on 10 September 1999 «http://www.europarl.eu.int/experts/en/default.htm»

Romano Prodi's nomination as new President of the Commission was approved by the European Parliament on 5 May and the process of selecting and screening the 20 new Commissioners began on 21 July. A new Commission site has been set up at «http://europa.eu.int/comm/index_en.htm» which includes reports of the screening process. Details of the proposals for reform of the Commission are at «http://europa.eu.int/comm/reform/index_en.htm» including the new code of conduct and rules of procedure.

The Directorates-General are now referred to by name rather than by number to make them more easily identifiable by the public and some areas of responsibility have been reallocated. The new layout is shown on the List of Directorates-General and Services at «http://europa.eu.int/comm/dgs_en.htm»

Many improvements have been made to the Europa server, including a section on policies of the EU «http://europa.eu.int/pol/index-en.htm» which gives access to legal texts, implementation and information sources.

The European Council and the Presidency

Germany held the Presidency from January to June 1999 «http://www.eu-praesidentschaft.de/»

The Cologne European Council was held on 3–4 June 1999. A declaration on security and defence, a common strategy for Russia and the European Employment Pact were adopted.

Conclusions in *Bulletin of the EU* 6-1999 pp. 7–37 «http://europa.eu.int/council/off/conclu/june99/june99_en.htm»

Finland held the Presidency from July to December 1999 «http://www.presidency.finland.fi/frame.asp»

The European Council held a special meeting on 15–16 October 1999 in Tampere on the creation of an area of freedom, security and justice in the European Union «http://europa.eu.int/abc/doc/off/bull/en/9910/i1002.htm»

The Conclusions of the Finnish Presidency in Helsinki 10–11 December 1999 «http://europa.eu.int/council/off/conclu/dec99/dec99_en.htm»

The Court of Auditors

Annual report concerning the financial year 1998 was published in *OJ* C349 3.12.1999

Four special reports were issued in 1999; all are available from the Court's website at «http://www.eca.eu.int/»

The European Parliament

The fifth elections to the European Parliament took place in June 1999. Although there was a record number of candidates (10,000), turnout in many countries was low «http://www2.europarl.eu.int/election/»

Other Institutions

Each of the European institutions publishes an annual report; all are available on paper and, in most cases, online from Institutions on the Europa server «http://europa.eu.int/inst-en.htm»

II. Internal Policy Developments

Agriculture

Income insurance in European agriculture (*European economy*. Reports and studies, no.2/1999) ISBN 92-828-6755-2 cat.no.CM-21-99-957-EN-C

Prospects for agricultural markets 1999–2006 (CAP reports) «http://europa.eu.int/comm/dg06/publi/caprep/prospects/index_en.htm»

Business

Enhancing tourism's potential for employment (*COM*(99) 205)

Financial services action plan: progress report (*COM*(99) 630)

Report on concerted action with Member States in the field of enterprise policy (*COM*(99) 569)

Report on the evaluation of the 3rd multi-annual programme for SMEs in the EU (1997–2000) (*COM*(99) 319)

White Paper on Commerce ISBN 92-828-6572-x cat.no. CT-20-99-438-EN-C (originally issued as *COM*(99) 6)

Your Business and the Euro: a strategic guide (with interactive CD-ROM) ISBN 92-828-6077-9 cat.no. CT-16-98-910-EN-Y

Competition

Buyer power and its impact on competition in the food distribution sector of the EU ISBN 9282879380 cat.no. CV-25-99-649-EN-C

The importance of monitoring state aid to ensure that Member States of the European Union do not allow unfair competition and an emphasis on the international dimension is demonstrated by a number of reports.

The 7th survey on state aid in the EU was published (*COM*(1999) 148)

A report on state aid to the steel industry (*COM*(1999) 94) and a 12th report monitoring Art. 95 ECSC steel aid cases (*COM*(1999) 481)

Report on the application of the agreement between the EU and the US regarding the application of their competition laws (*COM*(1999) 439)

State aid and the single market (*European economy*. Reports and studies series, No. 3, 1999) ISBN 92828-7055-3 cat.no.CM-22-99-587-EN-C

Report on the application of EC state aid law by the Member State courts «http://europa.eu.int/comm/dg04/aid/en/app_by_member_states/index.htm»

A radical 'White Paper on modernisation of the rules implementing Articles 85 and 86 of EC Treaty' proposes that national competition authorities should take over the role of implementing EC competition rules (*COM*(1999) 101); also published in *OJ* C132 «http://europa.eu.int/comm/dg04/entente/en/wb_modernisation.pdf»

Consumers

Green Paper on liability for defective products was adopted on 28 July with the intention of assessing the need for changing existing legislation. (*COM*(1999) 396) «http://europa.eu.int/comm/dg15/en/update/consumer/99-580.htm»

Culture

Kaleidoscope programme report 1996–98 ISBN 9282842177

Economic and Monetary Issues

1999 annual economic report: the EU economy at the arrival of the euro; promoting growth, employment and stability (*COM*(99) 7). Reprinted in *European economy*, No. 67 (1999) ISSN 0379-0991 cat.no. CM-AR-99-001-EN-C

Commission's recommendations for the broad guidelines of the economic policies of the Member States and the Community (*COM*(99) 143. Reprinted in *European economy*, No. 68 (1999) ISSN 0379-0991 cat.no.CM-AR-99-002-EN-C together with texts related to the European Employment Pact

Both the above documents are available as pdf files from «http://europa.eu.int/comm/economy_finance/document/docum_en.htm/»

Economic and structural reform in the EU (Cardiff II) (*COM*(99) 61)

Economic reform: report on the functioning of Community product and capital markets; response to the Cardiff European Council (*COM*(99) 10)

Risk capital: implementation of the action plan; proposals for moving forward (*COM*(99) 493)

On 1 January a single European currency was introduced in the 11 countries participating in EMU. The European Central Bank («http://www.ecb.int/») began to issue a monthly bulletin, available on paper and online. ISSN 1561-0136

The impact of the changeover to the euro on Community policies, institutions and legislation; duration of the transitional period related to the introduction of the euro (Euro papers, No. 33–34). (Second report was also issued as (*COM*(99) 174))

Education, Training and R&D

Intercultural education in the EU: local, regional and interregional activities, examples of good practice (Committee of the Regions) ISBN 9282875962

Report on the implementation, results and overall assessment of the European Year of Lifelong Learning (1996) (*COM*(99) 447)

Report on the initial implementation phase of the Socrates programme, 1995–1997 (*COM*(99) 60)

Energy

In April the Commission adopted its second report on harmonization requirements *COM*(1999) 164

and in May its second report on the state of liberalization of energy markets *COM*(1999) 198

In April a working paper was adopted looking at ways of increasing the contribution of renewable energy *SEC*(1999) 470

In December both the Altener II programme on renewable energy sources and the SAVE II programme on promotion of energy efficiency were adopted *COM*(1999) 560 *COM*(1999) 558

Economic foundations for energy policy (*Energy in Europe* special issue, December 1999) ISBN 92-828-7529-6 cat.no. CS-24-99-114-3N-C)

EU energy outlook to 2020 (*Energy in Europe* special issue, November 1999) ISBN 92-828-7533-4 cat.no. CS-24-99-130-EN-C

Security of supply was an issue addressed, for example in the following documents: Security of EU gas supply (*COM*(99) 571)

Strengthening the northern dimension of European energy policy (*COM*(99) 548)

A large number of documents were published in 1999 by the Thermie Project of the Energy Directorate of the Commission on research into alternative energy sources.

Environment

The Commission made continued efforts towards the integration of environmental concerns into other policy areas. See, e.g:

Fisheries management and nature conservation in the marine environment *COM*(1999) 363 final

Directions toward sustainable agriculture *COM*(1999) 22 final

Single market and the environment *COM*(1999) 263 final

Integrating environment and sustainable development into economic and development co-operation policy *COM*(1999) 499 final

In addition to a large number of detailed legal instruments, a number of framework documents were published, including:

Preparing for implementation of the Kyoto protocol *COM*(1999) 230 final

Amended proposal for a European Parliament and Council directive establishing a framework for community action in the field of water policy *COM*(1999) 271 final

Proposal for a decision of the European Parliament and of the Council on a Community framework for co-operation to promote sustainable urban development *COM*(1999) 557 final

Most of these documents are available in full text from the Environment Directorate website at «http://europa.eu.int/comm/environment/docum/index.htm»

The subject of environmental impact assessment continues to be of crucial importance, as shown by these recent reports:

Database on environmental taxes in the EU Member States plus Norway and Switzerland: evaluation of effects of environmental taxes ISBN 92-828-5178-8 cat.no.CR-18-98-324-EN-C

Groundwater quality and quantity in Europe (European Environment Agency. Environmental assessment report, No. 3) ISBN 92-9167-146-0 cat.no.GH-18-98-607-EN-C

A handbook on environmental assessment of regional development plans and EU structural funds programmes: final report ISBN 92-828-5133-8 cat.no.CR-18-98-130-EN-C

A number of documents were issued by the European Consultative Forum on the Environment and Sustainable Development. Further details available from its website at «http://europa.eu.int/comm/environment/forum/home.htm»

The European Environment Agency produced a large number of reports (complete list available at «http://themes.eea.eu.int/everything.php»)

including, in June, a report entitled 'Environment in the European Union at the turn of the century' «http://themes.eea.eu.int/toc.php?toc=39179»

Fisheries

In April the Commission adopted a proposal for a regulation to widen the dialogue on effects of the Common Fisheries Policy (CFP) *OJ* L187, 20.7.99

A proposed regulation adopted in October aims to establish a framework for collection of data for managing the CFP *COM* (1999) 541

followed in November by a proposal setting out arrangements for the financing of Members States' expenditure in carrying out the CFP *COM*(1999) 551 final

The regulation setting Total Allowable Catches for 2000 was adopted in December *OJ* L341, 31.12.1999

Report from the Commission to the Council and the European Parliament on the application of the Community system for fisheries and aquaculture in 1996–1998 *COM* (2000) 15

Health

Fourth report on the integration of health protection requirements in Community policies (1999) (*COM*(99) 587)

'Best practice': state of the art and perspectives in the EU for improving the effectiveness and efficiency of European health systems ISBN 9282879348 cat.no. CE-24-99-259-EN-C

Health and safety at work in Europe: reference texts (Employment and social affairs) ISBN 9282875075 cat.no.CE-10-97-170-EN-C

Health and safety at work in Europe – where next? (Employment and social affairs) ISBN 9282873773

Health technology assessment in Europe: the challenge of co-ordination (Employment and social affairs) ISBN 9282876292 cat.no. CE-23-99-007-EN-C

Interim report … on the implementation of Community action … in the field of public health (*COM*(99) 463)

Progress achieved in relation to public health protection from the harmful effects of tobacco consumption (*COM*(99) 407)

Report on the evaluation of the 2nd action plan of the 'Europe against cancer' programme 1990–1994, plus 1995 (*COM*(99) 408)

Information Society

Public sector information: a key resource for Europe; Green Paper on public sector information in the information society (*COM*(99) 585)

Internal Market

Assessment of the single market plan June 1997–December 1998 (*COM*(99) 74)

Justice and Home Affairs

The adoption of the Amsterdam Treaty incorporated the questions of visas, asylum, immigration and judicial co-operation in civil matters into the framework of the EC Treaty.

Europol took up its full activities on 1 July 1999. «http://www.europol.nl/home.htm»

Affirming fundamental rights in the EU: Report of the Expert Group on Fundamental Rights (Employment and social affairs) ISBN 92-828-6605-x cat.no. CE-21-99-181-EN-C

Communication on the implementation of measures to combat child sex tourism (*COM*(99) 262)

First European meeting of the main partners in the fight against child sex tourism (proceedings of a conference in Brussels, 24–25 November 1998) ISBN 92-828-7463-X cat.no. CT-18-99-669-3A-C

Communication on the special measures concerning the movement and residence of citizens of the Union which are justified on grounds of public policy, public security or public health (*COM*(99) 372)

Countering racism, xenophobia and anti-semitism in the candidate countries (*COM*(99) 256)

Social Policy and the Labour Market

The 1999 employment guidelines: Council resolution of 22 February 1999

Communication on a EU action plan to combat drugs (2000–2004) (*COM*(99) 239)

Communication on certain Community measures to combat discrimination (*COM*(99) 564)

Community policies in support of employment (*COM*(99) 167)

The European Employment Pact – investing in people, was adopted by the European Council in June ISBN 92828-2194-3 «http://europa.eu.int/comm/dg05/empl&esf/empl2000/invest_en.pdf»

The modernization of public employment services in Europe: three key documents (employment and social affairs) ISBN 92828-7694-2 cat.no. CE-24-99-194-EN-C

The issue of an ageing population and the future provision of pensions was the subject of a number of publications, including:

Towards a Europe for all ages: promoting prosperity and intergenerational solidarity (*COM*(99) 221)

Towards a single market for supplementary pensions: results of the consultations on the Green Paper ... (*COM*(99) 134)

Structural Policy

European Development Fund (EDF): estimate of the contributions needed for expenditure in the 2000 financial year and forecast ... (*COM*(99) 688)

Evaluating socio-economic programmes (MEANS collection) (6 vol. set) ISBN 92-828-6626-2 cat.no. CX-10-99-000-EN-C

Transport

Communication on integrating conventional rail systems (*COM*(99) 617)

Communication on ... intermodality and intermodal freight transport in the EU (*COM*(99) 519)

Moving forward: the achievements of the European Common Transport Policy ISBN 92-828-7994-1 cat.no. C3-16-98-134-EN-C

Report on ... national road passenger transport services within a Member State (*COM*(99) 327)

Report ... on the procurement of air traffic management equipment and systems (*COM*(99) 454)

Report on ... the trans-European high-speed rail system (*COM*(99) 414)

Trans-European networks: 1998 annual report (*COM*(99) 410)

III. External Policies and Relations

Asia

The EU and Macau: beyond 2000 (*COM*(1999) 481)

Common Foreign and Security Policy (CFSP)

In the aftermath of the conflict in the former Yugoslavia and its neighbours, the Commission established a Stabilisation and Association Process for countries of south eastern Europe (*COM* (99) 235 – 26.05.1999 «http://europa.eu.int/comm/dg1a/see/com_99_235/index.htm»

More details are available from the EU/World Bank website Economic Reconstruction and Development in south east Europe «http://www.seerecon.org/»

The Council published a common strategy of the EU on Russia (*OJ* L157 24.06.1999 pp. 1–10)

The Commission reported on the Russian crisis and its impact on the new independent states and Mongolia (*COM*(1999) 8) and on relations with the South Caucasus, under the partnership and co-operation agreements (*COM*(1999) 272)

PHARE Programme annual report 1997 (*COM*(1999) 234)

TACIS annual report 1998 (*COM*(1999) 380

The Conclusions of the Finnish Presidency in Helsinki 10–11 December 1999 included important statements about the enlargement process and the common foreign and security policy. «http://europa.eu.int/comm/external_relations/news/12_99/doc_99_16.htm»

Developing Countries

Communication on a Community participation in the debt relief initiative for highly indebted poor countries (HIPC) (*COM*(99) 518)

The EC's response to the challenges of the International Conference on Population and Development: ICPD + 5, a 5-year review 1994–1998

Financial information on the European Development Funds (*COM*(99) 323)

Forests and development: the EC approach (*COM*(99) 554)

Guidelines for the participation to [sic] the 10th UN Conference on Trade and Development (*COM*(99) 451)

Integrating environment and sustainable development into economic and development co-operation policy: elements of a comprehensive strategy (*COM*(99) 499)

The status of OCTs [overseas countries and territories] associated with the EC and options for 'OCT 2000' (*COM*(99) 163) 2 vols.

A trade, development and co-operation agreement with South Africa was signed on 9 July (but not yet ratified because of disputes over spirits) (*OJ* L311, 4.12.1999) «http://europa.eu.int/comm/development/south_africa/agreement.pdf»

Enlargement

Report updating the Commission opinion on Malta's application for membership (*COM*(99) 69)

Regular reports from the Commission on progress towards accession of 13 applicant countries (including Cyprus, Malta and Turkey) were published as *COM*(1999) 501- 513. Also available on the Enlargement website at «http://europa.eu.int/comm/ enlargement/index.htm»

Enlargement and the reforms which will be necessary in the European institutions are two of the main topics on the agenda of the forthcoming Intergovernmental Confer- ence. Two Commission discussion documents on the subject were presented:

Adapting the institutions to make a success of enlargement (10 November 1999) (*COM*(2000) 34) also: *Bulletin of the EU*, Supplement 2/2000 ISBN 92-828-8897-5 cat.no. KA-NF-00-002-EN-C «http://europa.eu.int/igc2000/prep_igc_en.pdf»

The institutional implications of enlargement: Report to the European Commission – ('Dehaene–von Weizsäcker–Simon' report) (18 October 1999) «http://europa.eu.int/ igc2000/repoct99_en.htm»

External Trade

The Millennium Round of negotiations between WTO member countries took place in Seattle 30 November–3 December. Three reports put the EU's case:

The EU approach to the WTO Millennium Round (*COM*(99) 331)
EU-Millennium Round (3rd WTO Ministerial Conference, Seattle) (folder)
ISBN 92-828-6595-9 cat.no.CN-21-99-513-EN-C

'The Millennium Round: An Economic Appraisal' by Nigel Nagarajan (DG Finance. Economic papers, no.139) ECFIN/659/99

Latin America

The First EU–Latin America and Caribbean summit was held in Rio de Janeiro on 28– 29 June. The Rio declaration states the EU's intention to co-operate with Latin America in social, economic and political matters.

Bulletin of the EU 6-1999 pp.147–55 and later elaborated as Communication on a new EU–Latin America partnership on the eve of the 21st century (*COM*(1999) 105) «http://europa.eu.int/en/comm/dg1b/pol-orientations/en/en-projet.htm»

Communication on a Community action plan for the reconstruction of Central America (*COM*(1999) 201)

Mediterranean

Annual report of the MEDA programme 1998 (*COM*(99) 291)

Journal of Common Market Studies

Volume 38, Annual Review
September 2000

Books on European Integration

BRIAN ARDY
South Bank University
and
JACKIE GOWER
University of Kent at Canterbury

The following list includes all books submitted to the *Journal of Common Market Studies* during 1999, whether these were reviewed or not. Each book is entered only once even though, inevitably, some titles are of relevance to more than one section.

General Studies

Blair, A: *The European Union since 1945* (Harlow, Pearson Education, 1999, ISBN 0582368847) xv+384pp., pb £17.99.

Demain, F and Lejeune, Y (eds): *Annales d'études Européennes de l'Université Catholique de Louvain, 1998–1999* (Brussels, Bruylant, 1999, ISBN 2802712934) x+289pp., pb BEF 2,500.

Dinan, D: *Ever Closer Union: An Introduction to European Integration* (Basingstoke, Macmillan, 1999, 2nd edn, ISBN 0333732421) xii+598pp., pb £15.50.

Editions Delta: *Euro-Guide: Yearbook of the Institutions of the European Union and of the Other European Organisations* (Brussels, Editions Delta, 1999, ISBN 2802901354) 632pp., hb £130.00.

Edwards, G and Wiessala, G (eds): *The European Union: Annual Review 1998/1999* (Oxford, Blackwell Publishers, 1999, ISBN 0631215980) vi+254pp., pb £15.99 / US$32.95.

Lane, J E and Ersson, S: *Politics and Society in Western Europe* (London, Sage, 1999, 4th edn, ISBN hb 0761958614, pb 0761958622) vii+386pp., hb £55.00, pb £17.99.

McCormick, J: *Understanding the European Union: A Concise Introduction* (Basingstoke, Macmillan, 1999, ISBN hb 0333738985, pb 0333738993) xvii+251pp., hb £40.00, pb £12.99.

McCormick, J: *The European Union: Politics and Policies* (Oxford, Westview, 1999, 2nd edn, ISBN 081339032X) xvi+320pp., pb £17.50.

Mattli, W: *The Logic of Regional Integration: Europe and Beyond* (Cambridge, Cambridge University Press, 1999, ISBN hb 0521632277, pb 0521635365) ix+205pp., hb £35.00, pb £11.95.

Padgett, S: *Organizing Democracy in Eastern Europe: Interest Groups in Post-Communist Society* (Cambridge, Cambridge University Press, 1999, ISBN hb 0521651700, pb 0521657032) x+200pp., hb £35.00 US$57.95, pb £13.95 US$21.95.

Pennings, P, Keman, H and Kleinnijenhuis, J: *Doing Research in Political Science: An Introduction to Comparative Methods and Statistics* (London, Sage Publications, 1999, ISBN hb 0761951024, pb 0761951032) xi+368pp., hb £55.00, pb £16.99.

Pond, E: *The Rebirth of Europe* (Washington, D.C., Brookings, 1999, ISBN hb 0815771576, pb 0815771584) xiii+290pp., hb np, pb £20.95 $26.95.

Schulze, M S (ed): *Western Europe: Economic and Social Change Since 1945* (Harlow, Addison Wesley Longman, 1998, ISBN 0582291992) xiv+408pp., pb £19.99.

Stirk, P M R and Weigall, D (eds): *The Origins and Development of European Integration: A Reader and Commentary* (London, Cassell, 1999, ISBN hb 1855675161, pb 185567517X) xvi+336pp., hb £55.00, pb £18.99.

Tiersky, R (ed): *Europe Today: National Politics, European Integration, and European Security* (Maryland, USA, Rowman & Littlefield, 1999, ISBN hb 084768590X, 0847685918) x+492pp., hb £50.00, pb £18.95.

Weidenfeld, W and Wessels, W (eds): *Jahrbuch der Europäischen Integration 1997/98* (Bonn, Europa Union Verlag, 1998, ISBN 3771305659) 557pp., pb np.

Weidenfeld, W and Wessels, W(eds): *Jahrbuch der Europäischen Integration 1998/99* (Bonn, Europa Union Verlag, 1999, ISBN 3771305802) 560pp., pb np.

Government and Institutions

Anderson, J J (ed): *Regional Integration and Democracy* (Maryland, USA, Rowman & Littlefield, 1999, ISBN hb 0847690245, pb 0847690253) viii+334pp., hb $65.00 £45.00, pb £18.95 $24.95.

Banchoff, B & Smith, M P (eds): *Legitimacy and the European Union: The Contested Polity* (London, Routledge, 1999, ISBN hb 0415181887, pb 0415181895) x+226pp., hb £45.00, pb £17.99.

Coombes, D: *Seven Theorems in Search of the European Parliament* (London, Federal Trust, 1999, ISBN 0901573701) vii+70pp., pb £9.99.

Duina, F G: *Harmonizing Europe: Nation-States Within the Common Market* (New York, State University of New York Press, 1999, ISBN 0791441784) xvi+176pp., pb £14.75 $18.95.

Dyson, K and Featherstone, K: *The Road to Maastricht: Negotiating Economic and Monetary Union* (New York, Oxford University Press, 1999, ISBN hb 0198280777, pb 019829638X) xxiii+859pp., hb £75.00, pb £25.00.

Endo, K: *The Presidency of the European Commission Under Jacques Delors: The Politics of Shared Leadership* (Basingstoke, Macmillan, 1999, ISBN 0333721012) xx+260pp., hb £45.00.

Héritier, A: *Policy-Making and Diversity in Europe: Escape from Deadlock* (Cambridge, Cambridge University Press, 1999, ISBN hb 0521652960, pb 0521653843) vi+113pp., hb £35.00, pb £11.95.

Hocking, B (ed): *Foreign Ministries: Change and Adaptation* (Basingstoke, Macmillan, 1999, ISBN hb 033369242X, pb 0333692438) xiv+281pp., hb £45.00, pb £16.99.

Joerges, C and Vos, E (eds): *EU Committees: Social Regulation, Law and Politics* (Oxford, Hart Publishing, 1999, ISBN 190136268X) xxxiii+410pp., hb £30.00.

Jopp, M, Maurer, A and Schmuck, O (eds): *Die Europäische Union nach Amsterdam: Analysen und Stellungnahmen zum Neuen EU-Vertrag* (Bonn, Institut für Europäische Politik, 1998, ISBN 3771305640) 361pp., pb np.

Jopp, M, Maurer, A and Schneider, H (eds): *Europapolitische Grundverständnisse im Wandel: Analysen und Konsequenzen für die Politische Bildung* (Bonn, Institut für Europäische Politik, 1998, ISBN 3771305691) 571pp., pb np.

Laffan, B, O'Donnell, R and Smith, M: *Europe's Experimental Union: Rethinking Integration* (London, Routledge, 1999, ISBN hb 041510260X, pb 0415102618) xii+244pp., hb £55.00, pb £17.99.

Lord, C: *Democracy in the European Union* (Sheffield, Sheffield Academic Press / UACES, 1998, ISBN 1850758689) 148pp., pb £10.95.

MacCormick, N: *Questioning Sovereignty* (New York, Oxford University Press, 1999, ISBN 0198268769) x+210pp., hb £40.00.

McLaughlin, A M and Maloney, W A: *The European Automobile Industry: Multi-Level Governance, Policy and Politics* (London, Routledge, 1999, ISBN 0415113296) xii+256pp., hb £50.00.

Martin, R: *The Regional Dimension in European Public Policy: Convergence or Divergence?* (Basingstoke, Macmillan, 1999, ISBN 0333746716) xx+197pp., hb £42.50.

Miller, W E, Pierce, R, Thomassen, J, Herrera, R, Holmberg, S, Esaiasson, P and Wessels, B: *Policy Representation in Western Democracies* (New York, Oxford University Press, 1999, ISBN 0198295707) x+180pp., hb £40.00.

Ojanen, H: *The Plurality of Truth: A Critique of Research on the State and European Integration* (Aldershot, Ashgate, 1998, ISBN 1840144025) xii+377pp., hb £42.50.

Pinder, J (ed): *Foundations of Democracy in the European Union: From the Genesis of Parliamentary Democracy to the European Parliament* (Basingstoke, Macmillan, 1999, ISBN 0333774701) xii+151pp., hb £42.50.

Radaelli, C M: *Technocracy in the European Union* (London, Addison Wesley Longman, 1999, ISBN 0582304938) x+174pp., pb £12.99.

Scharpf, F: *Governing in Europe: Effective and Democratic?* (New York, Oxford University Press, 1999, ISBN hb 0198295456, pb 0198295464) viii+243pp., hb £40.00, pb £15.99.

Shapiro, I: *Democratic Justice* (London, Yale University Press, 1999, ISBN 0300078250) xiii+333pp., hb £20.00.

Shapiro, I and Hacker-Cordón, C (eds): *Democracy's Value* (Cambridge, Cambridge University Press, 1999, ISBN hb 0521643570, pb 0521643880) xiii+201pp., hb £35.00 $49.95, pb £12.95 $18.95.

Shapiro, I and Hacker-Cordón, C (eds): *Democracy's Edges* (Cambridge, Cambridge University Press, 1999, ISBN hb 0521643562, pb 0521643899) xiii+297pp., hb £35.00 $54.95, pb £12.95 $19.95.

Smith, D A, Solinger, D J and Topik, S C (eds): *States and Sovereignty in the Global Economy* (London, Routledge, 1999, ISBN hb 0415201195, pb 0415201209) xiii+288pp., hb £55.00, pb £18.99.

Smith, J: *Europe's Elected Parliament* (Sheffield, Sheffield Academic Press / UAC-ES, 1999, ISBN 1850759995) 198pp., pb £10.95.

van Deth, JW (ed): *Comparative Politics: The Problem of Equivalence* (London, Routledge, 1998, ISBN 0415192455) xii+278pp., hb £60.00.

Westlake, M: *The Council of the European Union* (London, John Harper Publishing, 1999, 2nd edn, ISBN 0953627802) xxv+417pp., hb £41.50.

Internal Policies and the Law

Ackers, L: *Shifting Spaces: Women, Citizenship and Migration within the European Union* (Bristol, Policy Press, 1999, ISBN hb 186134127X, pb 1861340389) vii+343pp., hb £45.00, pb £18.99.

Arnull, A: *The European Union and its Court of Justice* (Oxford, Oxford University Press, 1999, ISBN hb 0198258984, pb 0198298811) lxxxiii+593pp., hb £65.00, pb £29.99.

Bache, I: *The Politics of European Union Regional Policy: Multi-Level Governance or Flexible Gatekeeping?* (Sheffield, Sheffield Academic Press / UACES, 1998, ISBN 1850758638) 172pp., pb £10.95.

Beaumont, P and Walker, N (eds): *Legal Framework of the Single European Currency* (Oxford, Hart Publishing, 1999, ISBN 184113001X) xx+204pp., hb £30.00.

Dashwood, A and Ward, A (eds): *The Cambridge Yearbook of European Legal Studies: Volume One 1998* (Oxford, Hart Publishing, 1999, ISBN 1841130885) xxxvii+313pp., hb £55.00.

Dickie, J: *Internet and Electronic Commerce Law in the European Union* (Oxford, Hart Publishing, 1999, ISBN 1841130311) xxii+154pp., pb £30.00.

Hantrais, L (ed): *Gendered Policies in Europe: Reconciling Employment and Family Life* (Basingstoke, Macmillan, 1999, ISBN 0333739825) xii+228pp., hb £42.50.

Ibañez, A G: *The Administrative Supervision and Enforcement of EC Law: Powers, Procedures and Limits* (Oxford, Hart Publishing, 1999, ISBN 1841130567) xliv+356pp., hb £35.00.

Jones, C A: *Private Enforcement of Antitrust Law in the EU, UK and USA* (Oxford, Oxford University Press, 1999, ISBN 0198268688) xliii+263pp., hb np.

Keppenne, J P: *Guide des aides d'état en droit communautaire: réglementation, jurisprudence et pratique de la Commission* (Brussels, Établissements Émile Bruylant, 1999, ISBN 2802712306) xvi+693pp., pb BEF 3,800.

Levy, D A: *Europe's Digital Revolution: Broadcasting Regulation, the EU and the Nation State* (London, Routledge, 1999, ISBN 0415171962) xvi+208pp., hb £55.00.

Lott Jr, J R: *Are Predatory Commitments Credible? Who Should the Courts Believe?* (Chicago, University of Chicago Press, 1999, ISBN 0226493555) x+173pp., hb £20.50.

Magnette, P: *La citoyenneté Européenne* (Brussels, Brussels University Press, 1999, ISBN 2800412224) 249pp., pb BEF 850 FF 157.

Mathijsen, P S R F: *A Guide to European Union Law* (London, Sweet and Maxwell, 1999, 7th edn, ISBN 0421635002) lxxxii+537pp., pb £26.00.

Nehl, H P: *Principles of Administrative Procedure in EC Law* (Oxford, Hart Publishing, 1999, ISBN 1841130087) xx+214pp., hb £27.50.

Rider, B A K and Andenas, M (eds): *Developments in European Company Law: Vol 2/1997: The Quest for an Ideal Legal Form for Small Businesses* (London, Kluwer Law International, 1999, ISBN 9041196978) xviii+171pp., hb £43.00.

Taylor, P M: *EC and UK Competition Law and Compliance* (London, Sweet and Maxwell, 1999, ISBN 042168030X) l+602pp., hb £75.00.

Tupman, B and Tupman, A: *Policing in Europe: Uniform in Diversity* (Exeter, Intellect Books, 1999, ISBN 1871516900) iv+107pp., pb £9.95.

Tuytschaever, F: *Differentiation in European Law* (Oxford, Hart Publishing, 1999, ISBN 1841130729) xxxiv+298pp., hb £30.00.

United Nations: *Bilateral Investment Treaties in the Mid-1990s* (Geneva, United Nations, 1998, ISBN 9211124301) xii+305pp., pb $46.00.

Vos, E: *Institutional Frameworks of Community Health and Safety Regulation: Committees, Agencies and Private Bodies* (Oxford, Hart Publishing, 1999, ISBN 1901362744) xlvi+360pp., hb £30.00.

Weiler, J H H: *The Constitution of Europe: 'Do the New Clothes Have an Emperor?' and Other Essays on European Integration* (Cambridge, Cambridge University Press, 1999, ISBN hb 0521584736, pb 0521585678) xvi+364pp., hb £40.00, pb £14.95.

Wrench, J, Rea, A and Ouali, N (eds): *Migrants, Ethnic Minorities and the Labour Market: Integration and Exclusion in Europe* (Basingstoke, Macmillan, 1999, ISBN 0333682793) xii+274pp., hb £45.00.

Zito, A R: *Creating Environmental Policy in the European Union* (Basingstoke, Macmillan, 1999, ISBN hb 0333722140) xii+225pp., hb £42.50.

External Relations and Developments

Brack, D, Grubb, M and Windram, C: *International Trade and Climate Change Policies* (London, Royal Institute of International Affairs, 1999, ISBN 1853836206) xxiii+140pp., pb £15.95.

Bretherton, C and Vogler, J: *The European Union as a Global Actor* (London, Routledge, 1999, ISBN hb 0415150523, pb 0415150531) xii+316pp., hb £60.00, pb £18.99.

Cameron, F: *The Foreign and Security Policy of the European Union: Past, Present and Future* (Sheffield, Sheffield Academic Press / UACES, 1999, ISBN 1841270016) 158pp., pb £10.95.

Cosgrove-Sacks, C (ed): *The European Union and Developing Countries: The Challenges of Globalization* (Basingtoke, Macmillan, 1999, ISBN 0333718356) xxiii+365pp., hb £55.00.

de Wilde d'Estmael, T: *La dimension politique des relations économiques extérieures de la Communauté Européenne* (Brussels, Etablissements Emile Bruylant, 1998, ISBN 2802711954) xvii+445pp., pb BEF 2,900.

Dent, C M: *The European Union and East Asia: An Economic Relationship* (London, Routledge, 1999, ISBN hb 0415171997, pb 0415172004) xvii+316pp., hb £65.00, pb £21.99.

Duke, S: *The Elusive Quest for European Security: From EDC to CFSP* (Basingstoke, Macmillan, 1999, ISBN 0333777980) xvii+406pp., hb £50.00.

Hocking, B and McGuire, S (eds): *Trade Politics: International, Domestic and Regional Perspectives* (London, Routledge, 1999, ISBN hb 0415193567, pb 0415193575) xx+316pp., hb £60.00, pb £19.99.

King, R, Lazaridis, G and Tsardanidis, C (eds): *Eldorado or Fortress? Migration in Southern Europe* (Basingstoke, Macmillan / St. Martin's Press, 1999, ISBN 0333747909) xiv+351pp., hb £52.50.

Lavendex, S: *Safe Third Countries: Extending the EU Asylum and Immigration Policies to Central and Eastern Europe* (Budapest, Central European University Press, 1999, ISBN 9639116440) xii+192pp., pb £13.95.

Lister, M (ed): *New Perspectives on European Union Development Cooperation* (Colorado, Westview, 1999, ISBN 0813337127) viii+175pp., hb £46.50.

Mace, G, Bélanger, L, *et al*: *The Americas in Transition: The Contours of Regionalism* (London, Lynne Rienner, 1999, ISBN 1555877176) x+297pp., hb £43.95.

Murray, P and Holmes, L: *Europe: Rethinking the Boundaries* (Aldershot, Ashgate, 1998, ISBN 1840140038) xii+179pp., hb £40.50.

Phinnemore, D: *Association: Stepping Stone or Alternative to EU Membership?* (Sheffield, Sheffield Academic Press / UACES, 1999, ISBN 1841270008) 168pp., pb £10.95.

Rotfeld, A D (ed): *Sipri Yearbook 1999: Armaments, Disarmament and International Security* (New York, Oxford University Press, 1999, ISBN 0198296460) xxxvi+772pp., hb £60.00.

Segal-Horn, S and Faulkner, D: *The Dynamics of International Strategy* (London, International Thomson Business Press, 1999, ISBN 1861520158) xi+286pp., pb £19.99.

van Brabant, J M (ed): *Remaking Europe: The European Union and the Transition Economies* (Lanham, Rowman & Littlefield, 1999, ISBN hb 0847693236, pb 0847693244) xix+269pp., hb $64.00, pb $23.95.

Zielinska-Gtebocka, A and Stepniak, A (eds): *EU Adjustment to Eastern Enlargement: Polish and European Perspective* (Gdansk, Fundacja Rozwoju Uniwersytetu Gdanskiego, 1998, ISBN 8386230479) 338pp., pb np.

Economic Developments in Europe and Beyond

Amtenbrink, F: *The Democratic Accountability of Central Banks: A Comparative Study of the European Central Bank* (Oxford, Hart Publishing, 1999, ISBN 1841130427) xlii+417pp., hb £55.00.

Andersen, T M, Hougarrd Jensen, S E and Risager, O (eds): *Macroeconomic Perspectives on the Danish Economy* (Basingstoke, Macmillan, 1999, ISBN 0333733312) xv+376pp., hb £66.00.

Audretsch, D B and Thurik, R: *Innovation, Industry Evolution, and Employment* (Cambridge, Cambridge University Press, 1999, ISBN 0521641667) vii+321pp., hb £30.00 / $64.95.

Baldwin, R E, Cohen, D, Sapir, A and Venables, A (eds): *Market Integration, Regionalism and the Global Economy* (Cambridge, Cambridge University Press, 1999, ISBN hb 0521641810, pb 0521645891) xix+344pp., hb £45.00 $74.95, pb £16.95 $27.95..

Barrell, R and Pain, N (eds): *Innovation, Investment and the Diffusion of Technology in Europe: German Direct Investment and Economic Growth in Postwar Europe* (Cambridge, Cambridge Univevrsity Press, 1999, ISBN hb 0521620872, pb 0952621371) ix+194pp., hb £35.00, pb £18.50.

Begg, D, Halpern L, and Wyplosz, C: *Monetary and Exchange Rate Policies, EMU and Central and Eastern Europe, Forum Report of the Economic Policy Initiative No. 5* (London, Centre for Economic Policy Research, 1999, ISBN 1898128413) xiv+108pp., pb £25.00.

Begg, I and Grimwade, N: *Paying for Europe* (Sheffield, Sheffield Academic Press / UACES, 1998, ISBN 1850758581) 200pp., pb £10.95.

Bergman, L, Brunekreeft, G, Doyle, C, von de Fehr, N H M, Newbery, D M, Pollitt, M and Régibeau, P: *A European Market for Electricity? Monitoring European Deregulation 2* (London, Centre for Economic Policy Research, 1999, ISBN 1898128421) xxiii+294pp., pb £30.00 $45.00.

Bishop, S and Walker, M: *The Economics of EC Competition Law: Concepts, Application and Measurement* (London, Sweet and Maxwell, 1999, ISBN 0421579404) xxxi+356pp., hb £95.00.

Caesar, R and Scharrer, H E (eds): *Die Europäische Wirtschafts und Währungsunion: Regionale und Globale Herausforderungen* (Bonn, Europa Union Verlag, 1998, ISBN 3771305713) 482pp., pb np.

Cobham, D and Zis, G (eds): *From EMS to EMU: 1979 to 1999 and Beyond* (Basingstoke, Macmillan, 1999, ISBN hb 0333770919, pb 031222799X) x+294pp., hb £45.00.

Cowie, H: *Venture Capital in Europe* (London, Federal Trust, 1999, ISBN 0901573868) 60pp., pb £12.95.

Cowling, K (ed): *Industrial Policy in Europe: Theoretical Perspectives and Practical Proposals* (London, Routledge, 1999, ISBN 0415204933) x+383pp., hb £65.00.

Danthine, J P, Giavazzi, F, Vives, X and von Thadden, E L: *The Future of European Banking, Monitoring European Integration No. 9* (London, Centre for Economic Policy Research, 1999, ISBN 1898128383) xxii+118pp., pb £25.00.

de Wit, B and Meyer, R: *Strategy Synthesis: Resolving Strategy Paradoxes to Create Competitive Advantage* (London, International Thomson Business Press, 1999, ISBN 1861523173) xvi+519pp., pb £22.99.

Deprez, J and Harvey, J T (eds): *Foundations of International Economics: Post Keynesian Perspectives* (London, Routledge, 1999, ISBN hb 041514650X, pb 0415146518) x+283pp., hb £60.00, pb £19.99.

Deutsche Bundesbank (ed): *Fifty Years of the Deutsche Mark: Central Bank and the Currency in Germany since 1948* (Oxford, Oxford University Press, 1999, ISBN 0198292546) xxvi+836pp., hb £50.00.

Duff, A: *The Unforeseeable Circumstances of Mr Gordon Brown* (London, Federal Trust, 1999, ISBN 0901573892) 32pp., pb £4.99.

Dyker, D A (ed): *The European Economy* (Harlow, Addison Wesley Longman, 1999, 2nd edn, ISBN 0582298032) xiii+439pp., pb £21.99.

El-Agraa, A M: *Regional Integration: Experience, Theory and Measurement* (Basingstoke, Macmillan, 1999, 2nd edn, ISBN 0333764609) xii+442pp., hb £60.00.

Eliassen, K A and Sjovaag, M (eds): *European Telecommunications Liberalisation* (London, Routledge, 1999, ISBN 0415187818) xx+298pp., hb £55.00.

Elliott, R, Lucifora, C and Meurs, D (eds): *Public Sector Pay Determination in the European Union* (Basingstoke, Macmillan, 1999, ISBN 0333745981) xx+350pp., hb £60.00.

Esping-Andersen, G: *Social Foundations of Post-industrial Economies* (New York, Oxford University Press, 1999, ISBN hb 0198742010, pb 0198742002) 207pp., hb £40.00, pb £15.99.

Frieden, J, Gros, D and Jones, E (eds): *The New Political Economy of the EMU* (Oxford, Rowman & Littlefield, 1998, ISBN hb 0847690180, pb 0847690199) ix+205pp., hb £51.00 $65.00, £18.95 $24.95.

Gabrisch, H and Pohl, R (eds): *EU Enlargement and its Macroeconomic Effects in Eastern Europe: Currencies, Prices, Investment and Competitiveness* (Basingstoke, Macmillan, 1999, ISBN 0333735498) xxiii+227pp., hb £47.50.

Gambardella, A and Malerba, F (eds): *The Organization of Economic Innovation in Europe* (Cambridge, Cambridge University Press, 1999, ISBN 0521643031) x+396pp., hb £45.00.

Haltiwanger, J, Manser, M E and Topel, R (eds): *Labor Statistics Measurement Issues* (Chicago, University of Chicago Press, 1999, ISBN 0226314588) xii+478pp., hb £47.95.

Heisenberg, D: *The Mark of the Bundesbank: Germany's Role in European Monetary Cooperation* (London, Lynne Rienner, 1998, ISBN 1555876897) x+214pp., hb £39.95.

Hood, N and Young, S (eds): *The Globalization of Multinational Enterprise Activity and Economic Development* (Basingstoke, Macmillan, 1999, ISBN 0333748816) xvi+418pp., hb £45.00.

Hughes Hallett, A, Hutchison, M M and Hougaard Jensen, S E: *Fiscal Aspects of European Monetary Integration* (Cambridge, Cambridge University Press, 1999, ISBN 052165162X) x+351pp., hb £45.00 $69.95.

Lamfalussy, A, Bernard, L D and Cabral, A J (eds): *The Euro-Zone: A New Economic Entity?* (Brussels, Bruylant, 1999, ISBN 2802713027) 153pp., pb BEF 1,600.

Lamoreaux, N R, Raff, D M G and Temin, P (eds): *Learning by Doing in Markets, Firms, and Countries* (London, University of Chicago Press, 1999, ISBN hb 0226468321, pb 0226468348) viii+347pp., hb £51.95, pb £17.95.

Loedel, P H: *Deutsche Mark Politics: Germany in the European Monetary System* (London, Lynne Rienner, 1999, ISBN 1555878350) xiv+261pp., hb £43.95.

McLoughlin, I: *Creative Technological Change: The Shaping of Technology and Organisations* (London, Routledge, 1999, ISBN hb 0415179998, pb 0415180007) xi+188pp., hb np, pb £19.99.

Martin, A, Ross, G, *et al.: The Brave New World of European Labor: European Trade Unions at the Millennium* (New York, Berghahn Books, 1999, ISBN hb 1571811672, pb 1571811680) xv+416pp., hb £50.00, pb £16.50.

Michie, J and Grieve Smith, J (eds): *Global Instability: The Political Economy of World Economic Governance* (London, Routledge, 1999, ISBN hb 0415202221, pb 041520223X) x+260pp., hb £55.00, pb £17.99.

Moore, L: *Britain's Trade and Economic Structure: The Impact of the European Union* (London, Routledge, 1999, ISBN hb 0415169208, pb 0415169216) xix+395pp., hb £65.00., pb £21.99.

Shipman, A: *The Market Revolution and its Limits: A Price for Everything* (London, Routledge, 1999, ISBN hb 0415157366, pb 0415157358) viii+493pp., hb £70.00, pb £22.99.

Sutcliffe, P (ed): *World Investment Report: 1999 Foreign Direct Investment and the Challenge of Development* (Geneva, United Nations, 1999, ISBN 9211124409) xxxiv+541pp., pb £34.00 $49.00.

Taylor, J B (ed): *Monetary Policy Rules* (Chicago, University of Chicago Press, 1999, ISBN 0226791246) ix+447pp., hb £49.00.

Trebilcock, M J and Howse, R: *The Regulation of International Trade* (London, Routledge, 1999, 2nd edn, ISBN hb 0415184975, pb 0415184983) xii+612pp., hb £75.00, pb £22.99.

van der Linden, J: *Interdependence and Specialisation in the European Union: Intercountry Input–Output Analysis and Economic Integration* (Capelle, Labyrint Publication, 1999, ISBN 9072591615) viii+304pp., pb np.

Ward, H and Brack, D (eds): *Trade, Investment and the Environment* (London, Royal Institute of International Affairs, 1999, ISBN 1853836281) xxxviii+298pp., pb £18.95.

Member States

Allen, C S (ed): *Transformation of the German Political Party System: Institutional Crisis or Democratic Renewal?* (New York, Berghahn Books, 1999, ISBN 1571811273) xviii+265pp., hb £45.00.

Anderson, J: *German Unification and the Union of Europe* (Cambridge, Cambridge University Press, 1999, ISBN hb 0521643554, pb 0521643902) xii+227pp., hb £35.00, pb £12.95.

Anderson, P J and Weymouth, A: *Insulting the Public? The British Press and the European Union* (Harlow, Addison Wesley Longman, 1999, ISBN 0582317401) ix+230pp., pb £13.99.

Clemens, C and Paterson, W E (eds): *The Kohl Chancellorship* (London, Frank Cass, 1998, ISBN hb 0714648906, pb 0714644412) vii+166pp., hb £32.00, pb £14.50.

Corkill, D: *The Development of the Portuguese Economy: A Case of Europeanization* (London, Routledge, 1999, ISBN hb 0415145740) xxii+259pp., hb £60.00.

Forster, A: *Britain and the Maastricht Negotiations* (Basingstoke, Macmillan, 1999, ISBN 0333731700) ix+211pp., hb £42.50.

Lankowski, C (ed): *Breakdown, Breakup, Breakthrough: Germany's Difficult Passage to Modernity* (New York, Berghahn Books, 1999, ISBN 1571812113) xix+233pp., hb £35.00.

Lejeune, Y (ed): *La participation de la Belgique à l'élaboration et à la mise en œuvre du droit Européen* (Brussels, Bruylant, 1999, ISBN 2802713159) 813pp., pb BEF 5,200.

Marsh, P T: *Bargaining on Europe: Britain and the First Common Market 1860–1892* (London, Yale University Press, 1999, ISBN 0300081030) viii+246pp., hb £22.50.

Merkl, P H (ed): *The Federal Republic of Germany at Fifty: The End of a Century of Turmoil* (Basingstoke, Macmillan, 1999, ISBN hb 0333725611, pb 0333770420) xv+373pp., hb £60.00, pb £19.50.

Padgett, S and Saalfeld, T (eds): *Bundestagswahl '98: End of an Era?* (London, Frank Cass, 1999, ISBN hb 0714650196, pb 0714680761) 214pp., hb £32.50, pb £16.50.

Pinder, J (ed): *Altiero Spinelli and the British Federalists* (London, Federal Trust, 1998, ISBN 0901573582) viii+141pp., hb £17.95.

Tannam, E: *Cross-Border Cooperation in the Republic of Ireland and Northern Ireland* (Basingstoke, Macmillan, 1999, ISBN 0333653955) ix+229pp., hb £42.50.

Index